A Phot

BI

OF NAMIBIA

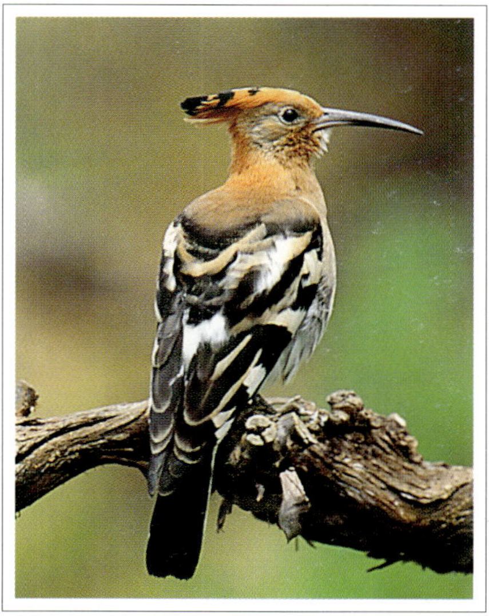

Ian and Jackie Sinclair

STRUIK

To Olga

Struik Publishers (Pty) Ltd
(a member of the Struik Publishing Group (Pty) Ltd)
Cornelis Struik House
80 McKenzie Street
Cape Town 8001

Reg. No.: 54/00965/07

First published in 1995

Managing editor: Tracey Hawthorne
Editor: Jane Maliepaard
Design Manager: Petal Muller
DTP: Gerhardt van Rooyen
Cartographer: Lyndall Hamilton
Reproduction by Hirt & Carter (Pty) Ltd, Cape Town
Printed and bound by Tien Wah Press (Pte) Ltd

ISBN 1 86825 730 4

Front cover: Crimsonbreasted Shrike (ABPL / Daryl Balfour)
Spine: female Violeteared Waxbill (J J Theron)
Back cover: Southern Yellowbilled Hornbill (Nigel Dennis)
Title page: African Hoopoe (Nigel Dennis)

Contents

Introduction

Namibia is a vast, mostly uninhabited country with an astounding range of habitats. The very name, Namibia, conjures up a visual image of wide, open stretches of desert, endless sand dunes and a coastline edged with the hulks and skeletons of wrecked ships.

This is true for only a part of the country, however; the remaining area is remarkably diverse. The lush and verdant riverine forest of the eastern and western Caprivi is an example.

Further west are the endless teak forests, so much like the miombo woodlands to the north. The enormous river systems in the north, which drain the Angola highlands, meet to form the Kavango River. Here, the papyrus-choked panhandle of the Okavango Delta holds all the enigma of that region with its attendant game and birdlife. Further west and south, the seasonally flooded lakes and pans hold a myriad waterbirds, and to the south lies the Etosha National Park with its flamingo population.

A rich mixture of bushveld and drier thornveld stretches to the horizon interspersed with impressive dry mountain ranges until the desert edge reveals itself in its true starkness. Dry gravel plains give way to mountainous sand dunes and to a foggy coastline sparsely interrupted with bays and estuaries, oases for all kinds of birds.

Offshore is the cold and grey Benguela Current, an oceanic upwelling that provides a food source for huge populations of local seabirds and those visitors from both polar regions. Namibia is indeed one of the most fascinating birding countries in Africa with a huge wealth of endemic or near-endemic birds.

There are many fieldguides to southern African birds which include all those found in Namibia plus a few hundred more. This photographic guide excludes all the extraneous species and depicts those birds that are frequently seen in Namibia or that can be found with a little effort.

Emphasis has been placed on birds very typical of Namibia, and on those readily seen from roadsides, perched on telephone poles, and found in parks, reserves and even suburban gardens.

Virtually wherever you are in Namibia you will see birds and the challenge then arises to identify them correctly. Even the most remote and hostile areas of the Namib Desert contain birds, and an alert observer will soon find larks, coursers and korhaans beautifully camouflaged in the dunes and gravel fields.

Learning to identify birds is a long and slow process and it takes years of experience to develop the skills needed to tell the obscure species from the 'little brown jobs'; herein lies the challenge and the fascination of birding. Most beginners are put off by the enormous variety of shorebirds, seabirds, pipits, warblers and larks. This should not be a consideration in the early stages of birding. First familiarize yourself with the large, more obvious birds. When the identification of the first hundred or more species is accomplished, the rest become easier with time.

How to use this book

This pocket-sized book has been designed primarily for use in the field, but if you peruse it at leisure you will reap further benefits. By looking at the photographs frequently you will be able to remember the bird. For example, if you have looked at the photograph of the Lilacbreasted Roller (see page 78) many times you will instantly recognize the bird the very first time you encounter it in the field. This applies to most other birds depicted in this guide except for the unremarkable or nondescript species.

It also helps to know which species belong to which families; the thumbnail silhouettes at the top of each page are intended as a guide, allowing quick location of the bird families as you flick through the book. The photographs have been chosen to show the birds' most obvious identifying features. Where there is a marked difference, for example, between the sexes, or between breeding and non-breeding plumage, more than one photograph has been included.

An up-to-date, colour, distribution map accompanies each species entry. Each bird is ascribed both its English and scientific names and its Roberts' number (Maclean, 1994). The length (L) of the bird (from bill tip to outstretched tail) is also given, except in the case of the Ostrich where the height (H) is given.

The text is brief and to the point and the *italicized* phrases highlight the diagnostic features; knowing the most obvious field characters of a bird aids quick identification. Birds that are similar in size or have similar colouring, and are likely to be confused, are grouped for purposes of comparison. A knowledge of calls, either learnt in the field or from tapes, is also recommended. The call of a species is, however, only mentioned in the text if it is characteristic of the bird.

The habitat in which a bird is likely to occur often reveals its identity. A full-colour habitat map, showing the major vegetation zones within the region, appears on page 141. There is also an introduction to birding etiquette, a guide to further reading, a glossary of birding terms used in this book, as well as a diagram showing the major parts of a bird. An index of common names concludes this easy-to-use guide.

Ostrich *Struthio camelus* (1) H 2 m

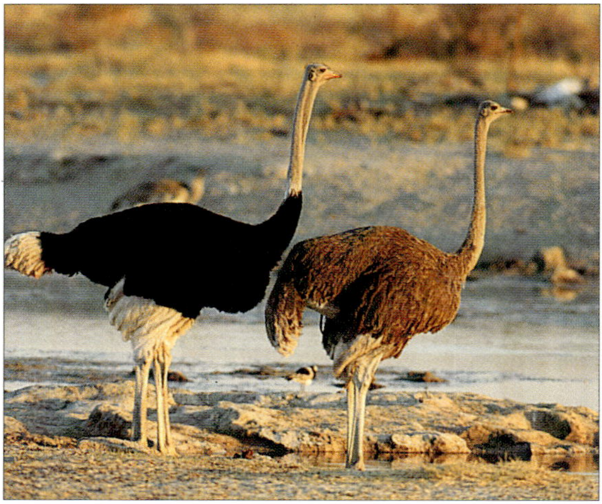

MAY CRAIG-COOPER

Male (left) and female (right)

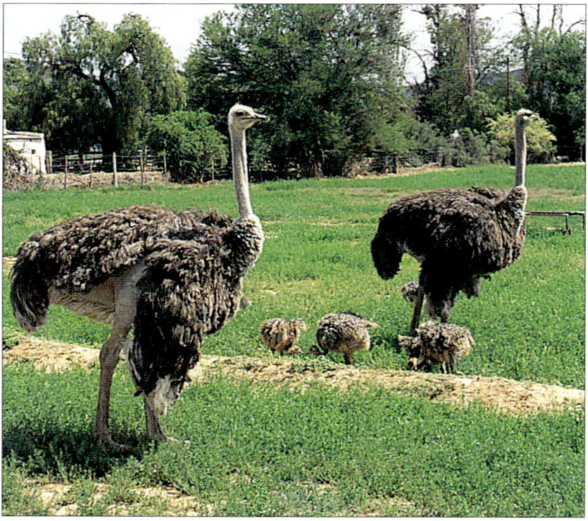

SIL/NIGEL J DENNIS

Females and immatures

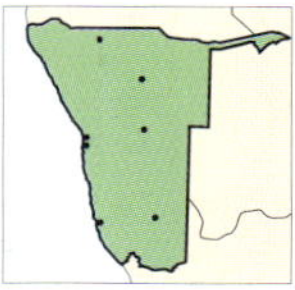

This is the *largest* bird in Namibia and, indeed, in the world. It is unlikely to be misidentified. The male is black and white; females and immatures are greyish brown and white. If seen alone, the young bird might be mistaken for a korhaan but can be distinguished by its very thick legs and flattened bill. A nocturnal booming call is made by the male and sounds like a lion's roar. Domestic and feral in most regions, the only genuine wild populations occur in the northern parts.

Great Crested Grebe *Podiceps cristatus* (6) L 50 cm

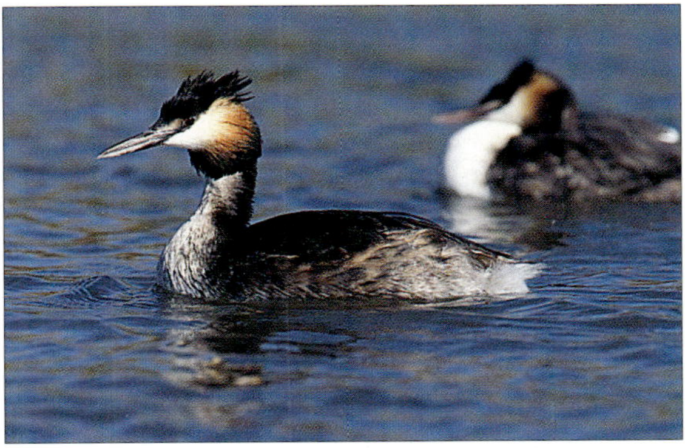

ABPL/NIGEL J DENNIS

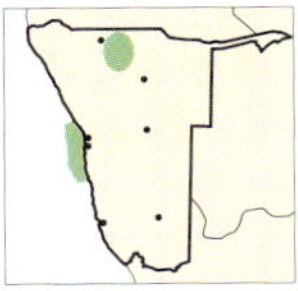

The breeding adult is unmistakable with its *dark double crest and a rufous-edged ruff* on the sides of the head. The female has a paler ruff. Both ruff and crest are less pronounced in the non-breeding adult. In flight a pale wing bar is visible. The juvenile has black and white striping on the head. The call is a barking 'rah-rah-rah' and various growls and snarls. Uncommon and thinly distributed in Namibia, it is found on open stretches of permanent freshwater, at the coast and on salt pans.

Blacknecked Grebe *Podiceps nigricollis* (7) L 28 cm

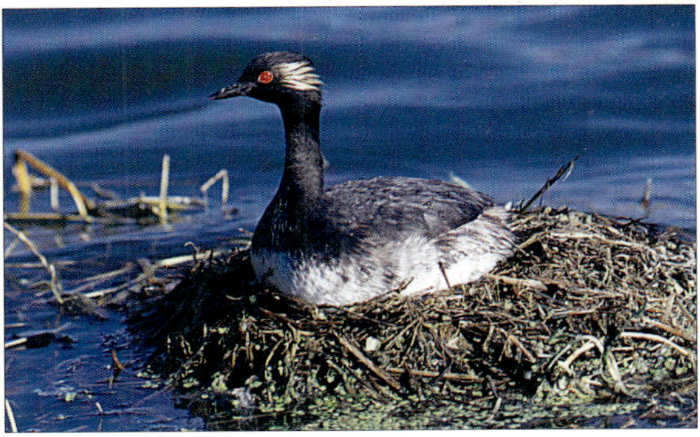

T D LONGRIGG

Breeding adult

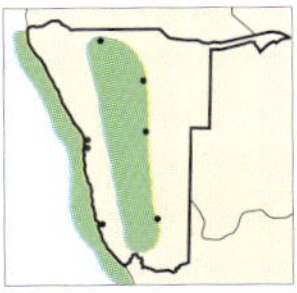

Smaller than the Great Crested Grebe but larger than the Dabchick, the breeding adult of this species has a black head and throat, and *conspicuous golden ear tufts*. The throat and cheeks of the non-breeding adult and immature are *whitish*, not greyish as in the Dabchick. Normally silent, it gives a soft, mellow trill during display. Common on coastal salt pans and close inshore in sheltered bays, it occurs inland during seasonal flooding of wetlands and frequents reed-fringed ponds.

Dabchick *Tachybaptus ruficollis* (8) L 20 cm

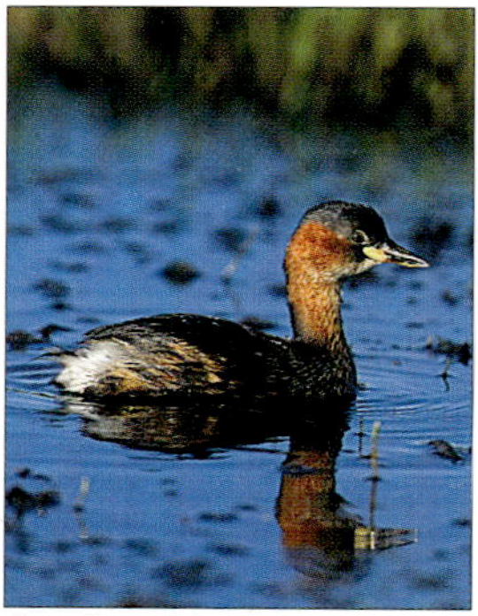

SIL/NIGEL J DENNIS

Breeding adult

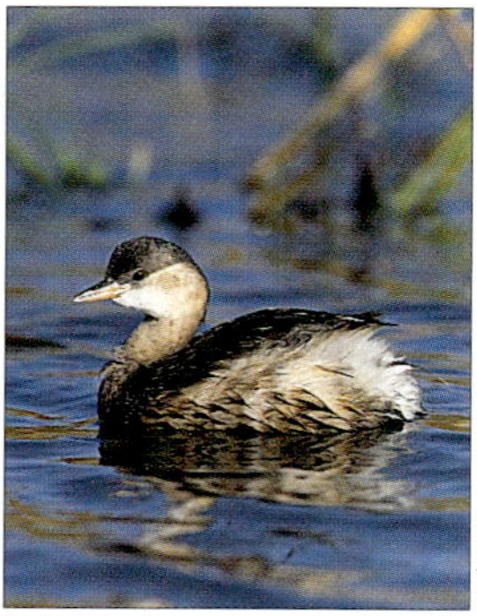

SIL/NIGEL J DENNIS

Non-breeding adult

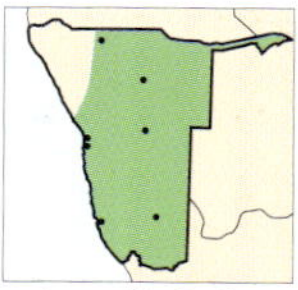

This is one of the smallest aquatic birds in Namibia. The *pale creamy spot at the base of the bill* is diagnostic. During the breeding season this dark grebe has *chestnut sides to the neck*. Non-breeding adults and immatures are greyish brown, but immatures may show black and white stripes on the cheeks. Its call is a noisy, often-heard, whinnying trill. It dives frequently, often emerging with just the head showing above water. It is common on most permanent freshwater wetlands.

Blackbrowed Albatross *Diomedea melanophris* (12) L 90 cm

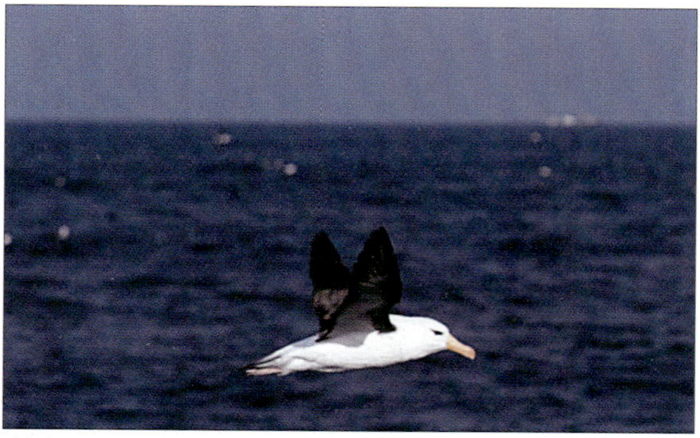

IAN SINCLAIR

Adult

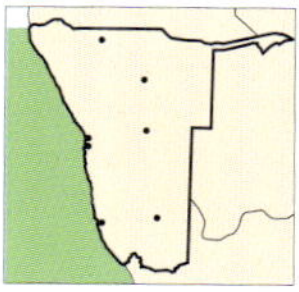

The adult has a diagnostic *yellow bill with a reddish tip, and a white underwing with broad black borders*. Immatures have a grey, black-tipped bill, and varying amounts of grey on the head and sides of the neck which sometimes join to form a collar. The underwing of the immature is darker but lightens with age. It grunts and squawks when fighting over food. Most common during winter on the deep-sea trawling grounds off the coast, it ventures close inshore during strong winds.

Southern Giant Petrel *Macronectes giganteus* (17) L 90 cm

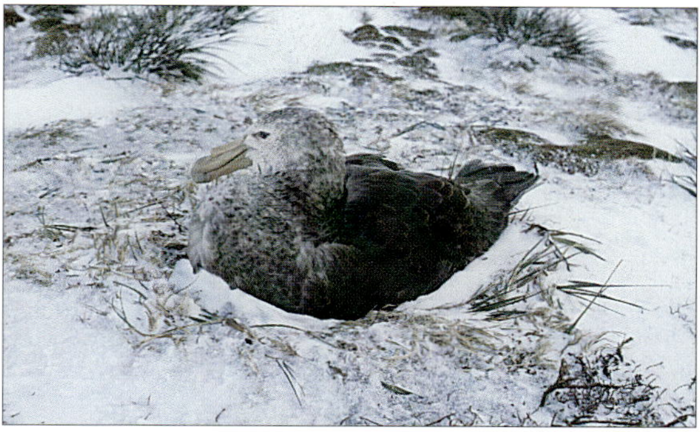

IAN SINCLAIR

Adult

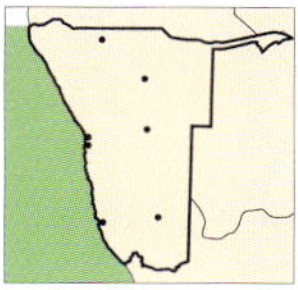

Unlike the otherwise similar Northern Giant Petrel, this species has an all-white phase. When the dark brown phase is seen close inshore near seal colonies, the *powerful, lumbering flight and hump-backed appearance* aid identification. At close range the *dark green, not brown, bill tip* distinguishes this species. Immatures are dark, becoming lighter with age. It emits harsh grunts when squabbling over food and is a common to uncommon year-round visitor, usually in winter.

Whitechinned Petrel *Procellaria aequinoctialis* (32) L 54 cm

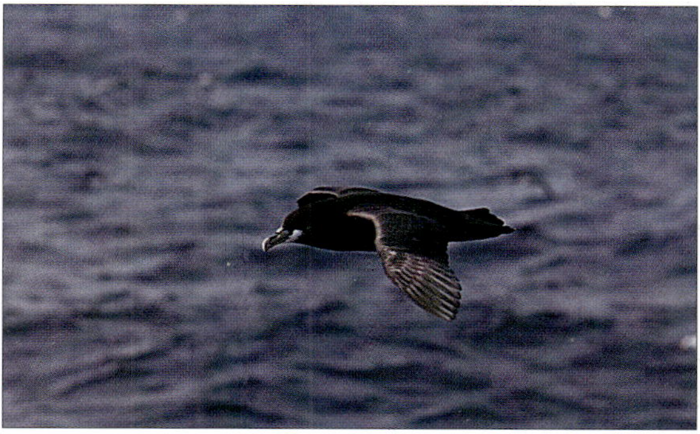

IAN SINCLAIR

Adult

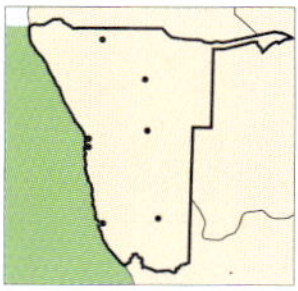

It is considerably larger than all the other dark brown petrels. The diagnostic *white chin and long, robust, pale greenish bill* with its black saddle are visible at close range. It has a towering, careening flight action high above the waves, regularly venturing close inshore around the coast where it can be seen, quite frequently, following fishing trawlers. Normally silent, it will utter a fast 'tititit' when alarmed. It is a common year-round visitor, but more regularly seen during winter.

Eastern White Pelican *Pelecanus onocrotalus* (49) L 180 cm

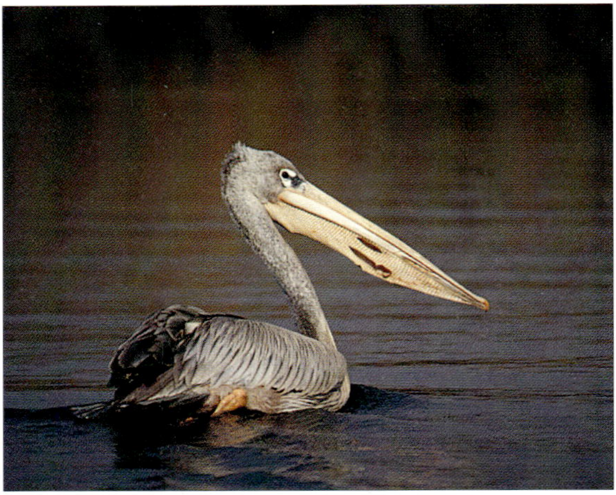

ABPL/TIM LIVERSEDGE

Immature

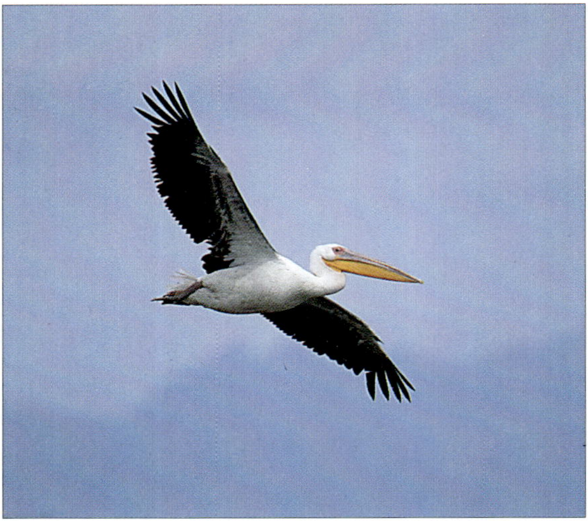

NIGEL J DENNIS

Adult

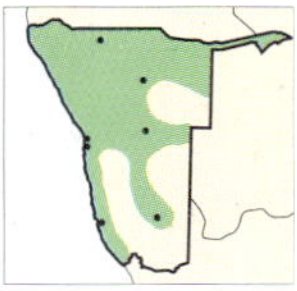

This is a large white bird with *contrasting black primary and secondary feathers* and *a bright yellow pouch*. It assumes a pinkish flush in the breeding season. Immatures are dark brown; the young birds lighten progressively with age. Guttural sounds can be heard from the breeding colonies, otherwise they are silent. They are frequently seen flying in 'V' formation, and habitually fish in groups. The Eastern White Pelican occurs in coastal estuaries and close inshore between Sandwich Harbour and Swakopmund. It is seen less often on freshwater.

Sooty Shearwater *Puffinus griseus* (37) L 46 cm

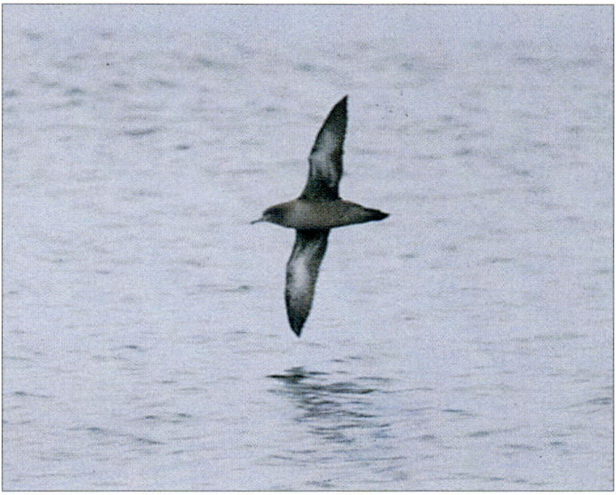

JOHN MARCHANT

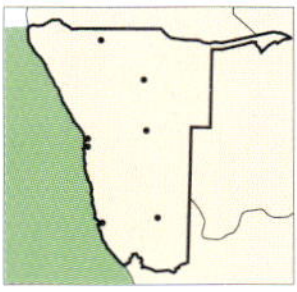

The diagnostic *silvery linings to the underwings* differentiate this bird from all other dark shearwaters. The sexes are alike. Its flight is swift and direct with rapid wing beats interspersed with short glides when the bird banks over the waves and flashes its silvery underwings. It is seen in coastal waters throughout the year where it forages on small shoaling fish. It is silent at sea. The Sooty Shearwater is the most common shearwater over these coastal waters.

Cape Gannet *Morus capensis* (53) L 85 cm

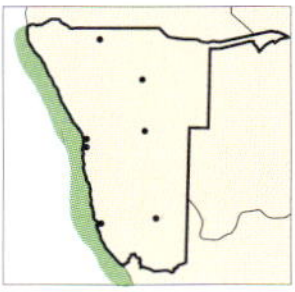

In the adult, the all-white plumage contrasts with the black flight feathers and the *black pointed tail*. It has a long, pale grey, *dagger-shaped bill*. The nape and the sides of the neck are straw yellow. The immature is a dark brown version of the adult, progressing through mottled brown and white stages. A 'warrra-warrra-warrra' call is uttered when feeding in flocks at sea as well as at breeding colonies. It is seen regularly along the coast, although it does not range very far out to sea, and breeds on islands off the Namibian coast.

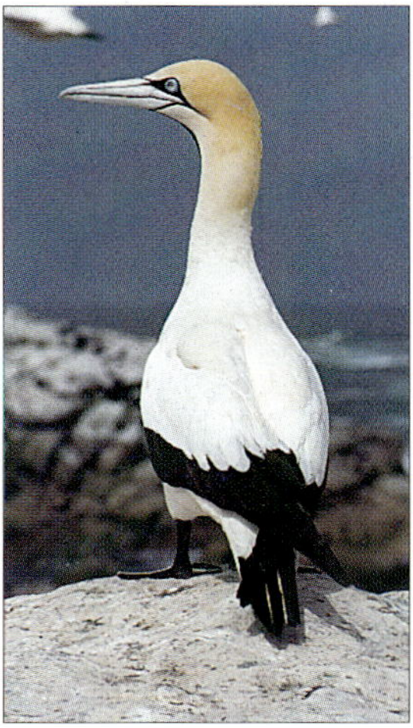

ROY JOHANNESSON

Whitebreasted Cormorant *Phalacrocorax carbo* (55) L 90 cm

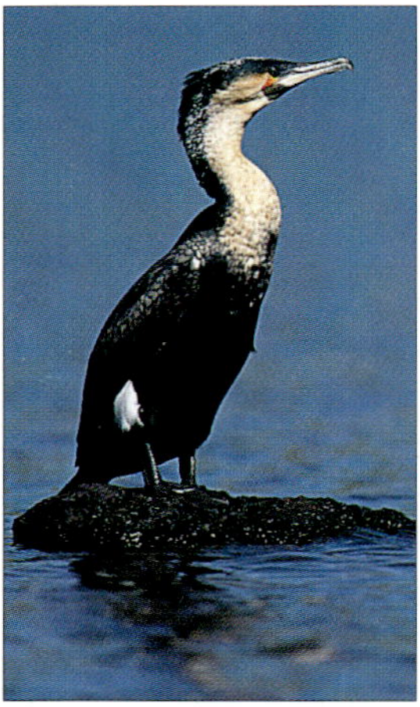

NIGEL J DENNIS

Adult

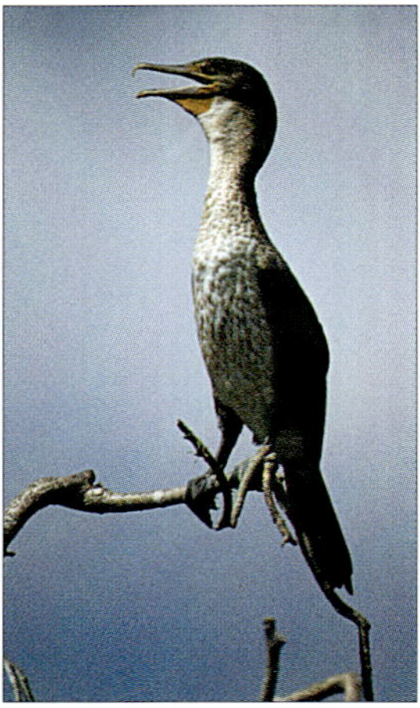

DR & MRS MANFRED REICHARDT

Immature

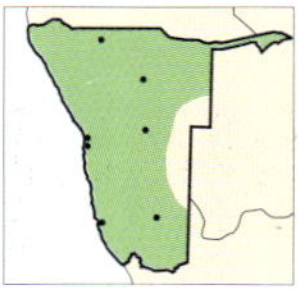

This is by far the largest cormorant in the region. The adult has glossy black plumage, a *white breast and throat, and a bright yellow patch at the base of the bill*. In the breeding season it shows white flank patches. The immature is dark brown and has variable amounts of white on the underparts. It is normally silent but utters grunts and squeals during the breeding season. A common coastal bird, it avoids feeding over the ocean, preferring sheltered bays and inland freshwater areas.

Cape Cormorant *Phalacrocorax capensis* (56) L 65 cm

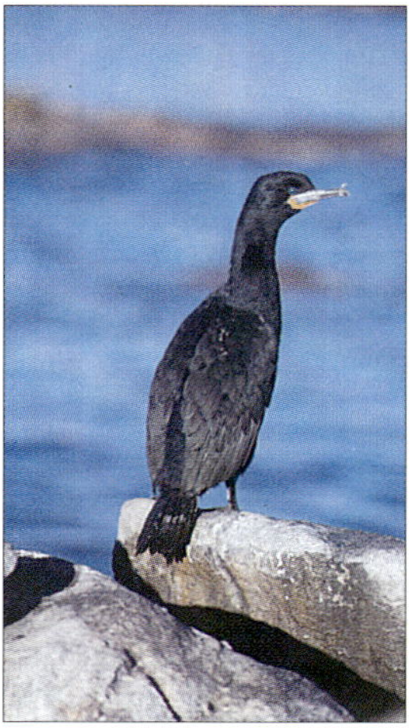

IAN SINCLAIR

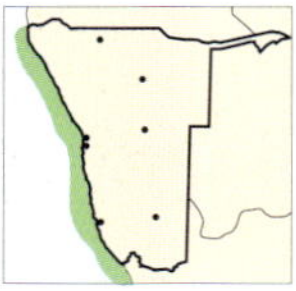

This species is intermediate in size between the Bank and Crowned cormorants. The adult has glossy *blue-black plumage* with a *bright yellow-orange patch at the base of the bill.* The patch brightens during the breeding season. Immatures are a dowdy brown with slightly paler underparts. Various 'gaaaa' and 'geeee' noises are uttered during the breeding season. It is the most abundant marine cormorant in the region, and is found in large concentrations on breeding platforms along the coast or flying in straight lines to and from feeding areas.

Bank Cormorant *Phalacrocorax neglectus* (57) L 76 cm

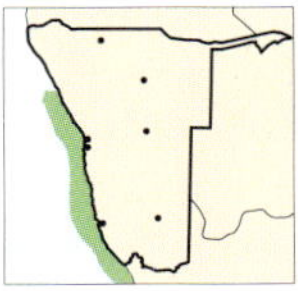

It is larger and more robust than the Cape Cormorant, from which it differs by having *dull black plumage and a thick, woolly-textured neck,* and by lacking the pale patch at the base of the bill. It has a *small tuft of erectile feathers on the forehead*, which looks like a small, rounded crest. It shows white flecks on the head and a diagnostic white rump during breeding. The immature lacks white flecks on the head and has a duller eye. Its call is a wheezy 'wheeee', given when the bird alights near its nest. It is found on coastal waters and offshore islands.

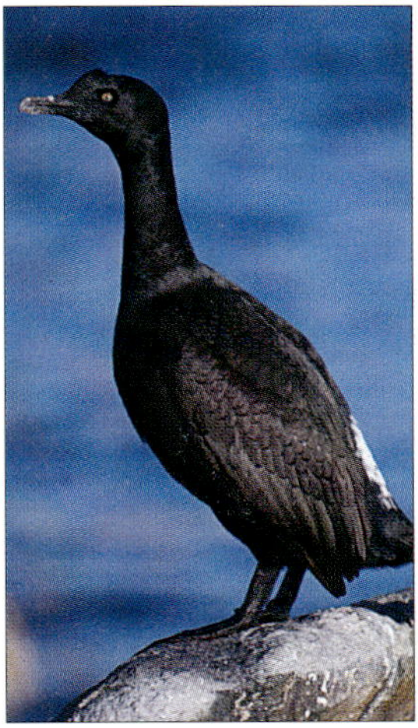

IAN SINCLAIR

Reed Cormorant *Phalacrocorax africanus* (58) L 52 cm

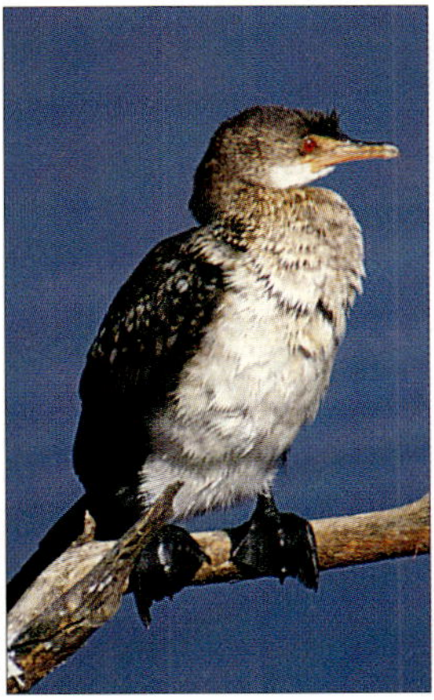

ABPL/JOAN RYDER

Immature

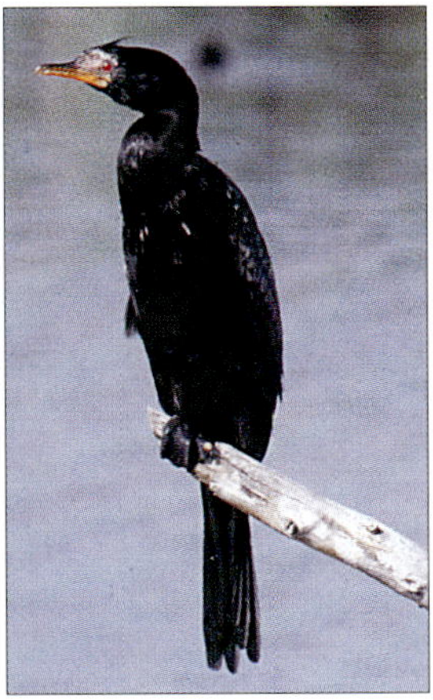

DR & MRS MANFRED REICHARDT

Adult

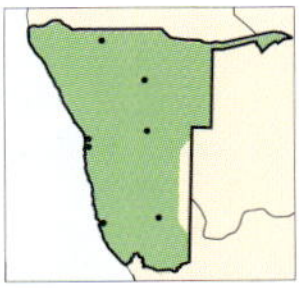

This small black cormorant has *pale spotting on the back*. The tail is *long and unmarked* and is proportionately longer than that of the Whitebreasted Cormorant. In breeding plumage the adult shows a yellow-orange face patch and throat, and displays a small, erectile crest on the forehead. The immature bird is brownish grey above with white underparts. It roosts and breeds colonially. It is silent, except for cackles and hisses at breeding colonies, and frequents freshwater dams, lakes and rivers. It is rarely seen at the coast.

Crowned Cormorant *Phalacrocorax coronatus* (59) L 50 cm

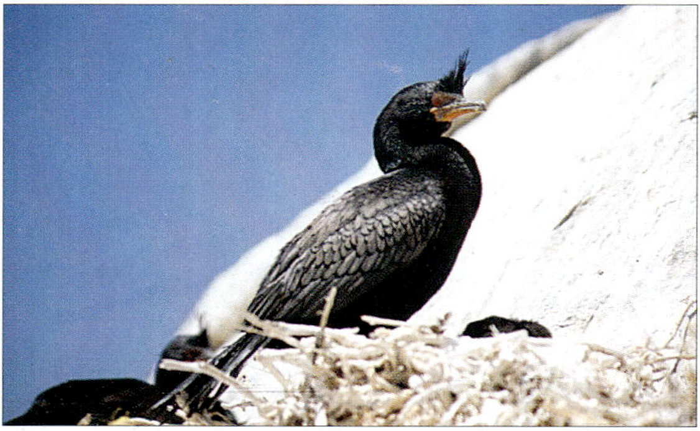

IAN SINCLAIR

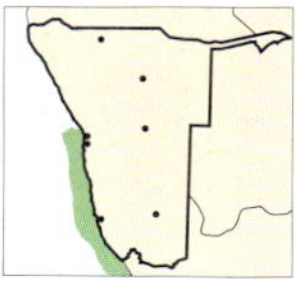

This cormorant resembles the Reed Cormorant but differs by having a much shorter tail, an *orange-red face and throat patch in breeding plumage* and a longer, more pronounced erectile crest. The immature differs from the immature Reed Cormorant by having brown, not white, underparts. It is usually silent except for hisses and grunts at the nest in breeding colonies. It is uncommon and thinly distributed along the coast, favouring rocky shorelines.

African Darter *Anhinga rufa* (60) L 80 cm

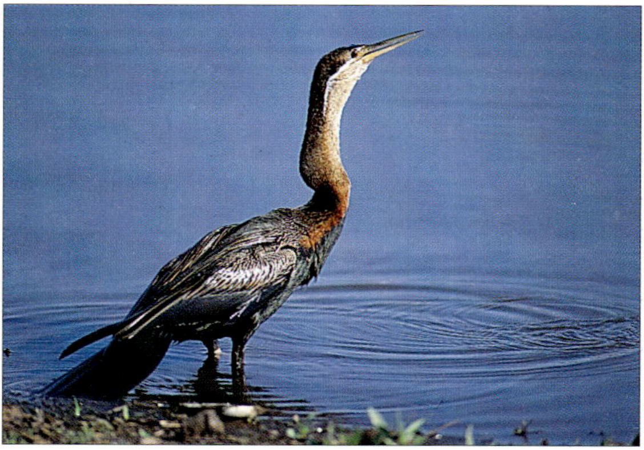

PETER CRAIG-COOPER

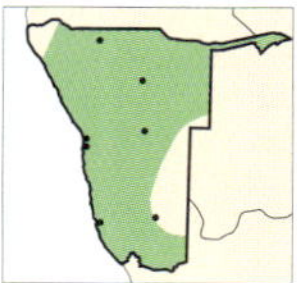

It resembles a cormorant but has a *long, egret-like neck* with a slender head and an *elongated, pointed bill*. The adult male in breeding plumage shows a rufous head and neck with a long white stripe running from the eye on to the neck. Females and nonbreeding males are pale brown on the face and the throat. The immature has a white head which darkens with age. Its call is a distinctive croaking. It is uncommon to common in the wetter regions of the north.

Grey Heron *Ardea cinerea* (62) L 100 cm

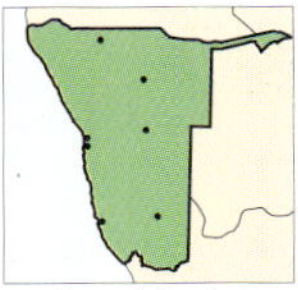

This is a large, long-legged, greyish heron, with *a white head and neck*, and a *black eye-stripe* which ends on the nape in a wispy black crest. Its *bill is dagger shaped and yellow*. The immature lacks the eye-stripe and crest and has a darker bill and yellow upper legs. In flight the adult can be distinguished from the Blackheaded Heron by having a uniform grey underwing. Its call is a harsh 'kraauunk'. This bird is mostly solitary except when breeding. It is common in coastal regions and inland freshwater areas.

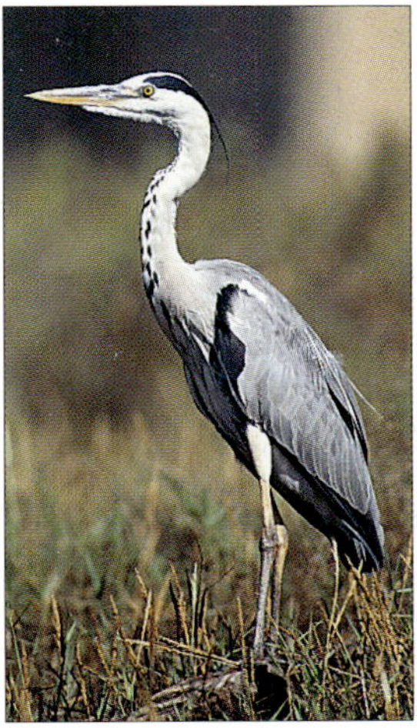

PETER CRAIG-COOPER

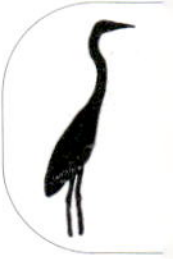

Blackheaded Heron *Ardea melanocephala* (63) L 96 cm

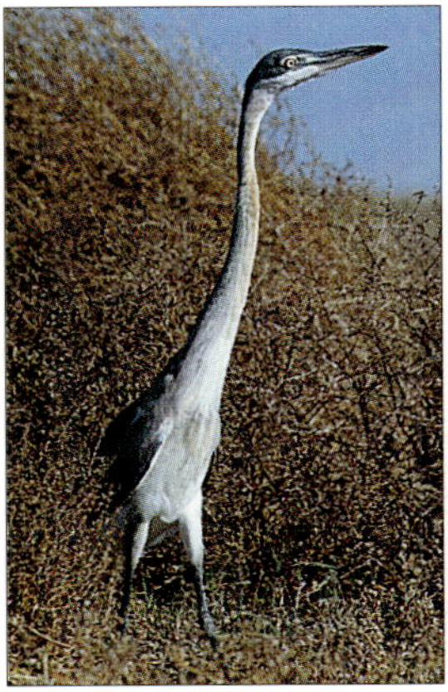

COLIN URQUHART

Immature

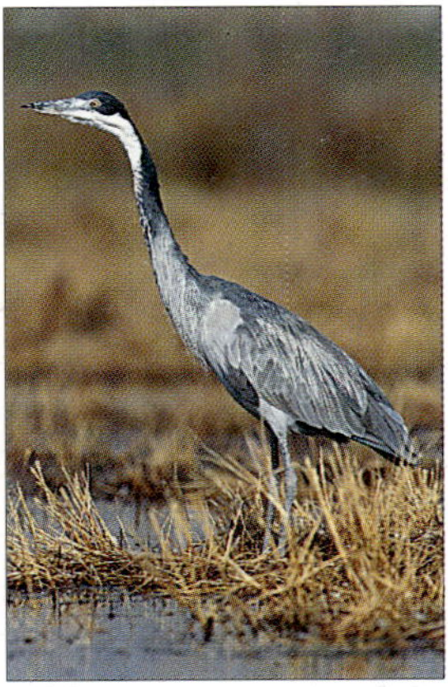

NIGEL J DENNIS

Adult

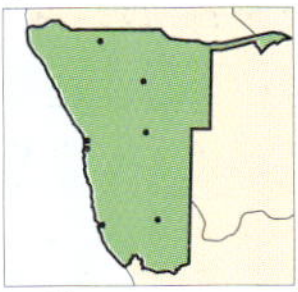

The *black-topped head and hindneck contrast with the white throat*, rendering this heron unmistakable. The immature is grey, not black, on the head and neck and can be distinguished from the immature Grey Heron by its dark legs and thighs. In flight the *contrasting black and white underwing* distinguishes it from the Grey Heron which has a uniform grey underwing. It has a loud 'aaaaark' call, and various hoarse cackles and bill clapping at the nest. More often seen stalking through open grasslands than near water, it is thinly distributed throughout Namibia but is more common in the north.

Little Egret *Egretta garzetta* (67) L 65 cm

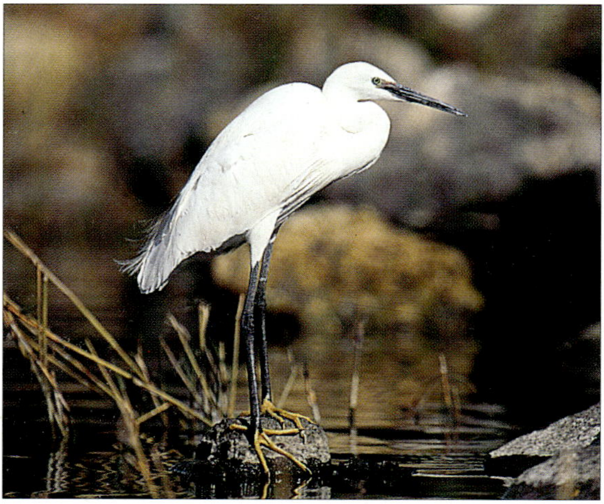

NIGEL J DENNIS

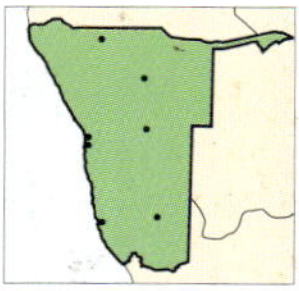

This small white heron is distinguished from all other herons in Namibia by having *black legs and contrasting yellow toes. The bill is slender and always black.* It feeds by dashing to and fro in shallow water, stabbing at its prey. In breeding plumage it shows white head plumes and aigrettes on the lower back. Immatures lack plumes and aigrettes. Its call is a harsh 'waaark', similar to that of other egrets. It occurs in coastal and freshwater areas, breeding in colonies in reed beds.

Cattle Egret *Bubulcus ibis* (71) L 54 cm

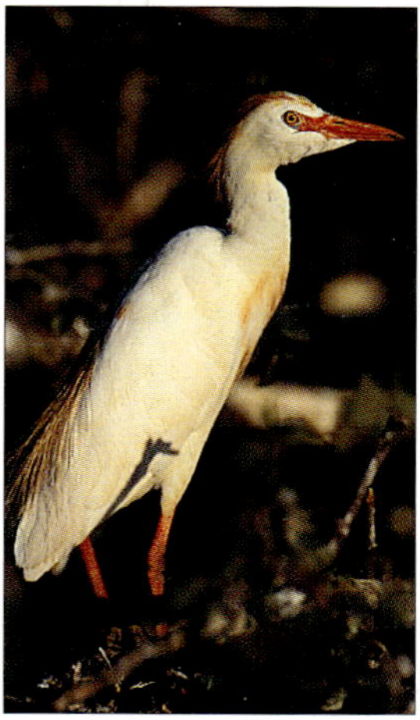

W R TARBOTON

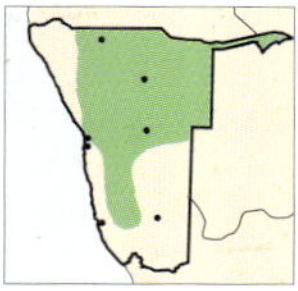

This species is often seen following cattle or game. The *breeding bird* has a *red bill and buff plumes on the head, breast and mantle, and a noticeably shaggy bib and throat,* giving it a distinct jowl. The legs are red at the start of the breeding season. Non-breeding and immature birds are white with the legs varying from dark brown (never black) through to yellowish green. A highly gregarious bird with a typical heron-like 'aaaark' or 'pok-pok' call, it is common in the north but absent from the very driest regions.

Hamerkop *Scopus umbretta* (81) L 56 cm

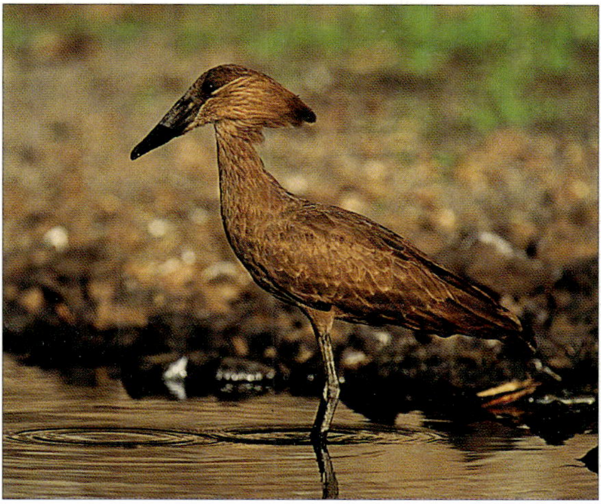

SIL/NIGEL J DENNIS

Adult

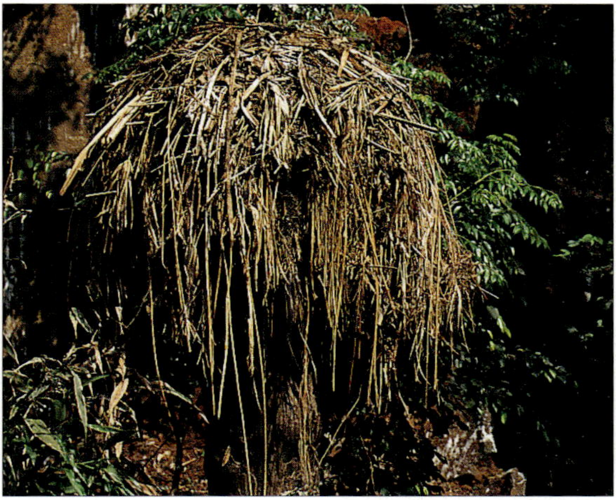

SIL/NIGEL J DENNIS

Hamerkop nest

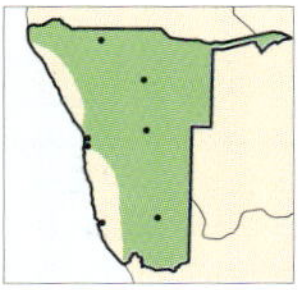

The *hammer-shaped profile of its head* renders this bird unmistakable. It is dark brown with long legs, a heavy crest and a large black bill. In flight it has a finely barred tail that lends it a hawk-like appearance, but the long bill and legs preclude any confusion with birds of prey. It builds an enormous domed nest, usually in a tree or on a cliff, with a small round entrance which faces downwards from one end of the structure. It has a sharp 'kiep' call in flight. Normally associated with freshwater dams, lakes and rivers, it is found in swampy regions and seasonally flooded areas, and is more abundant in the north.

Abdim's Stork *Ciconia abdimii* (85) L 76 cm

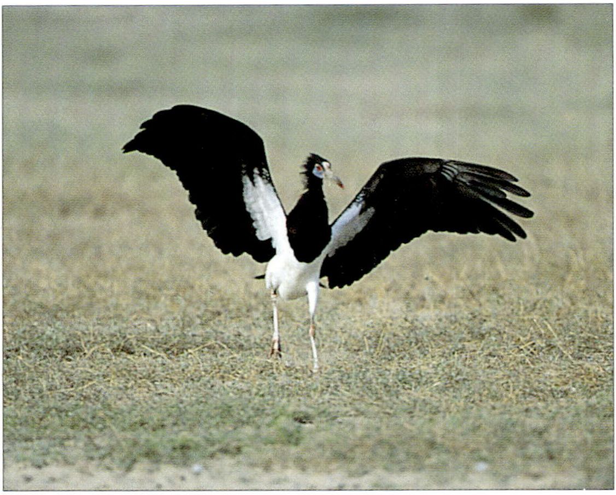

ABPL/NIGEL J DENNIS

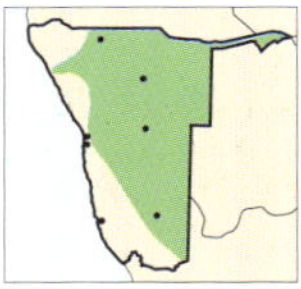

This is a black and white stork, distinguished from similar storks by its diagnostic *white lower back and rump*, as well as its *greenish legs with a pink ankle, and a greenish bill*. At close range the red joints and blue face of this stork are visible. The immature has a dark red bill and is duller than the adult. Abdim's Stork is normally silent but has a weak, two-noted whistle at roosts. This common summer visitor often occurs in large flocks in open fields and agricultural lands.

Marabou Stork *Leptoptilos crumeniferus* (89) L 150 cm

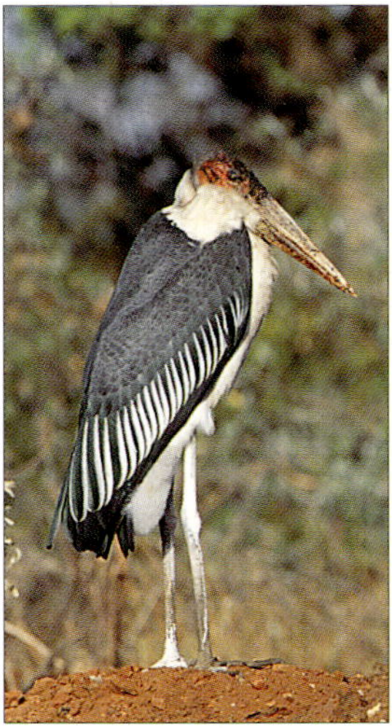

NIGEL J DENNIS

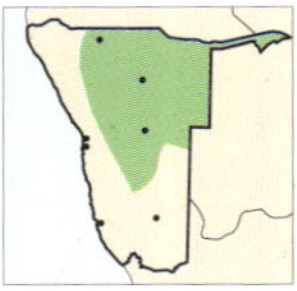

This huge bird with its *naked head and neck, massive bill* and *naked fleshy pink pouch* is primarily a scavenger. In flight the enormous black wings contrast with the white body and the head is tucked into the shoulders. The immature is very similar to the adult but its head and neck are covered with a sparse woolly down. It gives a low, hoarse croak when alarmed and claps its bill when displaying. The inflated pouch warns off other birds. This bird is usually seen in major game reserves, soaring with vultures or scavenging at lion kills. It is wide ranging over bushveld.

Sacred Ibis *Threskiornis aethiopicus* (91) L 90 cm

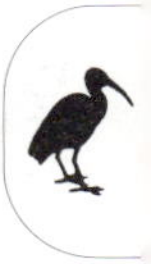

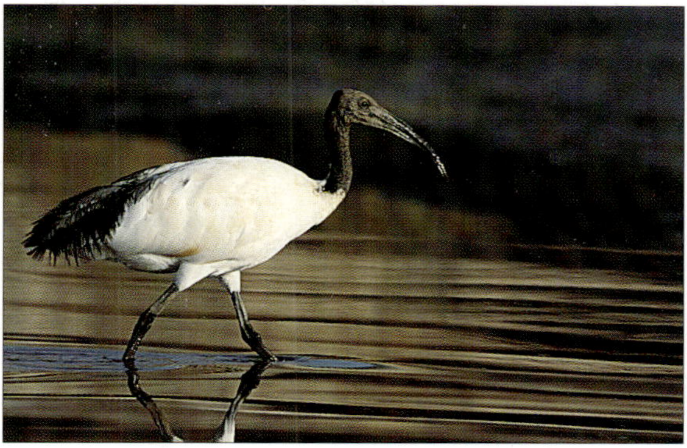

MAY CRAIG-COOPER

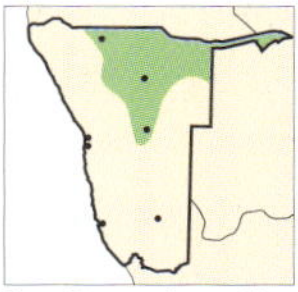

This white bird has *an unfeathered black head and neck, and a long, decurved black bill*. The flight feathers are black edged, giving the wings a narrow black border in flight. During breeding the naked skin on the underwing turns scarlet and the flank feathers yellow. The immature has white feathering on the neck. It is normally silent but croaks loudly at breeding colonies. It occurs singly or in small flocks near dams, vleis, pans, flooded grasslands and moist areas of the north.

African Spoonbill *Platalea alba* (95) L 90 cm

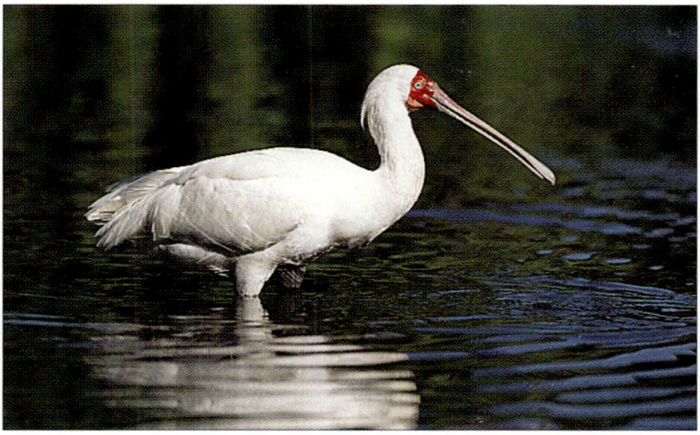

NIGEL J DENNIS

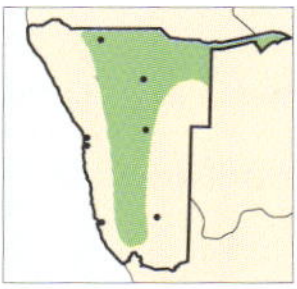

The *long, flattened, spoon-shaped red and grey bill* is diagnostic. *The legs, feet and face are bright red.* In flight it differs from egrets and herons by flying with its neck outstretched, not tucked into the shoulders. The bill is adapted for specialised feeding. It wades in shallow water, sweeping its partly open bill from side to side. Immatures are duller and have dark-tipped flight feathers and a pinkish bill. When alarmed it utters a low 'kaark'. It is found in freshwater lakes and estuaries, on seasonally flooded areas and more permanent wetlands in the north.

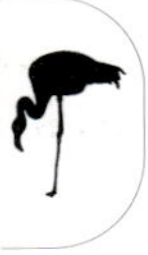

Greater Flamingo *Phoenicopterus ruber* (96) L 127 cm

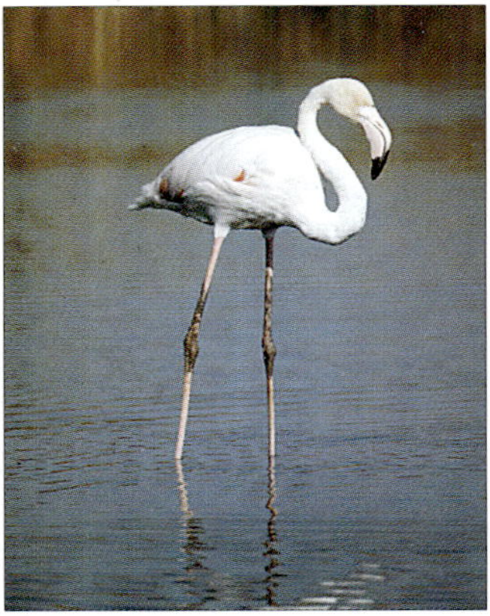

IAN DAVIDSON

Adult

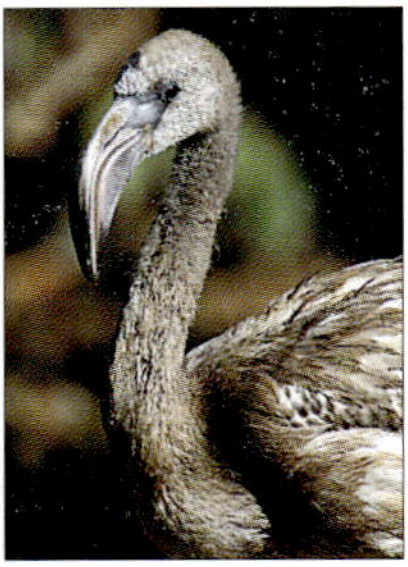

ABPL./NIGEL J DENNIS

Immature

This is a predominantly white bird with a small body in relation to its long legs and long neck. In flight it shows brilliant red patches on the fore-wings. In comparison with the Lesser Flamingo, it is larger, less red, and has a large diagnostic *pink bill with a black tip*. The immature is sandy brown, lacks the red in the wings and has a grey and black bill. The call is a goose-like honking. It is common in coastal areas and in Etosha, frequenting shallow freshwater lakes, salt pans and estuaries.

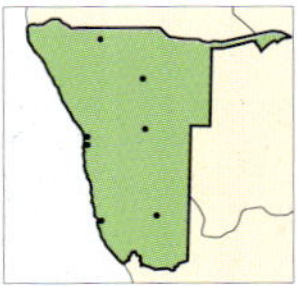

Lesser Flamingo *Phoenicopterus minor* (97) L 100 cm

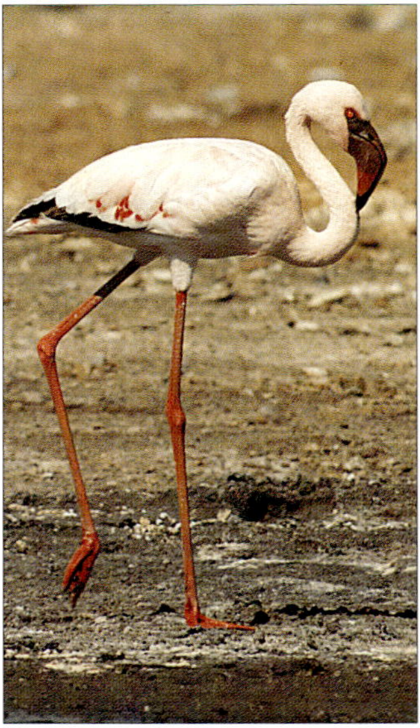

ALAN WEAVING

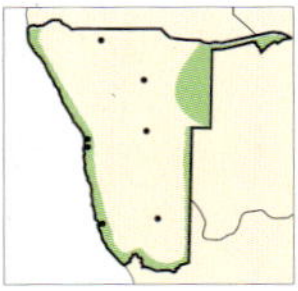

It is much smaller and redder than the Greater Flamingo. Its *dark red, black-tipped bill appears all black* when seen at a distance, further differentiating the two. The immature of this species is smaller than the immature Greater Flamingo, and has a darker, stubbier bill and greyish brown body. It is found in flocks together with the Greater Flamingo, at freshwater lakes, salt pans and estuaries. It is common in coastal regions and breeds at Etosha.

Egyptian Goose *Alopochen aegyptiacus* (102) L 70 cm

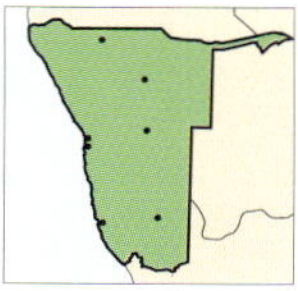

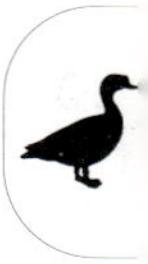

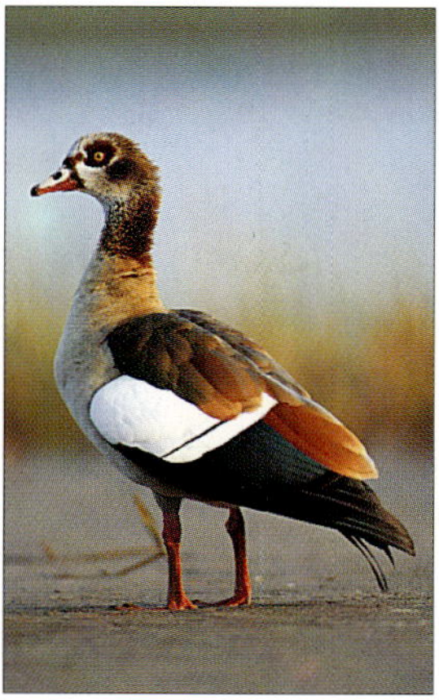

MAY CRAIG-COOPER

The *dark brown mask around the eye, white forewings and brown patch on the chest* are diagnostic of this small 'goose'. The neck and legs are longer than those of the South African Shelduck. A thin dark line through the white forewing is visible in flight. Immatures lack the brown mask around the eye and the brown breast patch. It is very noisy and aggressive in flocks, giving loud honking and hissing noises. It is common in freshwater habitats and coastal areas, but not found in dry parts.

South African Shelduck *Tadorna cana* (103) L 64 cm

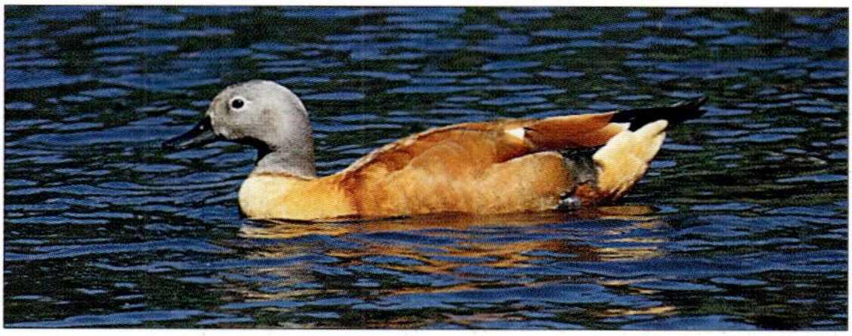

PETER CRAIG-COOPER

Male

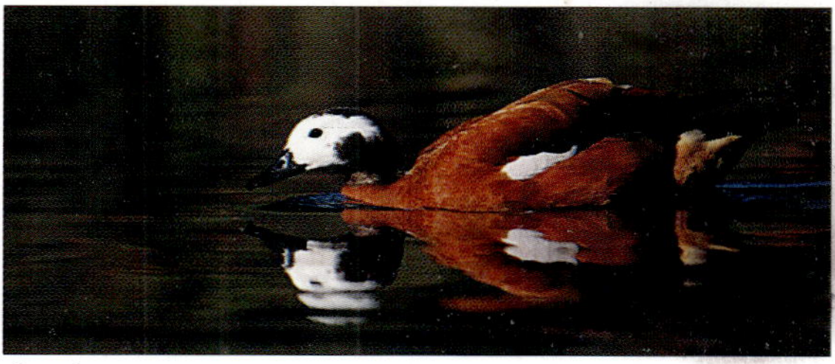

NIGEL J DENNIS

Female

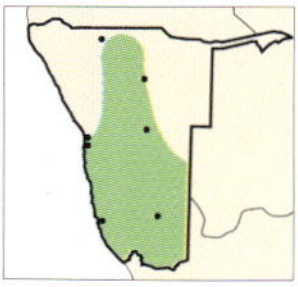

This is a *large, russet-coloured duck with a black bill and black legs*. The male has a diagnostic grey head; the female has a variable white and grey head. Both sexes show white forewings in flight but no black dividing line as seen in the Egyptian Goose. The immature resembles the adult. Its call consists of various honks and hisses. It frequents freshwater lakes and dams, salt pans and coastal areas but is often seen well away from water. It is more common in southern Namibia.

Cape Teal *Anas capensis* (106) L 46 cm

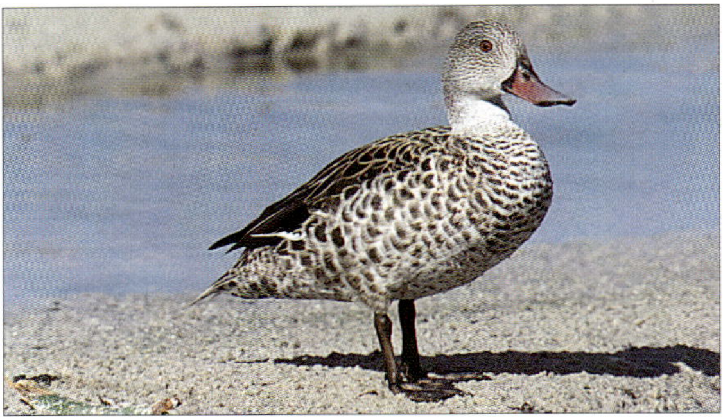

T D LONGRIGG

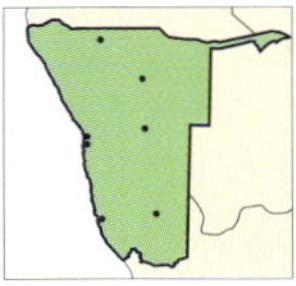

This is the palest duck in the region. It is easily identified by its *mottled greyish plumage and slightly upturned, pink bill.* In flight the wing pattern shows two broad white stripes bordering a small green speculum. The immature is pale grey. Its call is a thin, high-pitched whistle, usually given in flight. It usually occurs in mixed flocks. It occurs throughout the region, especially in drier areas, on any open stretch of fresh or saline water.

Redbilled Teal *Anas erythrorhyncha* (108) L 48 cm

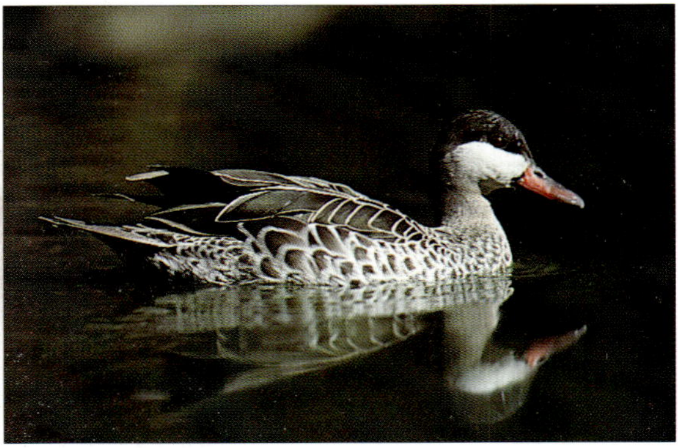

ABPL/ANTHONY BANNISTER

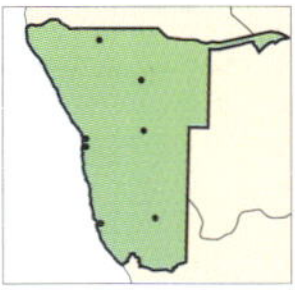

This medium-sized, brown and buff mottled duck has a diagnostic *dark cap, pale cheeks and a red bill.* Its dark cap distinguishes it from the paler Cape Teal. In flight it shows pale secondaries and a buff speculum. The immature bird is duller than the adult. The female's call is a soft quack; the male gives a soft, nasal whistle. The sexes are similar. This duck is very common and occurs in mixed flocks on large stretches of open freshwater.

Cape Shoveller *Anas smithii* (112) L 53 cm

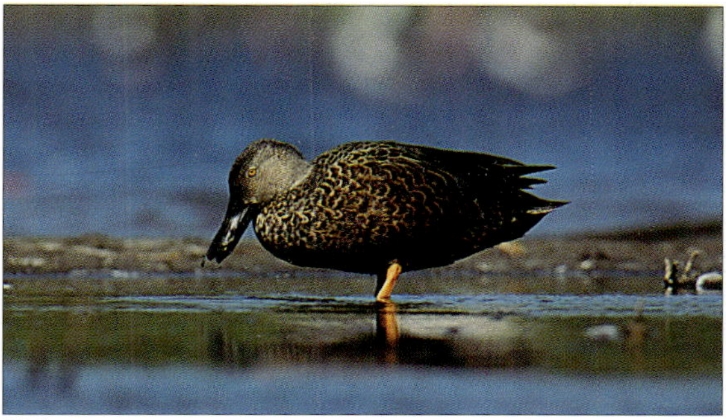

SIL/NIGEL J DENNIS

Male

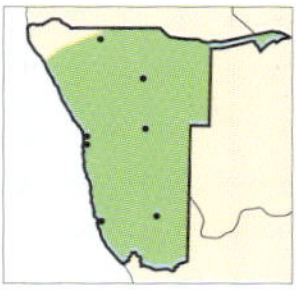

This duck is distinguished by its *black spatulate bill*, which appears longer than the head. The plumage is finely speckled grey brown and the *legs are a rich yellow orange*. In flight the *powder-blue forewings* are very conspicuous. The male has a paler head and yellower eyes than the female; overall, the female is darker than the male. Immatures resemble females. Its call is a 'quack' and continuous rasping. It occurs in small groups on freshwater, preferably with surface vegetation.

Knobbilled Duck *Sarkidiornis melanotos* (115) L 73 cm

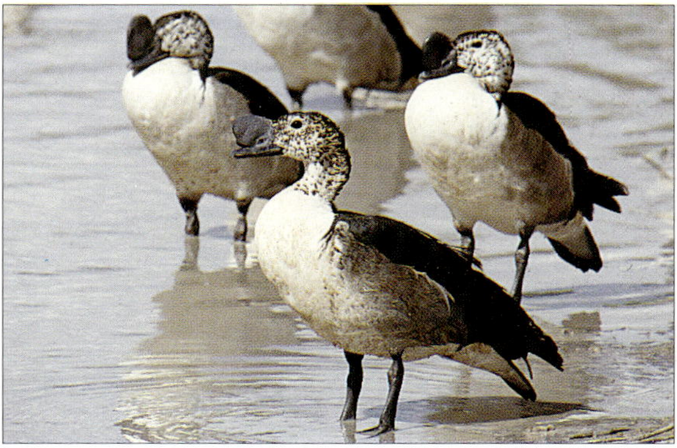

W R TARBOTON

Males

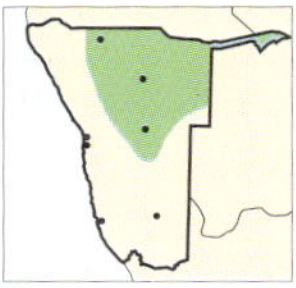

This large duck is unmistakable, with its *grey speckled head and contrasting blue-black and white plumage*. In flight the wings are black with no markings, although the female shows a little white on the lower back. The male is larger than the female, and when breeding it has a conspicuous comb on the bill. Immatures have dark speckling on the white areas. It utters a whistle but is usually silent. It is seen on any still freshwater body, and larger rivers in the north.

Secretarybird *Sagittarius serpentarius* (118) L 140 cm

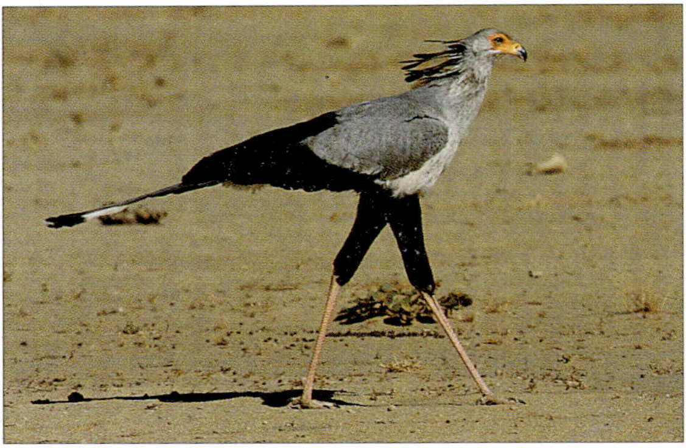

ABPL/LORNA STANTON

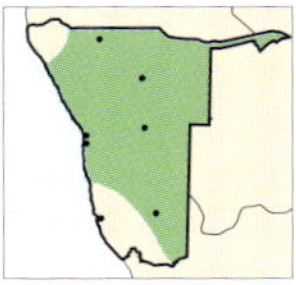

It might be mistaken for a stork or a crane when seen at long range but the *short hooked bill, the black partly feathered legs, and the black wispy nape plumes* should rule out any confusion. In flight the central tail feathers project well beyond the tail and legs. Immatures have a shorter tail and yellow, not red, facial skin. It utters a deep croak during aerial display. Pairs are often seen hunting over savanna and open grasslands. It is fairly common on the grassy plains of the north.

Blue Crane *Anthropoides paradisea* (208) L 100 cm

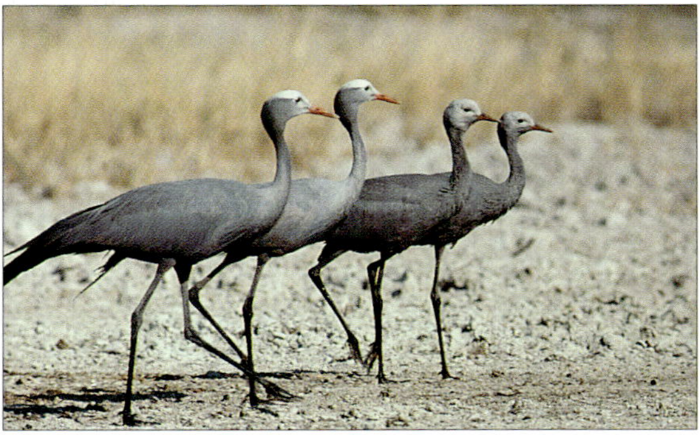

ABPL/CLEM HAAGNER

Adults and immatures

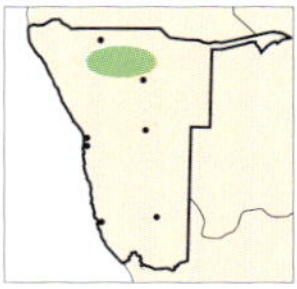

This greyish bird has an unusually *large head and a long, slender neck*. The tail is very short; the *drooping feathers* are elongations of the innerwing feathers. Immatures lack the long inner secondaries and are a paler grey. The call is a loud, nasal 'kraaank'. It performs a dancing display with the wings outstretched. Usually found in small groups or pairs in freshwater areas and open grasslands, it has also adapted to agricultural lands. It is confined mostly to Etosha and adjacent areas.

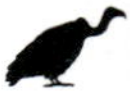

Whitebacked Vulture *Gyps africanus* (123) L 95 cm

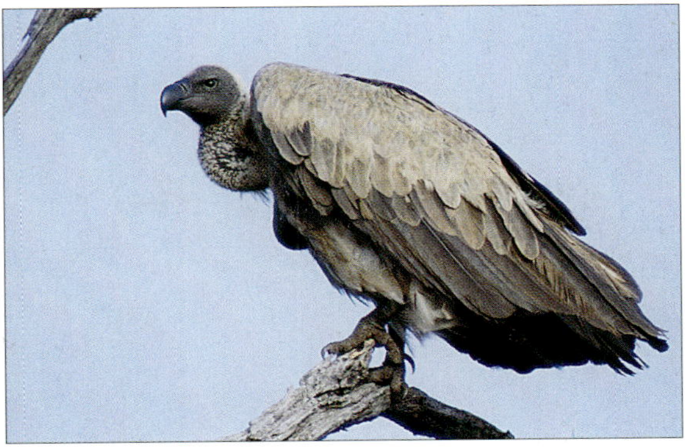

ALAN WEAVING

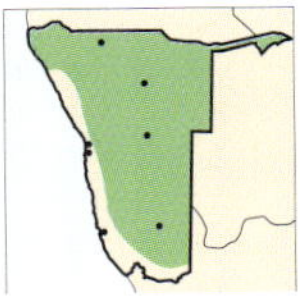

If seen from above the *white lower back* of this bird *contrasts with the dark upperwing*. Immatures are much darker than adults and show less contrast between the flight feathers and the wing linings. Its call is a harsh cackling and it emits hissing noises when feeding at the nest. It is most frequently seen in flight, riding thermals or searching the ground for kills. It occurs in open savanna parkland and is found most commonly over bushveld and in larger game reserves.

Lappetfaced Vulture *Torgos tracheliotus* (124) L 100 cm

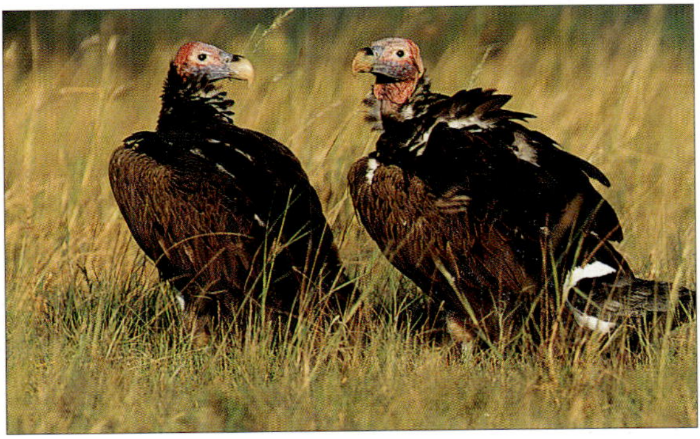

ABPL/NIGEL J DENNIS

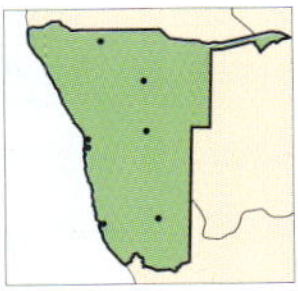

This, the most common vulture in the Namib Desert, has a diagnostic *bare, red-skinned face and throat*. It is identified in flight by the white thighs and white bar running along the forepart of the underwing. Immatures are dark brown all over. High-pitched whistles can be heard during display. It nests on treetops, solitarily or in small scattered colonies. It is found in thornveld, showing a preference for drier regions, but is rare outside major game reserves.

Black Kite *Milvus migrans* (126a) L 56 cm

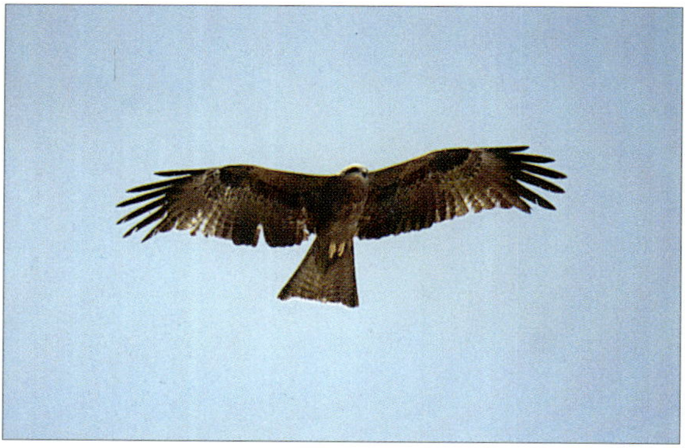

IAN DAVIDSON

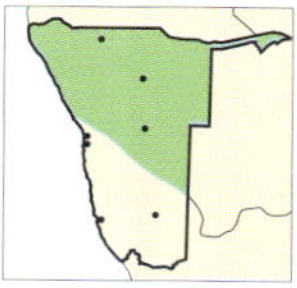

It differs from the very similar Yellowbilled Kite by its *grey-headed appearance, less deeply forked tail and the much smaller bill which is black* with a small yellow cere. The immature has buffy feather margins and is not separable from the immature Yellowbilled Kite. It emits a high-pitched, shrill, whinnying call. It is a common late-summer visitor, sometimes in mixed flocks of Yellowbilled Kites, falcons and eagles. Its diverse habitats include forest edges, savanna and semi-desert.

Yellowbilled Kite *Milvus parasitus* (126b) L 56 cm

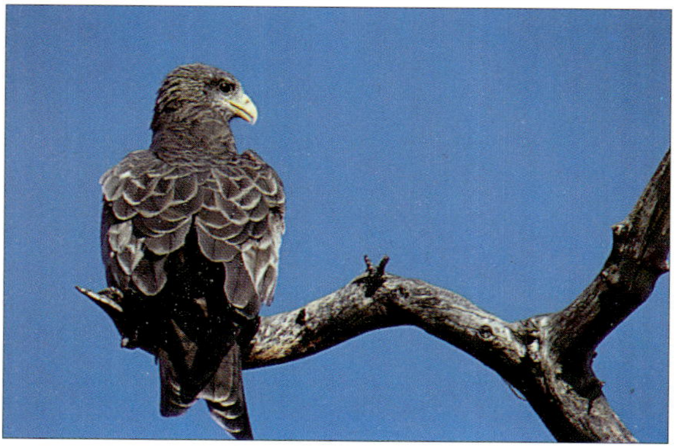

PETER CRAIG-COOPER

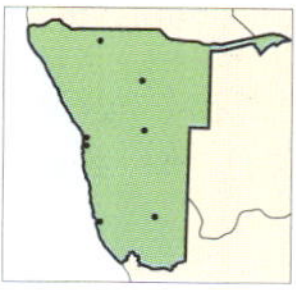

This kite is often seen patrolling roads, and frequents towns and cities. It differs from the Black Kite by having a *bright yellow bill and a more deeply forked tail*. It can be distinguished from other birds of prey by its forked tail which it twists in flight, from the horizontal to the near vertical, as it manoeuvres through the air. The immature has buffy feather margins and is not readily distinguished from the immature Black Kite. Its call is a whinnying 'kleeeuw' trill.

Blackshouldered Kite *Elanus caeruleus* (127) L 33 cm

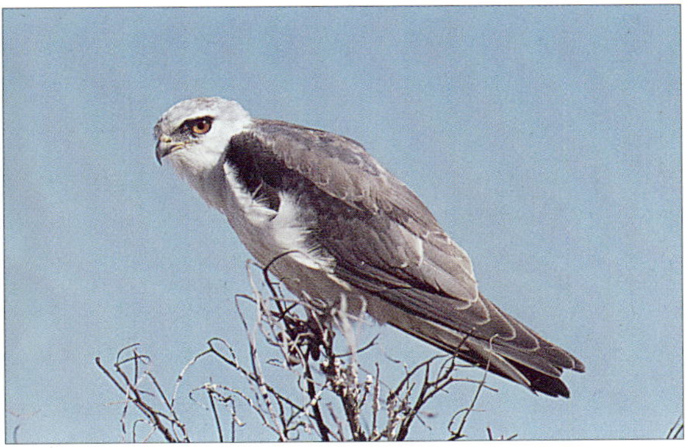

T D LONGRIGG

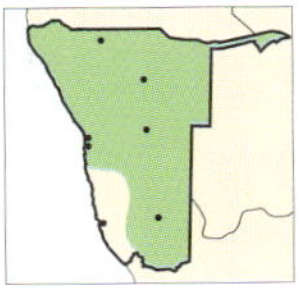

This is a small, conspicuous grey and white raptor with a diagnostic *black shoulder patch and a deep cherry-red eye*. It is commonly seen hovering, or sitting on telephone poles flicking its white tail up and down. The immature is more buffy than the adult, with a brown and buff barred back. It emits high-pitched whistles and harsher 'kek-kek-kek' sounds. Common in all but extreme desert areas, from mountainous regions to open thornveld, it is also often seen in agricultural lands.

Verreaux's Eagle *Aquila verreauxii* (131) L 75-95 cm

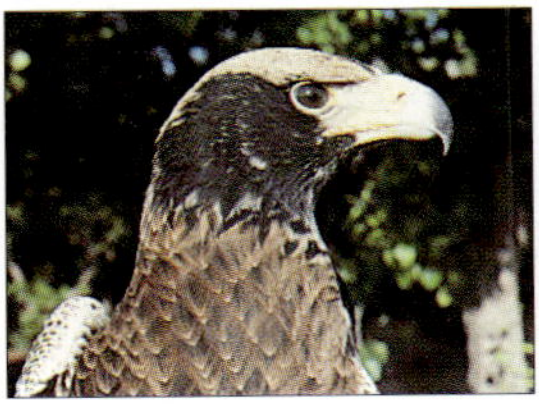

J VAN JAARSVELD

Immature

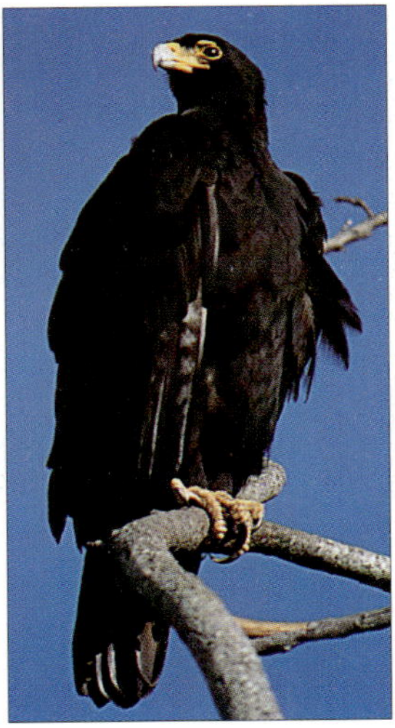

J C PATERSON-JONES

Adult

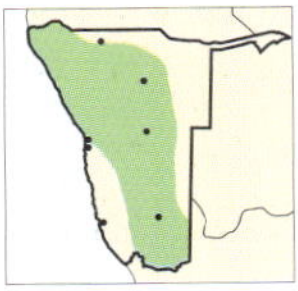

This eagle is unmistakable with its *diagnostic white 'V' on the mantle, and a white back*. The sexes are alike, but the female is larger and more extensively white on the back. The in-flight wing shape is narrower at the base, broadening out at the central secondaries. The immature has a diagnostic rufous crown and nape, contrasting with a darker face and throat. It prefers mountainous and rocky regions frequented by its major prey, dassies.

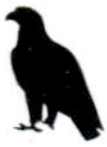

Tawny Eagle *Aquila rapax* (132) L 65-80 cm

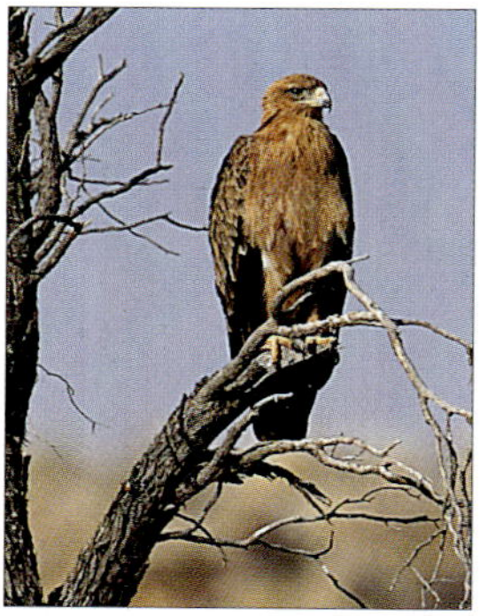

ABPL/NIGEL J DENNIS

Dark form

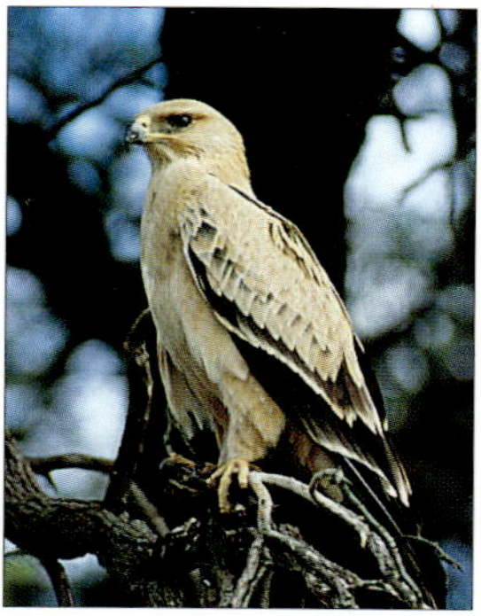

PETER CRAIG-COOPER

Pale form

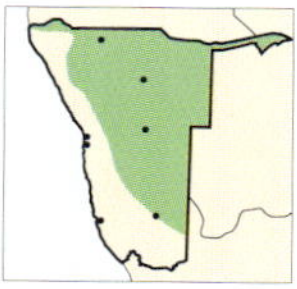

At close range this eagle has a *diagnostic yellow gape, extending to below the middle of the pale eye*. The *unbarred to faintly barred tail* is also diagnostic in this species. The plumage is variable in colour, ranging from streaked dark brown to pale buff. The female is usually darker than the male. The immature is rufous brown, fading to buff as it develops into a sub-adult. It seldom calls, except for a sharp 'kyow' bark. It is found in thornveld and semi-desert.

African Hawk Eagle *Hieraaetus fasciatus* (137) L 66-74 cm

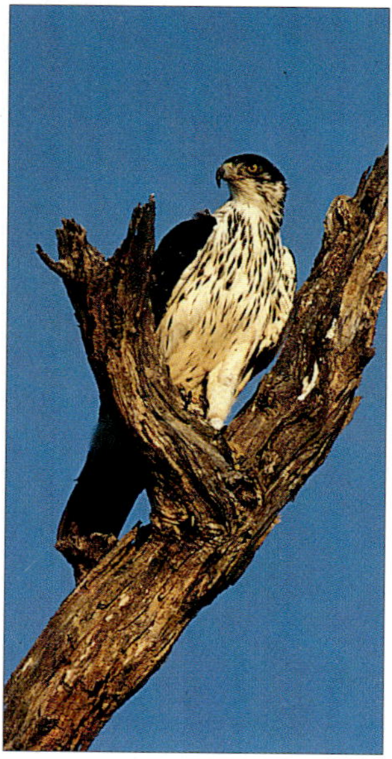

ABPL/LORNA STANTON

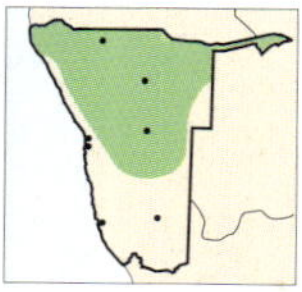

It is easily identified in flight by its *mainly white underwing with black edgings to the wing linings and dark brown upperwing with white panels at the base of the primaries*. Immatures are russet below, lightly streaked with black, and also show mainly white underwing character. During courtship a musical 'klee-klee-klee' call is given. Characteristically found in pairs, they often hunt and perch together. It frequents open thornveld, woodland and savanna in hilly, rugged country. It is common but thinly distributed, and mostly absent from the south.

Martial Eagle *Polemaetus bellicosus* (140) L 78-83 cm

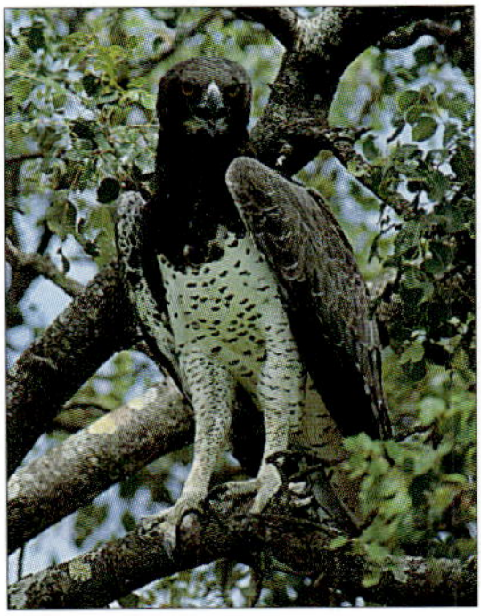

K S BEGG

Adult

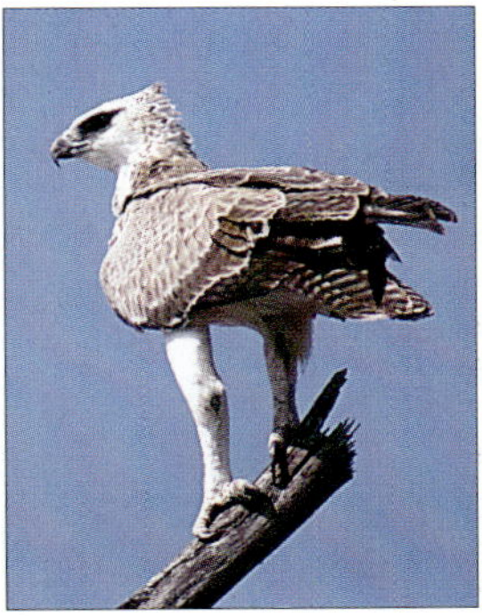

ALAN WEAVING

Immature

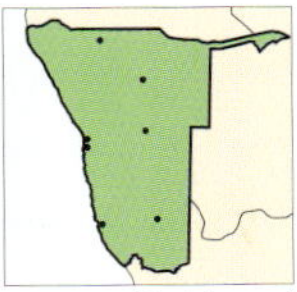

This huge bird has a diagnostic *dark head, throat and upper breast, combined with a white, lightly spotted breast and belly, and a very dark underwing*. Immatures have white 'trousers' and uniform underwings. During display the call is a rapid 'klooee-klooee-klooee'. Uncommon throughout the region, the Martial Eagle frequents a wide range of habitats, including savannah, forest edge and deserts, but is not found in extreme desert areas.

Blackbreasted Snake Eagle *Circaetus gallicus* (143) L 63-68 cm

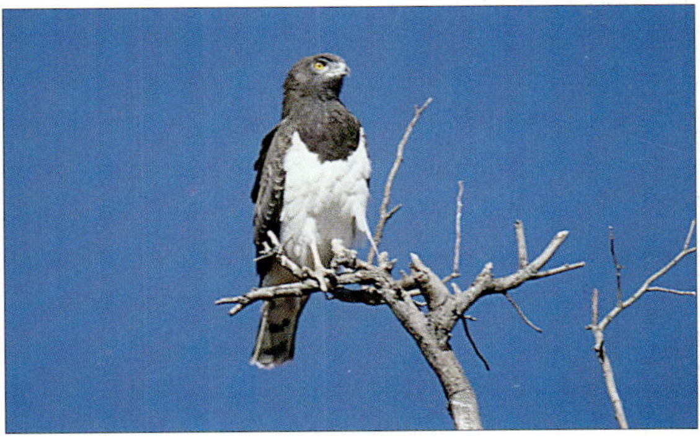

IAN DAVIDSON

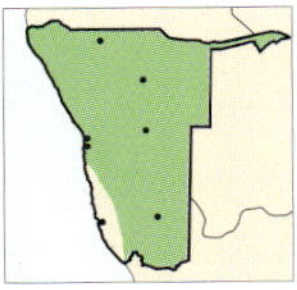

In flight this medium-sized raptor can easily be identified by its *white body and underwings, with its primaries and secondaries barred black, and its dark brown head and upper breast*. At rest it appears unusually large-headed, with huge, bright yellow eyes. The immature is a rich rufous colour with barred flight feathers and a uniform dark brown tail. It lacks the Martial Eagle's black spots on the lower breast and belly. Its call, a high-pitched 'kwo-kwo-kwo-kweeu', is seldom heard. It occurs commonly in habitats ranging from desert to savanna.

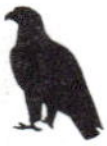

Bateleur *Terathopius ecaudatus* (146) L 55-70 cm

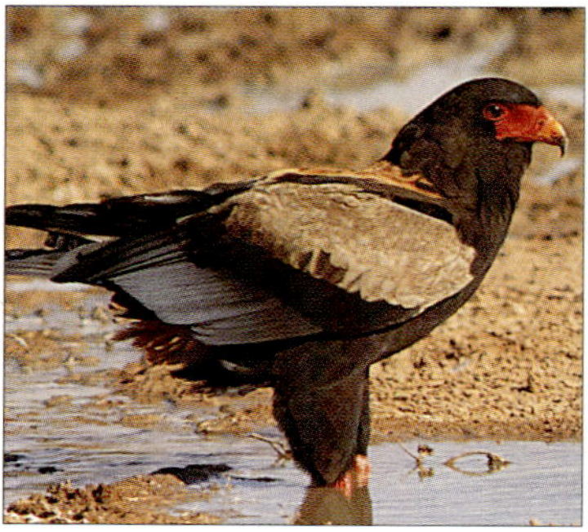

HEIN VON HÖRSTEN

Adult

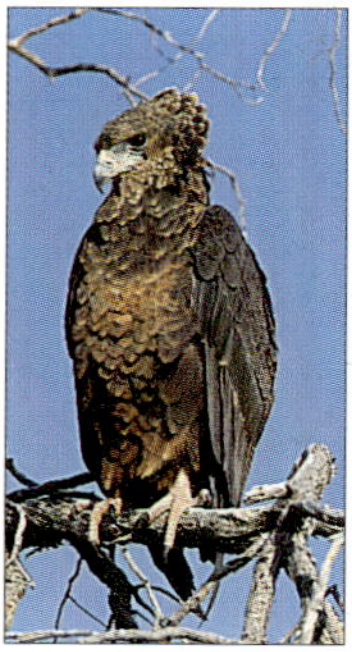

NIGEL J DENNIS

Immature

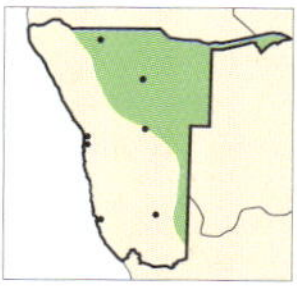

This is the most easily identified eagle of the region which, *in flight, appears to have virtually no tail*. With its long wings held slightly angled, and wings rarely flapping, it flies direct, canting from side to side. The *black, white and chestnut plumage,* combined with *long wings and a short tail,* render this bird unmistakable. The male has a broader black trailing edge to the wing than the female. The immature is a brown version of the adult with a slightly longer tail. Its call is a loud 'kow-wah' bark. It is found over open thornveld and semi-desert.

Steppe Buzzard *Buteo buteo* (149) L 45-50 cm

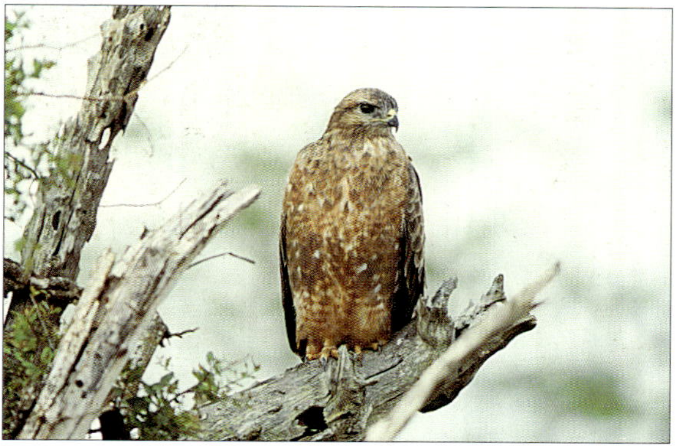

W R TARBOTON

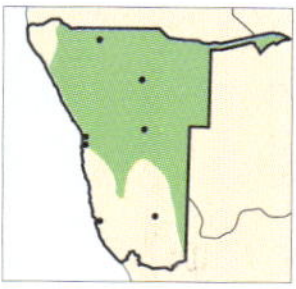

It is easily confused with many similar raptors in the region but most individuals show a *pale broad crescent across the breast*. Plumage coloration varies from pale brown to almost black. The immature is similar to the adult, but has yellow, not brown, eyes, and a narrower terminal tail bar. The call is a gull-like 'pee-ooo'. It is a common summer visitor, found in open country and seen perched on telephone poles along roads. It avoids deserts and well-wooded regions.

Augur Buzzard *Buteo augur* (153) L 45-53 cm

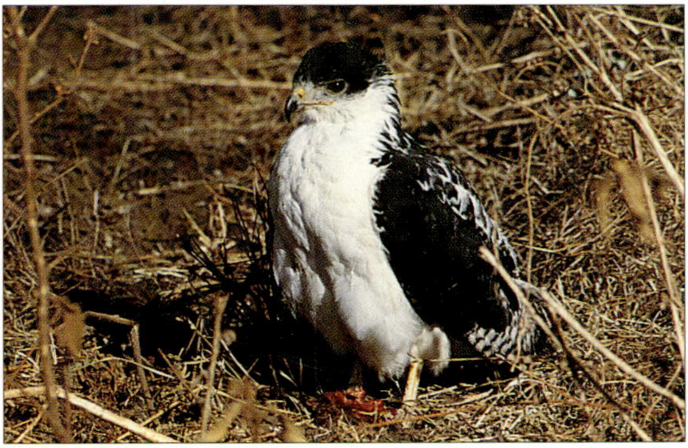

ABPL/BRENDAN RYAN

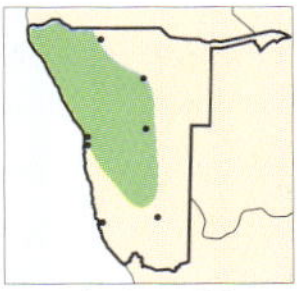

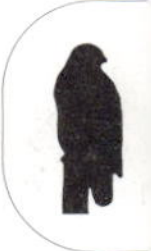

This buzzard differs from other buzzards by having a *white throat, breast and belly, and white wing linings*. The bill is black, and the cere, legs and feet are yellow. The female has black on the lower throat. Immatures are brown above and buffy below with darker brown streaking. The call is a harsh 'kow-kow-kow', given during display. It is commonly found in mountain ranges and hilly country in woodland, savanna and desert. It is also found to sea level in arid coastal Namibia.

Little Sparrowhawk *Accipiter minullus* (157) L 23-25 cm

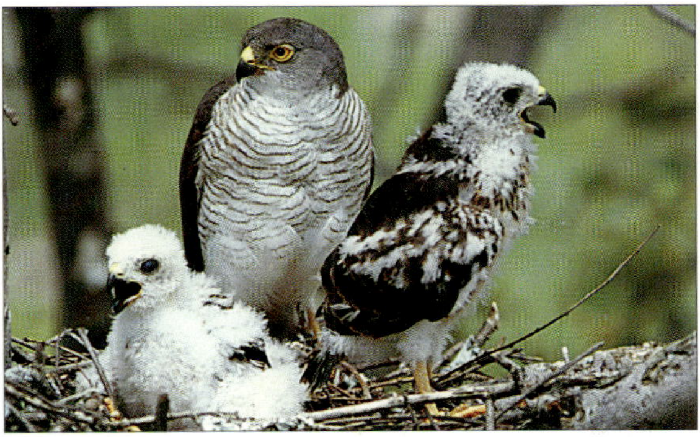

ABPL/CLEM HAAGNER

Adults and young

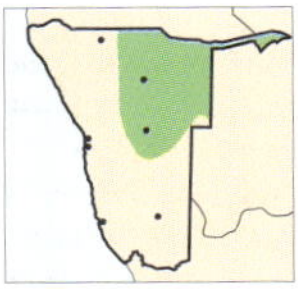

This is a tiny hawk with *a white rump and two white spots on its dark uppertail*. In flight the broad rounded wings and long tail are visible. The immature is brown above and has pear-shaped spots on its breast. During the breeding season the male utters a high-pitched 'keewik-keewik-keewik' call; the female has a softer 'kew-kew-kew' call. It prefers open woodland and has adapted to exotic plantations. It is absent from the drier regions but more common in the north.

Little Banded Goshawk *Accipiter badius* (159) L 28-30 cm

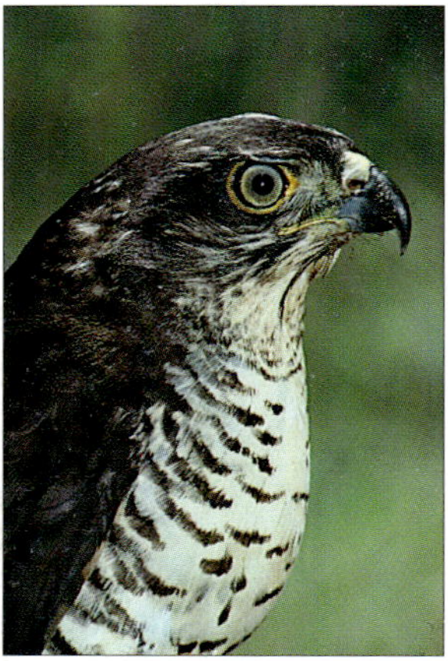

PETER CRAIG-COOPER

Immature

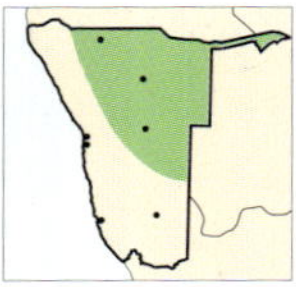

The Little Banded Goshawk differs from the Little Sparrowhawk by lacking the white rump and tail spots. It is distinguished by its *rufous barring below, cherry-red eye and yellow legs*. The immature is brown with a streaked breast and a barred belly. It avoids dense, evergreen forests and extremely dry regions. The male's call is a high-pitched 'keewik-keewik-keewik' and the female's call is a softer 'kee-uuu'. It is common in bushveld areas.

Gabar Goshawk *Micronisus gabar* (161) L 30-34 cm

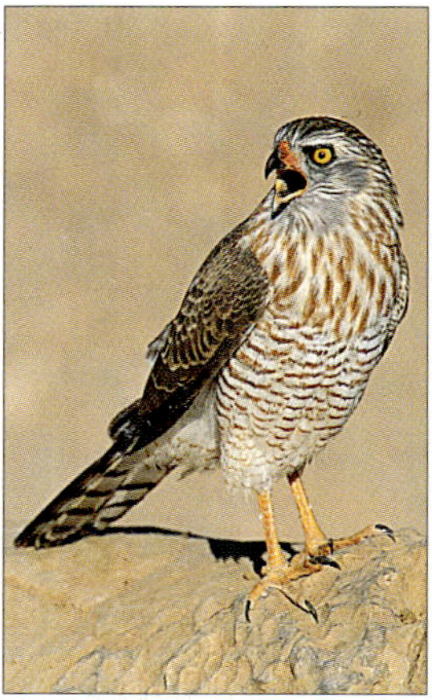

ABPL/NIGEL J DENNIS

Immature

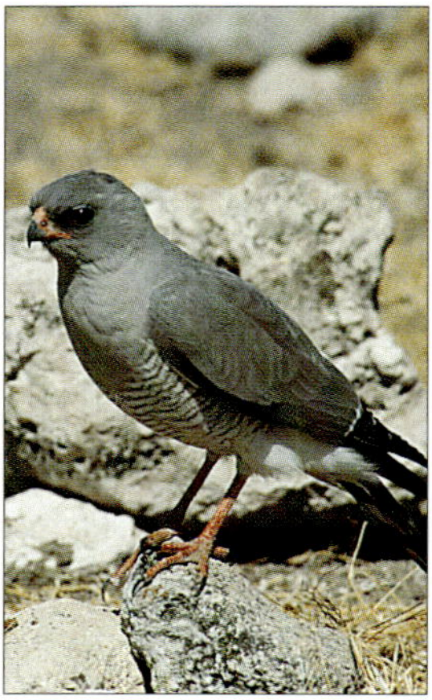

PETER CRAIG-COOPER

Adult

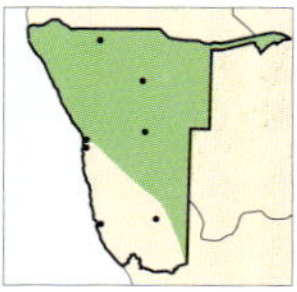

This goshawk, in its common grey form, is distinguished by its *white rump, grey throat and breast, and red eyes, cere and legs*. The uncommon black form can be identified by its red cere and legs. The immature has a rufous-streaked and mottled head and breast but also shows the white rump. It frequents savanna, especially thornveld and semi-arid habitats. The call is a high-pitched 'kik-kik-kik-kik-kik', given in display, but the bird is usually silent. It perches in the canopy, flying quickly from one tree to the next; it seldom soars. It is the most frequently seen small accipiter in the region.

Pale Chanting Goshawk *Melierax canorus* (162) L 54-63 cm

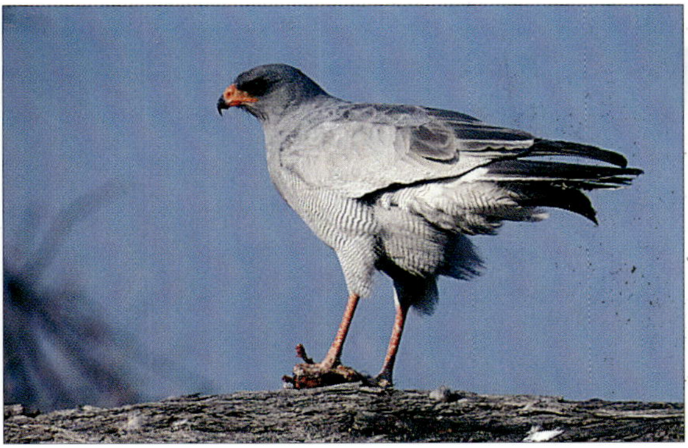

PETER CRAIG-COOPER

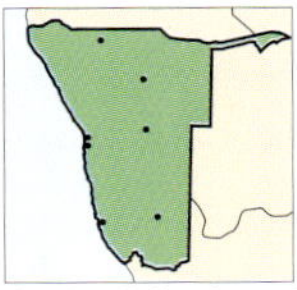

This species is much larger than the Gabar Goshawk and has proportionately longer legs. *In flight the upperparts show a white rump and white secondaries.* The adult is light grey above, but paler on the wing coverts. The immature is dark brown above and streaked and blotched with brown below. A chanting 'kleeuu-kleeuu-klu-klu-klu' call is given during the breeding season. It is the hawk commonly seen along roadsides in Namibia, from the drier areas to the bushveld.

Lanner Falcon *Falco biarmicus* (172) L 40-45 cm

PETER CRAIG-COOPER

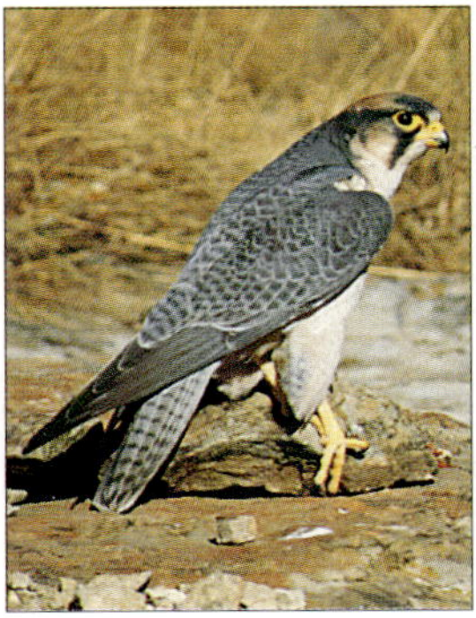

Adult

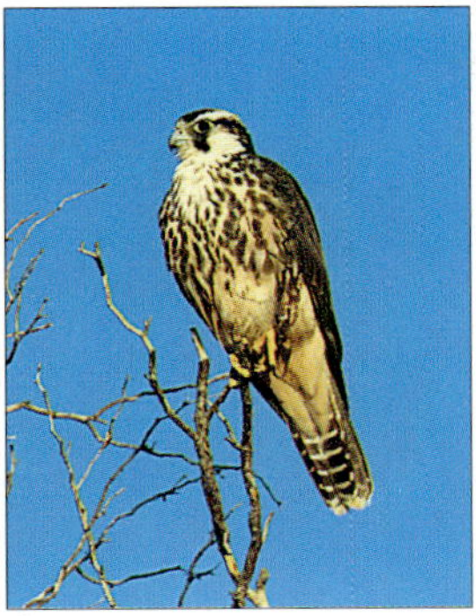

ABPL/NIGEL J DENNIS

Immature

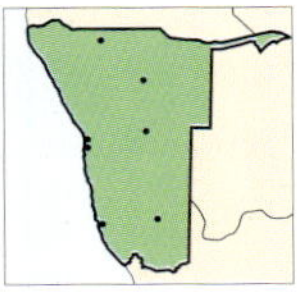

It is a medium-sized falcon with a *rufous forehead and crown, thin moustachial stripe and unmarked, pinkish breast.* In flight it shows relatively broad wings, rounded at the base and narrowing into points. The tail is longer, giving it a floppier flight action than that of smaller falcons. The immature has a buffy streaked crown and heavily streaked underparts. Its call is a harsh 'kak-kak-kak-kak-kak'. It is common in most areas, especially in the vicinity of water holes in game reserves.

European (Eurasion) Hobby *Falco subbuteo* (173) L 28-35 cm

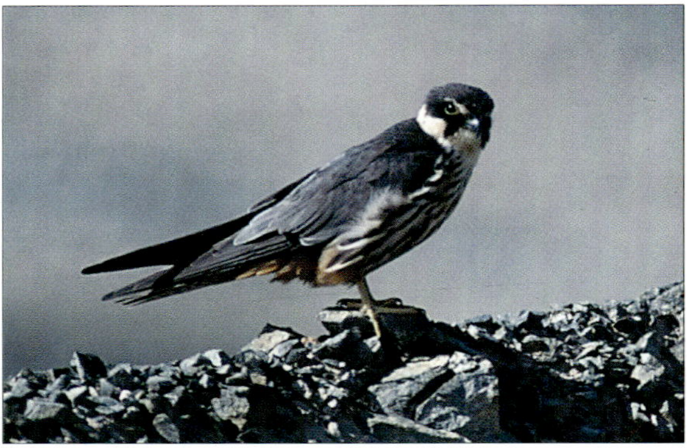
AQUILA/CONRAD GREAVES

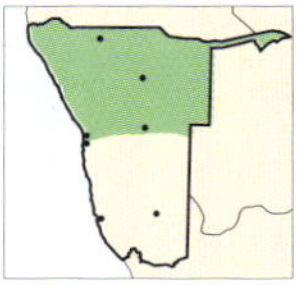

In flight the long, pointed wings and relatively short tail give this species a swift-like appearance. The *black head and moustachial stripe contrast boldly with the white throat.* It has a heavily streaked breast with conspicuous rufous leggings and vent. Immatures lack the rufous leggings and vent. It is silent in this region. It is found in open, broad-leafed woodland savanna and is mostly an uncommon, but sometimes common, summer visitor, chiefly in the north.

Rednecked Falcon *Falco chicquera* (178) L 30-36 cm

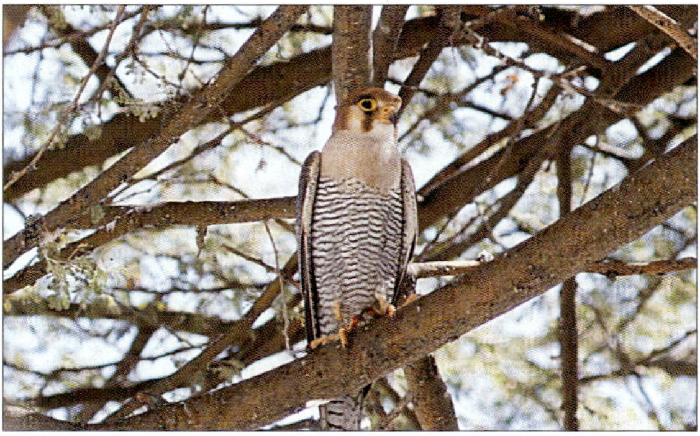
IAN DAVIDSON

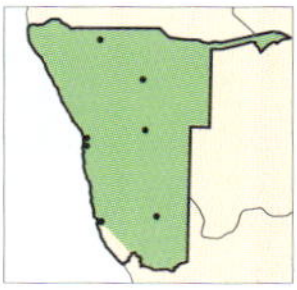

Small but unmistakable with a *chestnut crown and nape, dark brown moustachial stripes on its white cheeks,* and blue-grey upperparts with fine black barring on them. The grey tail is tipped with a broad black band; the white underparts are finely barred black and the breast has a rufous wash across it. Immatures have a dark brown head, two buff patches on the nape, and pale rufous underparts finely barred with brown. Its breeding call is a shrill 'ki-ki-ki-ki'. It occurs in palm savanna and arid thornveld, and is common but thinly distributed in Namibia.

Greater Kestrel *Falco rupicoloides* (182) L 36-40 cm

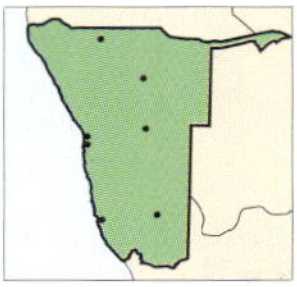

At close range the diagnostic *whitish eye* is obvious. It is larger and paler brown than the Rock Kestrel with a whitish underwing, a grey barred tail and a paler head without moustachial stripes. The immature has a rufous barred tail and a dark eye. Although usually silent, during display a shrill, repeated 'kee-ker-rik' is given. It perches on telephone poles, fences, dead trees or low rocks, hunting from its perch. It is found throughout the drier regions, including the desert, as well as in more open bushveld.

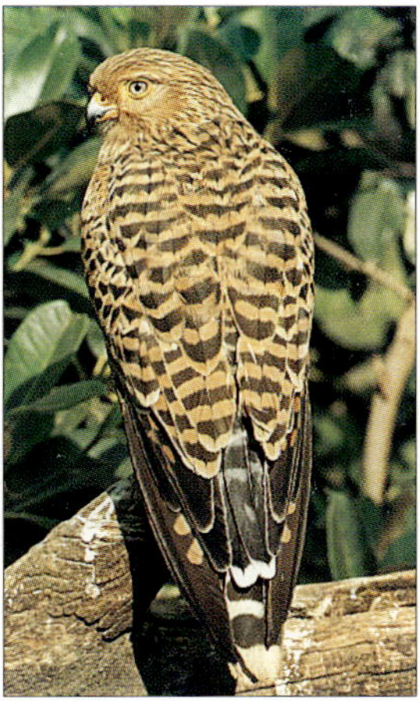

RAYMONDE JOHANNESSON

Rock (Common) Kestrel *Falco tinnunculus* (181) L 33-39 cm

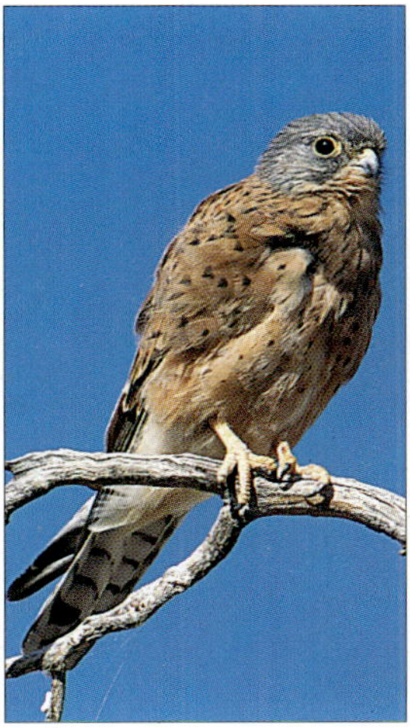

NIGEL J DENNIS

Male

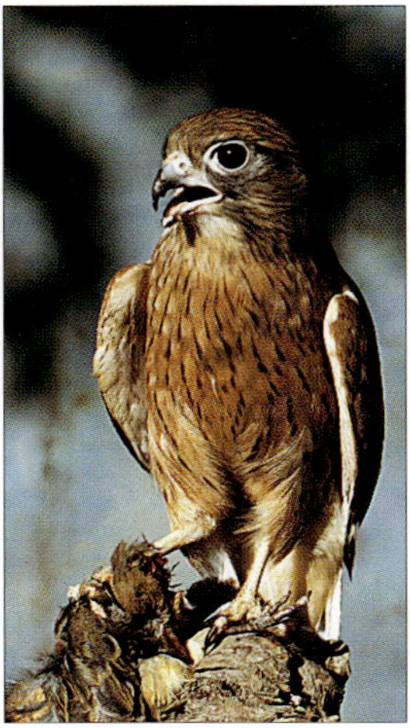

ROY JOHANNESSON

Female

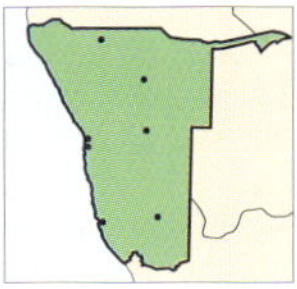

The *male* Common Rock Kestrel *has a spotted chestnut back and wings, with a spotted and barred underwing*. The *female has narrow bands on the tail* which the male lacks. Both sexes have a *grey head*. The immature lacks blue-grey on the head and the tail. This bird has a high-pitched 'kik-kik-kik-kik' call. It occurs in a diverse range of habitats but is usually seen in mountainous, rocky terrain. It is common but thinly distributed throughout Namibia.

Pygmy Falcon *Polihierax semitorquatus* (186) L 18-20 cm

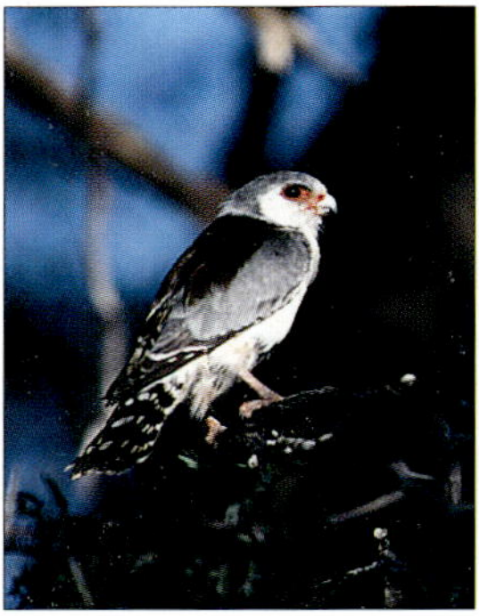

ABPL/CLEM HAAGNER

Female

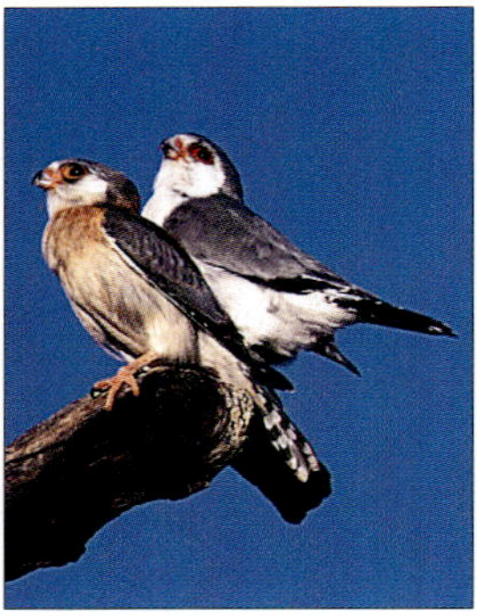

ABPL/LORNA STANTON

Male (front) and female (back)

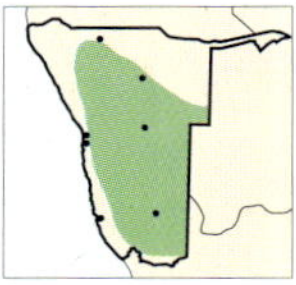

The distinctive feature of this falcon is its *very small size*. Shrike-like in appearance and manner, it sits very upright on an exposed perch and hawks insects and lizards. The upperparts of the male are grey and the underparts white. The female has a deep chestnut back. The white rump is conspicuous in flight. The immature is similar to the female but has a dull brown back. Its call is a noisy 'chip-chip' and 'kik-kik-kik-kik'. It occurs in dry thornveld and semi-desert regions.

Orange River Francolin *Francolinus levaillantoides* (193) L 35 cm

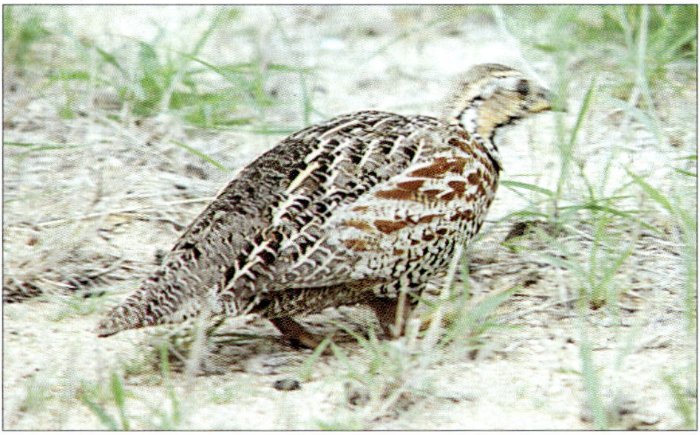

TRANSVAAL MUSEUM

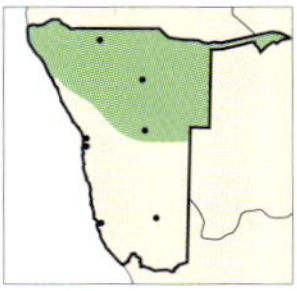

In Namibia this species may be confused with only the smaller Hartlaub's Francolin but it differs by having *dark stripes on the head with deep red spotting and stripes on the breast and underparts*. In flight it shows chestnut primaries. Immatures resemble the adults. The call is a distinctive, melodious, oft-repeated 'kibitele', usually given at dawn. It frequents grassy and bush-covered hillsides and gullies and is common in the central and northern areas of the region.

Redbilled Francolin *Francolinus adspersus* (194) L 35-38 cm

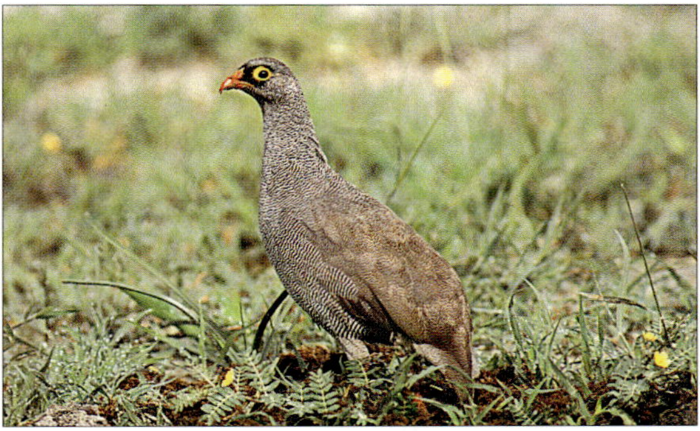

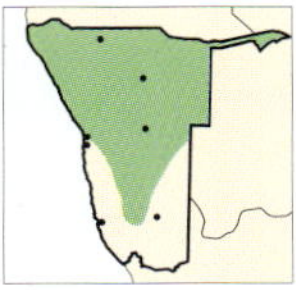

This is a dark francolin with a diagnostic *yellow eye-ring, and a dull red bill and legs.* It differs from other dark francolins by being more uniform in colour and slightly paler below, and by lacking any streaking or blotching. Immatures lack the yellow eye-ring. It has a loud, harsh 'chaa-chaa-chek-chek' call. It is found in dry thornveld and open broad-leafed woodland and wooded river beds in the desert. Less shy than other francolins, it is often seen feeding in the open.

Hartlaub's Francolin *Francolinus hartlaubi* (197) L 26 cm

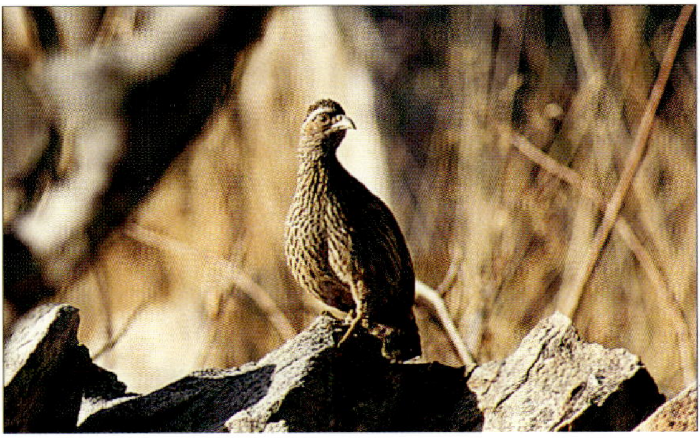

Male

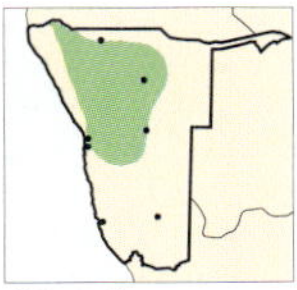

This is the smallest francolin in the region and is near-endemic to Namibia. The *dark cap and contrasting white eyebrow is distinctive in the male. It has a large decurved bill and pale underparts heavily streaked with brown.* The female and immature are dull brown, lacking any other distinguishing features. Its alarm call is a 'wak-ak-ak-ak'. It frequents rocky outcrops in hilly and mountainous regions, and is uncommon to common in some areas.

Helmeted Guineafowl *Numida meleagris* (203) L 56 cm

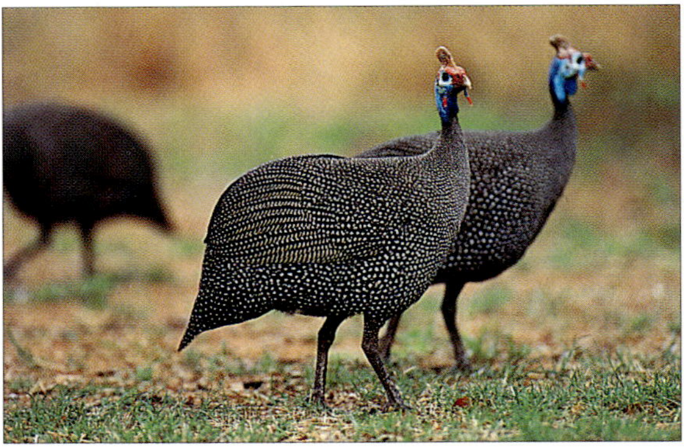

W R TARBOTON

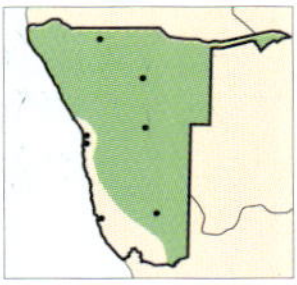

This is a familiar gamebird, easily distinguished by its *rotund grey body flecked with white, and naked blue and red head with a bare crown casque*. The male's casque is longer than that of the female. The immature has a less developed casque, and browner body coloration with the white flecking enlarged on the neck. It emits a loud 'krrdi-krrdi-krrdi-krrdi' call and a 'kek-kek-kek-kek' alarm note. It is common throughout the region but absent from extreme desert areas.

Namaqua Sandgrouse *Pterocles namaqua* (344) L 25 cm

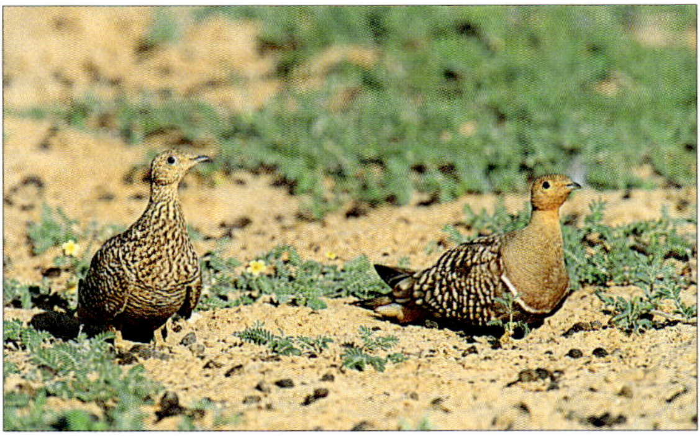

ABPL/NIGEL J DENNIS

Female (left) and male (right)

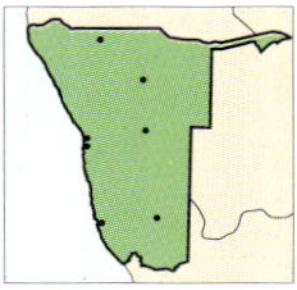

This is the only sandgrouse in the region with a *long pointed tail*. The male has a buff-spotted back and a white and chestnut breast band. The female is cryptically mottled and streaked with buff and brown. The immature is similar to the immature Doublebanded Sandgrouse but is more buffy yellow on the throat and breast and shows the pointed tail. In flight it gives a nasal 'kalke-ven' call, revealing its presence. It is common in grasslands, desert and semi-desert.

Burchell's Sandgrouse *Pterocles burchelli* (345) L 25 cm

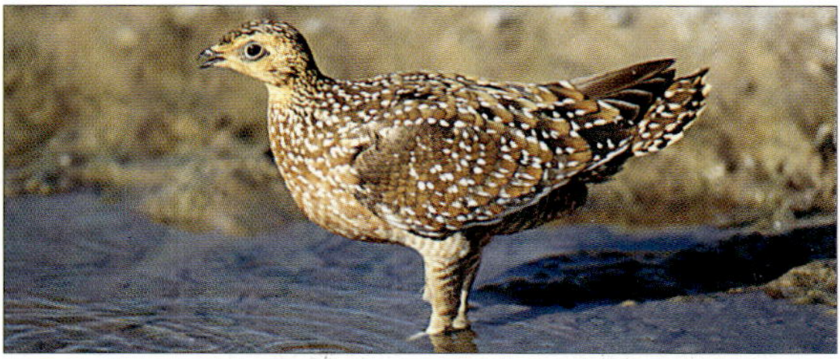

ALAN WEAVING

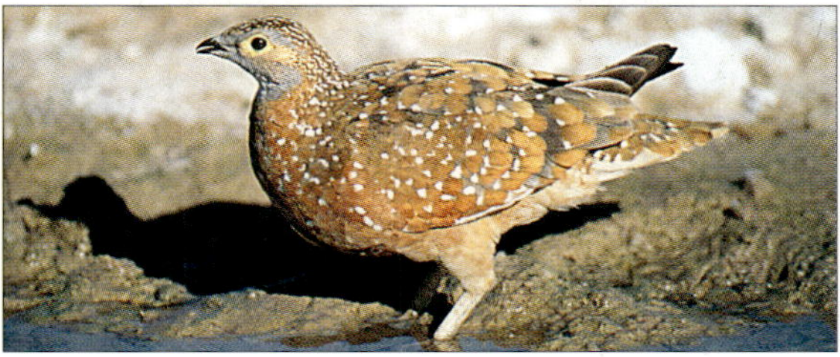

ALAN WEAVING

Above: female. Below: male

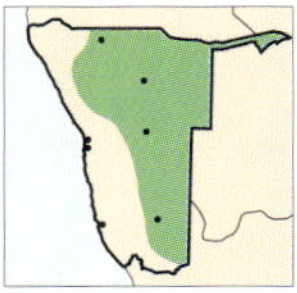

This small sandgrouse is easily identified by the combination of its *white-spotted cinnamon breast and belly, and its white-spotted back and wing coverts*. The female and the immature resemble the male but lack the blue-grey throat and are duller in colour. The call is a soft, mellow 'chup-chup, choop-choop', given in flight and around water holes, which are visited mid-mornings. It occurs in lightly wooded, dry areas and grass-covered sand dunes.

Doublebanded Sandgrouse *Pterocles bicinctus* (347) L 25 cm

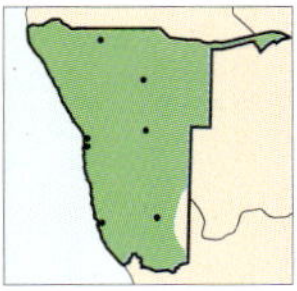

Similar to the Namaqua Sandgrouse, the *male of this species can easily be identified by its thin, black and white breast-band and the black and white markings on its head. The female and immature are distinguished by having a darker streaked crown, barred upper breast and a round tail*. It has a soft, whistling 'chwee-chee-chee' call. It frequents woodland and savanna areas. Flocks of Doublebanded Sandgrouse tend to gather at water holes just after sunset, sometimes in large numbers.

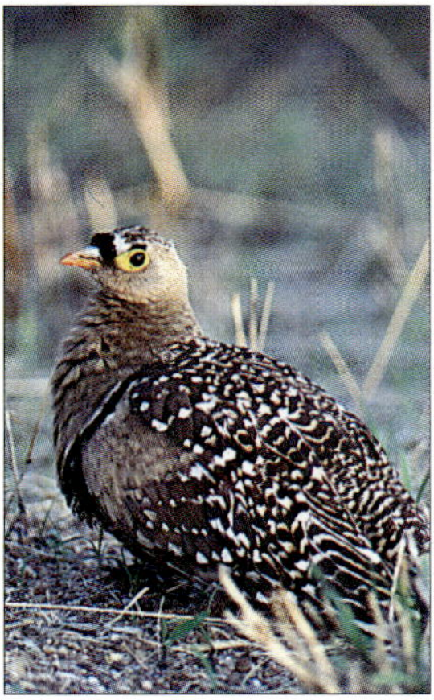

PETER PICKFORD

Black Crake *Amaurornis flavirostris* (213) L 20 cm

ABPL/CLEM HAAGNER

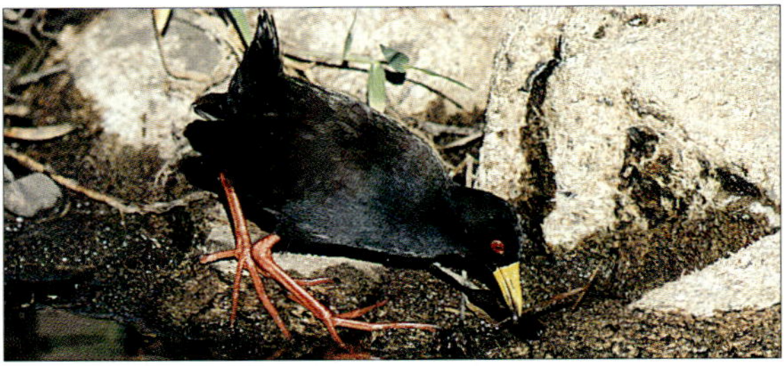

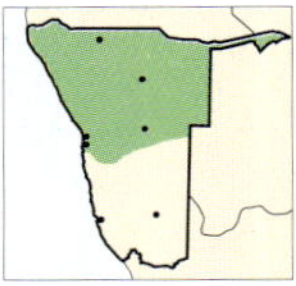

This is a small, furtive, *jet-black bird with a bright yellow bill, and red eyes and legs*. In the breeding adult the legs and feet are a brighter red. Immatures are greyish brown and have a black bill and dull red legs. Throaty 'chrrooo' and rippling trills are often heard. It occurs in marshes and swamps with a thick cover of reeds and other aquatic vegetation. It is more likely to venture from cover into the open at dawn or dusk, and is common on permanent wetlands in the north.

Common Moorhen *Gallinula chloropus* (226) L 32 cm

NIGEL J. DENNIS

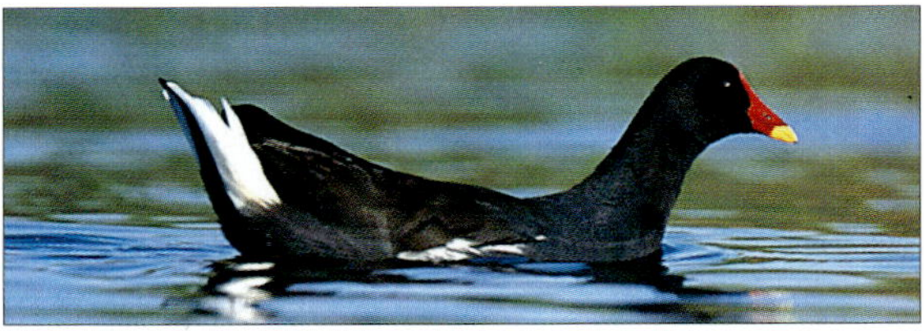

T D LONGRIGG

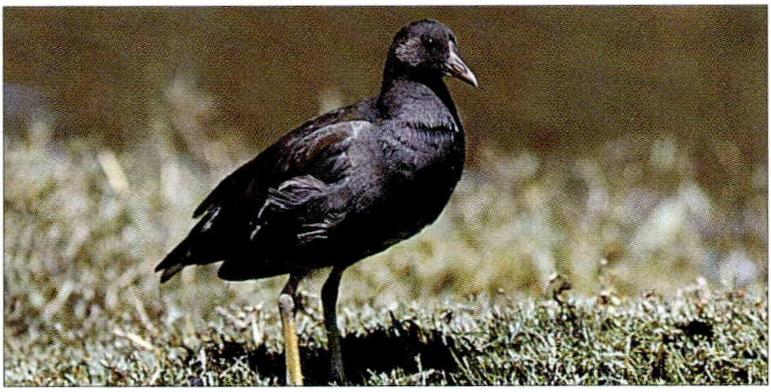

Above: adult. Below: immature

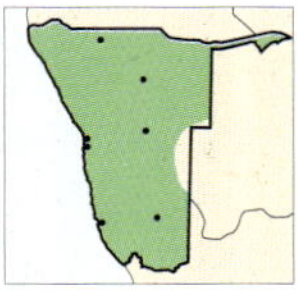

This bird is a *dull sooty black with green legs, a red frontal shield and a yellow tip to the bill*. The immature is a greyish brown version of the adult. Its call is a sharp 'krrik'. It swims freely on virtually any stretch of freshwater surrounded by a thick cover of reeds and grass. It is common in freshwater areas, both coastal and inland.

Redknobbed Coot *Fulica cristata* (228) L 44 cm

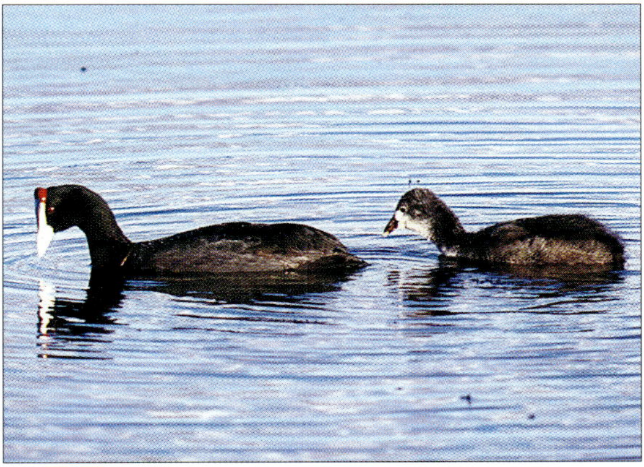

W R TARBOTON

Adult and young

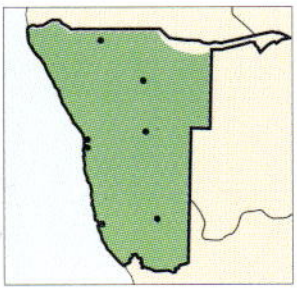

A medium-sized *matt black, duck-like bird with a white bill and a white unfeathered forehead.* It has two red knobs on the forehead which are more conspicuous in the breeding season. The immature is similar to the immature Common Moorhen but is dull brown and lacks white undertail coverts. Its call is a harsh, metallic 'claak'. It is found on virtually any stretch of freshwater, except in fast-flowing rivers. Common and nomadic in the area, it appears overnight at newly flooded areas.

Kori Bustard *Ardeotis kori* (230) L 135 cm

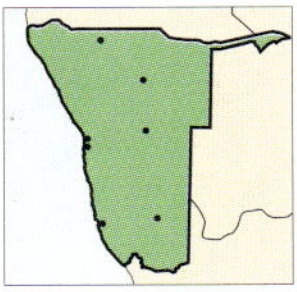

This heavy bird is *by far the largest bustard in the region.* Its *size and lack of any rufous on the hind neck and upper mantle, as well as long dark crest,* should rule out any confusion with regard to the much smaller Ludwig's Bustard also found in the region. It is reluctant to fly unless threatened. The female is similar to the male but noticeably smaller. The immature resembles the female. When displaying, the male emits a deep, resonant 'oom-oom-oom' call. It is usually found near the cover of trees in dry thornveld, grassland and semi-desert. It is common and conspicuous in Etosha.

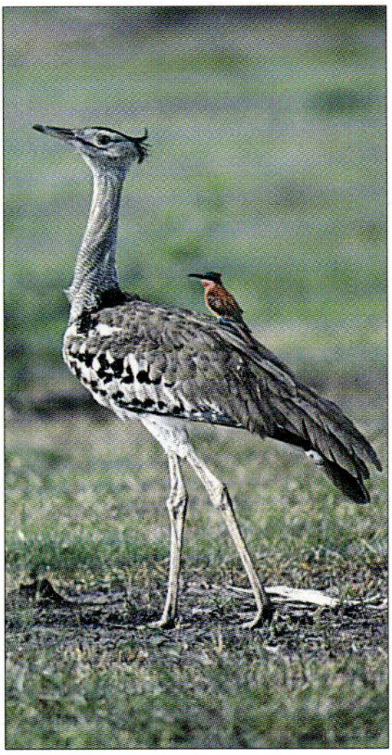

ABPL/CLEM HAAGNER

Ludwig's Bustard *Neotis ludwigii* (232) L 90 cm

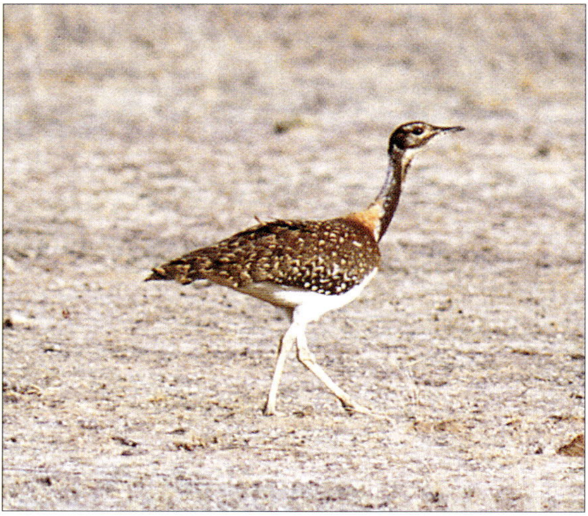

DR & MRS MANFRED REICHARDT

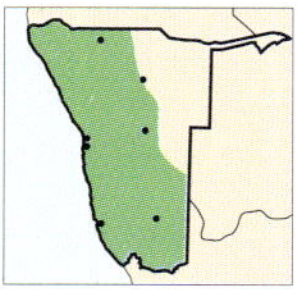

It is much smaller than the Kori Bustard and is readily distinguished by its *dark cap, throat and the front of the long neck*. The lower hindneck is deep russet. The female is noticeably smaller than the male. The displaying male inflates its throat, forming a conspicuous balloon of grey feathers. In flight it shows large expanses of white in the wings. It is uncommon and nomadic in Namibia, with populations moving from one region to another in response to rains.

Rüppell's Korhaan *Eupodotis rueppellii* (236) L 58 cm

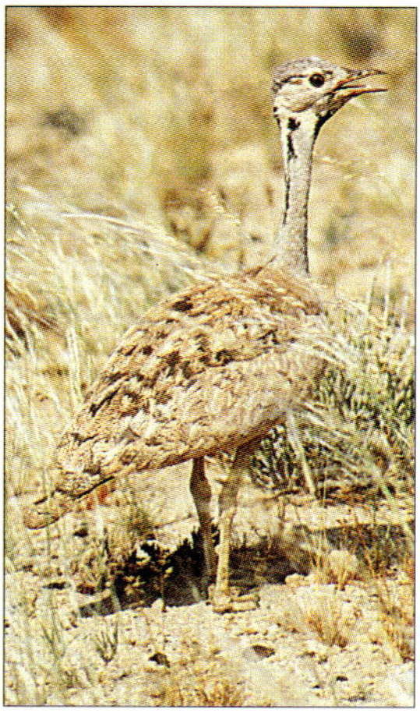

IAN SINCLAIR

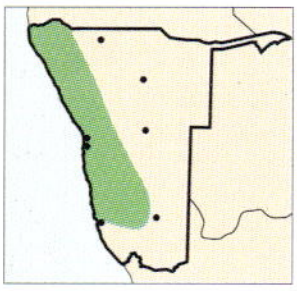

This bird is *pale pinkish-grey with a conspicuous black line running down the centre of the foreneck and extending onto the breast. It has contrasting black and white facial markings*. Immatures and females are not as boldly marked as the males, especially on the head and throat. Its call is a rasping, frog-like 'crrok-rrok-rrek', given at dawn and dusk. It occurs in Namibia where it is near-endemic to the Namib Desert. It is usually found in groups of two or three on gravel plains and in semi-scrub desert.

Redcrested Korhaan *Eupodotis ruficrista* (237) L 50 cm

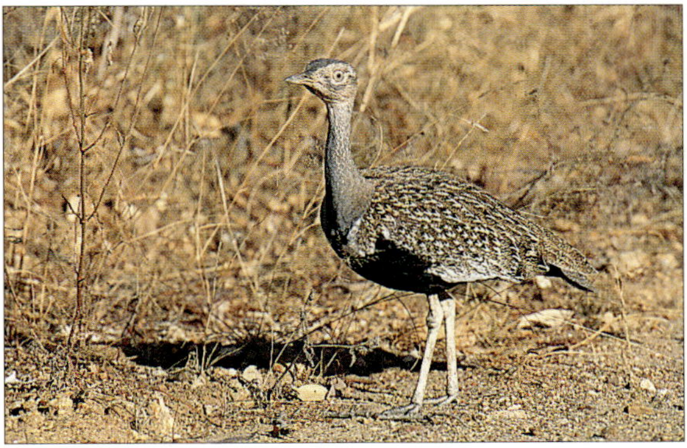

NIGEL J DENNIS

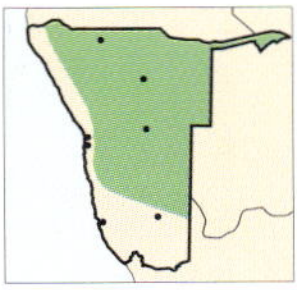

The erect, rufous crest is rarely seen unless a displaying male is observed. Both sexes have a *black belly, a thin neck, and chevron-shaped markings on the back*. The female bird has a mottled brown crown and neck. Immatures resemble the females. The male's call is a 'tic-tic-tic', finishing with a loud, whistling 'chew-chew-chew'. It is found in dry thornveld, thick bush and grassy areas adjoining thornveld. It is common in the bushveld areas of Namibia.

Northern Black Korhaan *Eupodotis afroides* (239b) L 52 cm

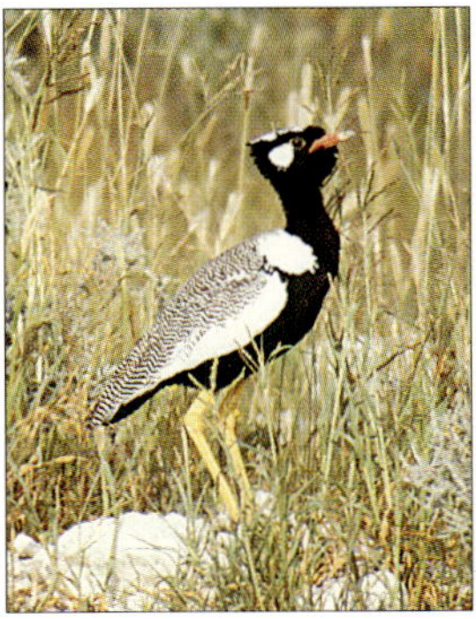

IAN SINCLAIR

Male

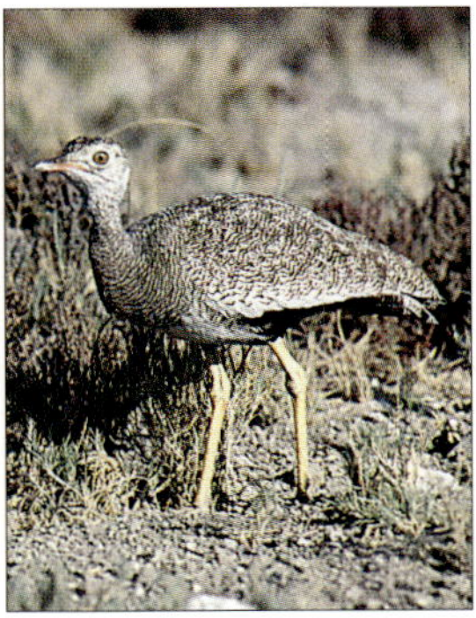

NIGEL J DENNIS

Female

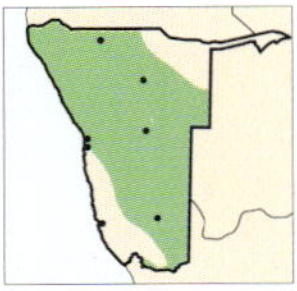

This bird can instantly be recognized by its *black head and body, brown barred upperparts and bright yellow legs*. In flight it shows white patches on the black primaries. The female resembles the Redcrested Korhaan but has a thicker neck, yellow, not olive, legs and obvious white wing patches in flight. In display flight, the male circles its territory, calling 'karrak, karrak, karrak'. It is common to abundant in some areas, especially open grassland and scrub, but absent from true desert.

African Jacana *Actophilornis africanus* (240) L 28 cm

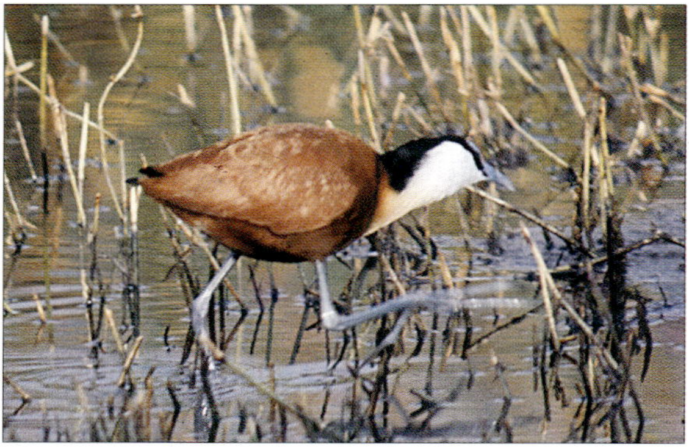

IAN SINCLAIR

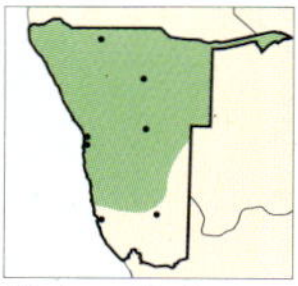

This is a *rufous bird with a darker belly, white neck and yellow upper breast*. The contrasting black and white head pattern highlights the *blue frontal shield and bill*. The very long toes and toenails allow the bird to walk over floating vegetation. Immatures are duller than adults and lack the frontal shield. Its call is a noisy, sharp, ringing 'krrrek' with a 'krrrrrk' flight call. It occurs in flooded grasslands and freshwater areas with floating vegetation, and is common in the moist regions of the north.

African Black Oystercatcher *Haematopus moquini* (244) L 44 cm

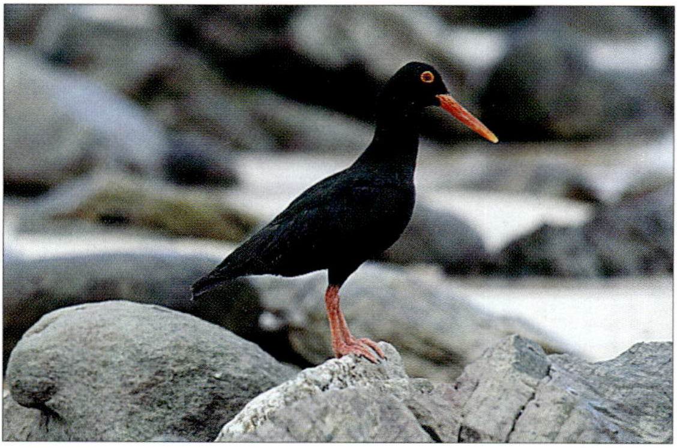

ALAN WEAVING

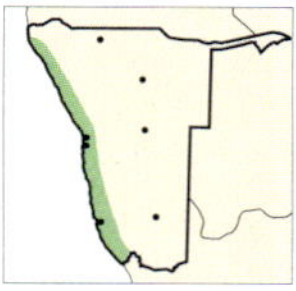

This *all-black, large wader* has an obvious *bright orange bill and eye-ring and dull pink legs*. Some adults have small white patches on the underparts, visible in flight. Adults have no wing markings. The immature is dowdier than the adult and has a less vivid orange bill which is tipped with brown. It has a 'klee-kleeep' call and a fast 'peeka-peeka-peeka' alarm call. Uncommon in Namibia, it is confined to the coastal regions of Walvis Bay, Swakopmund and offshore islands.

Common Ringed Plover *Charadrius hiaticula* (245) L 16 cm

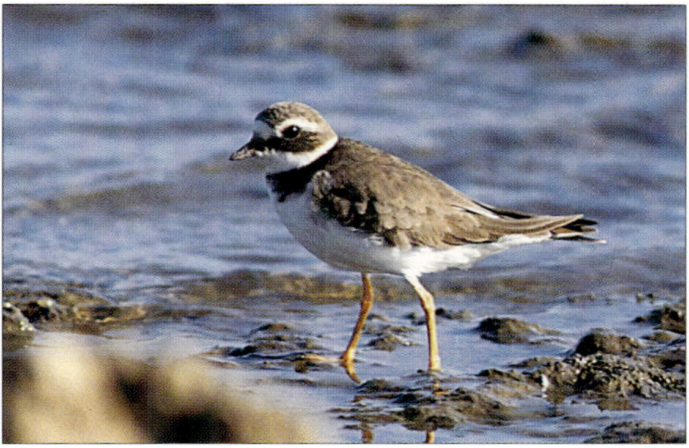

ALAN WEAVING

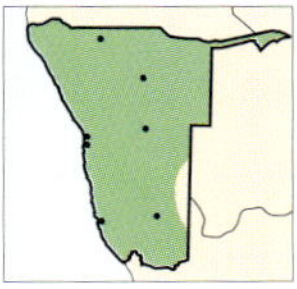

This is a *small, dark plover with short legs and a white collar above a blackish-brown breast band* which is often incomplete in non-breeding plumage. The legs are orange-yellow and the bill is usually orange at the base. In flight an obvious white wing bar can be seen. The immature has a duller plumage than the adult and its breast band is incomplete. The call is a fluty 'tooi'. It is found on coastal and inland wetlands, mainly during summer.

Whitefronted Plover *Charadrius marginatus* (246) L 18 cm

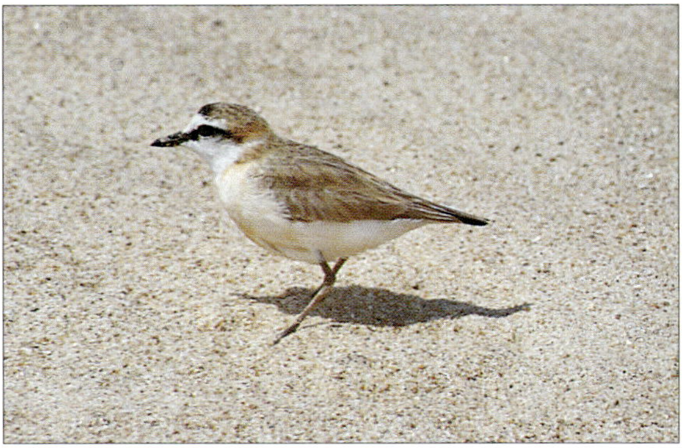

S M BLOOMFIELD

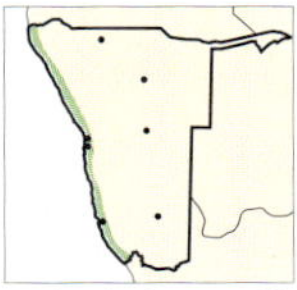

This is a small, very pale plover with a white collar and an incomplete breast band. It is paler than Kittlitz's Plover and lacks the black forehead markings but may have a thin black line through the eye and across the forehead. The immature lacks the dark markings on the head and is paler than the adult. It has a clear 'wiiit' call and a 'tukut' alarm call. It frequents sandy beaches and muddy coastal areas and is common along the Namibian coastal strip.

Chestnutbanded Plover *Charadrius pallidus* (247) L 15 cm

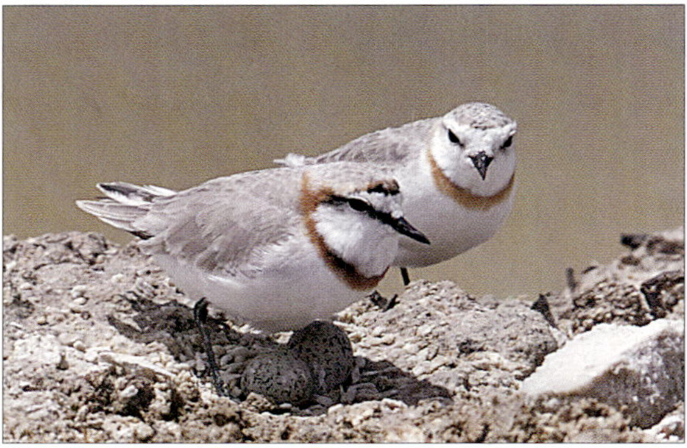

T D LONGRIGG

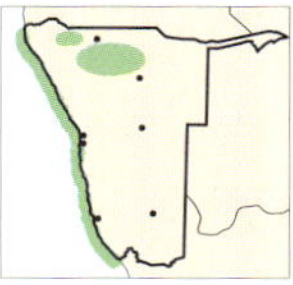

This is the smallest and palest plover in the region. The *thin chestnut breast band extends into a thin line on the crown in the male*. The male also has neat black markings on the forehead and lores. These markings are grey in the female. The immature has a duller, usually incomplete breast band and lacks the black and chestnut coloration. The call is a single 'tooit'. It frequents salt pans in summer; some birds move to estuaries and coastal wetlands in winter.

Kittlitz's Plover *Charadrius pecuarius* (248) L 16 cm

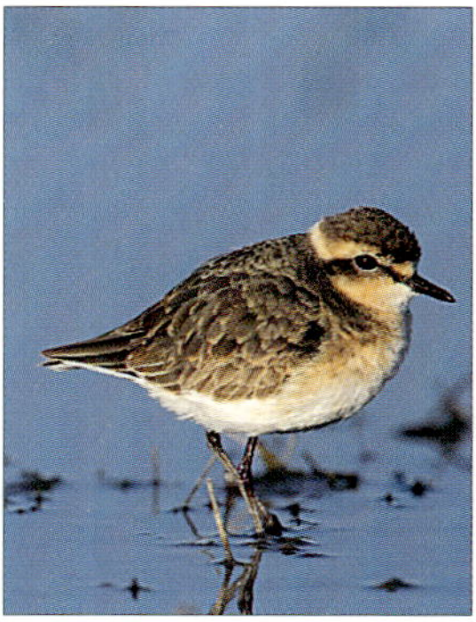

ABPL/NIGEL J DENNIS

Immature

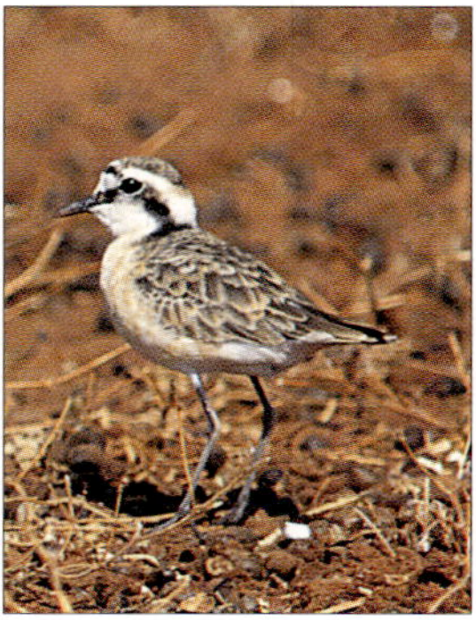

ABPL/BRENDAN RYAN

Adult

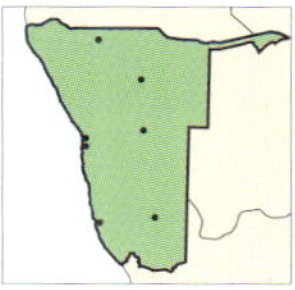

This small plover has a *black forehead line which extends behind the eye to the nape*. The head is less well marked in non-breeding plumage, with a pale buffy ring around the crown extending to the nape. The breast is creamy buff with a dark shoulder patch. The immature differs from the similar immature Whitefronted Plover by its buffy nape and dark shoulder. The call is a short, clipped 'kittip' trill. It is found on both coastal and inland wetlands and in dry, grassy areas.

Threebanded Plover *Charadrius tricollaris* (249) L 18 cm

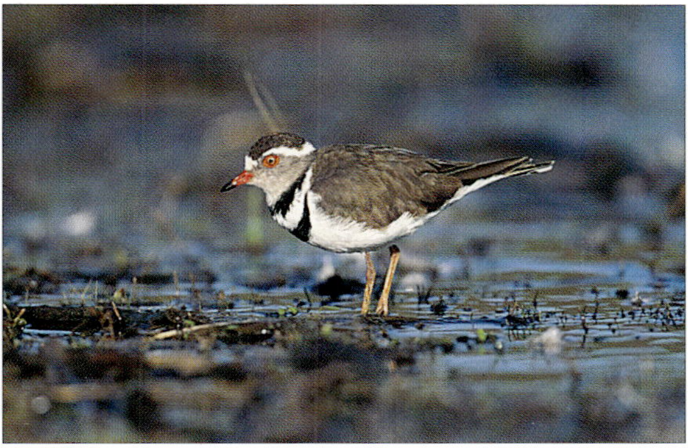

ABPL/NIGEL J DENNIS

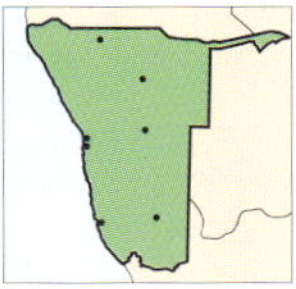

The *double black breast band, grey face and conspicuous red eye-ring and base of the bill* are diagnostic in this bird. In flight the tail shows white outer tips and edges, and a white terminal bar. The immature is a duller version of the adult, lacking the red eye-ring. The call is a penetrating, clear 'weet-weet' whistle. It is common throughout Namibia in most wetlands but prefers small waterbodies with sandy or pebbly margins. It is rare on the open coast.

Grey (Blackbellied) Plover *Pluvialis squatarola* (254) L 30 cm

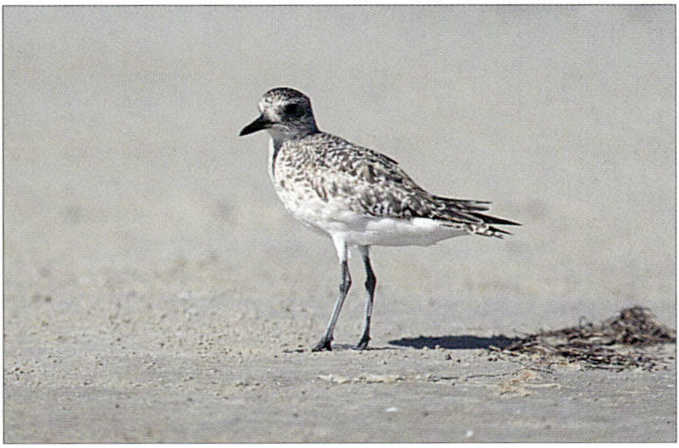

T D LONGRIGG

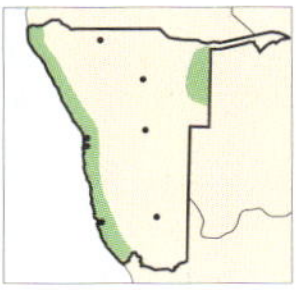

This medium-sized wader is *drab grey, and lightly speckled with white on the back and wing coverts.* In flight, from below, it shows black 'armpits' and, from above, a pale rump and white wingbar. The head is relatively large with a short black bill. In breeding plumage this bird has black underparts with a black and white spangled back. The call is a flutey 'tluuii', lower in pitch in the middle. It prefers open or rocky shorelines and coastal wetlands.

Crowned Plover *Vanellus coronatus* (255) L 30 cm

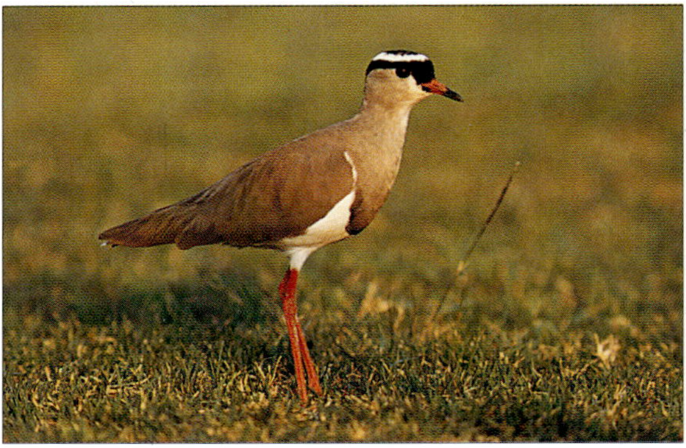

W R TARBOTON

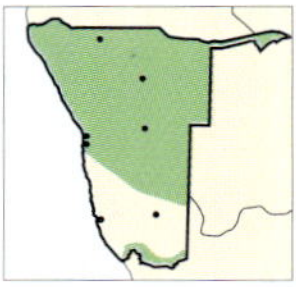

A large, readily identified plover with its *black cap interrupted by a white 'halo'. A black band separates the white belly from the sandy brown breast. The legs and basal part of the bill are a bright reddish* colour. The immature resembles the adult, but is less strikingly marked. A loud, grating 'kreeep' call is heard at night. It has no particular affinity for water, preferring drier grasslands, golf courses and playing fields. It is fairly common, but absent from the southern part of Namibia.

Blacksmith Plover *Vanellus armatus* (258) L 30 cm

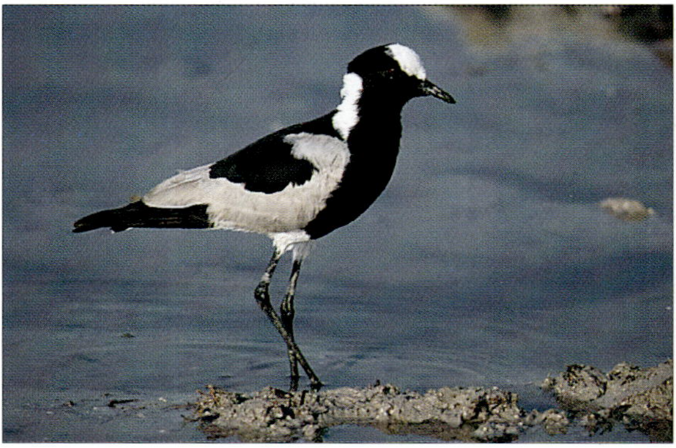

PETER CRAIG-COOPER

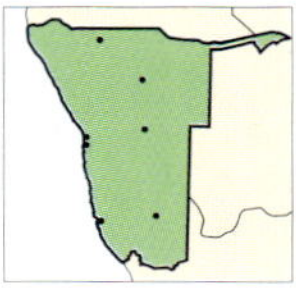

This *large black, white and grey bird* is the easiest plover to identify in southern Africa. It has an easily distinguishable bold wing pattern. The immature is a duller version of the adult with greyish brown feathers replacing the black. When alarmed, it gives a rapid, metallic 'tink tink' call. It occurs in damp areas at wetland edges and adjoining grasslands, seasonally flooded areas and coastal pools. It is common in many areas but especially the moist northern areas.

Ruddy Turnstone *Arenaria interpres* (262) L 23 cm

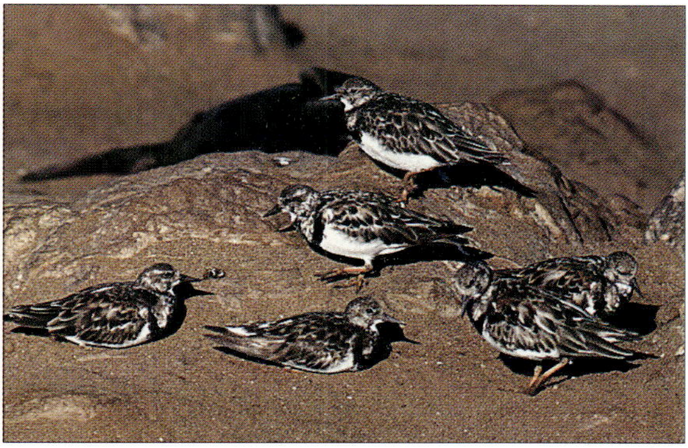

ABPL/CLEM HAAGNER

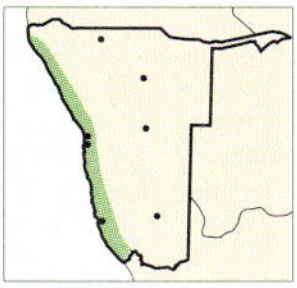

This stocky wader has a *short, black, slightly flattened and upturned bill. The legs are orange with darker joints.* In flight the upperparts show a distinctive dark and light pattern. In breeding plumage the head and neck have a clear black and white pattern and the wings and back are chestnut. The immature has browner underparts which are more heavily scaled. A hard 'kttuck' call is heard, especially in flight. It is a common summer visitor to the coast; some birds overwinter.

Common Sandpiper *Tringa hypoleucos* (264) L 19 cm

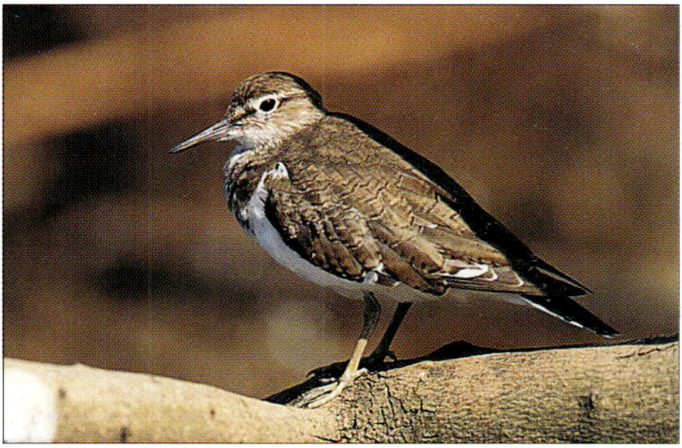

SIL/NIGEL J DENNIS

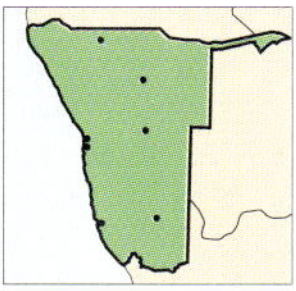

This small, usually solitary, wader is *uniformly brown showing a white shoulder in front of the closed wing, and having dull green legs.* It shows a prominent pale wing bar and barred sides to the dark tail. It has a peculiar habit of bobbing backwards and forwards between short bursts of running. The immature resembles the adult. The flight call is a characteristic 'ti-ti-ti'. It commonly occurs during summer in a wide range of Namibian wetlands.

Wood Sandpiper *Tringa glareola* (266) L 20 cm

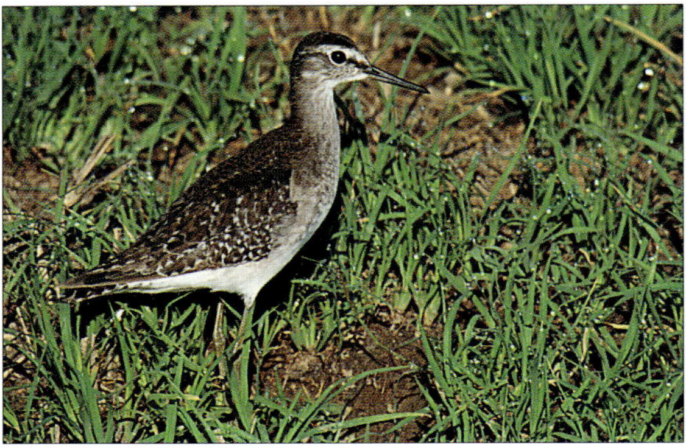

PETER CRAIG-COOPER

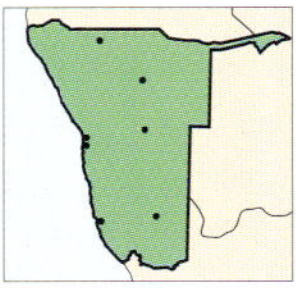

This sandpiper is similar in size to the Common Sandpiper but lacks the white shoulder and wing bar. It is identifiable by its *brownish back, well spotted with buff or white, white rump, pale grey underwing and greenish yellow legs*. The barred tail is visible in flight. Immatures resemble adults but are warmer brown above. It is a very vocal species with a high-pitched, slightly descending 'chiff-iff-iff' call. It is a common summer visitor to dams, vleis, bays and estuaries.

Common Greenshank *Tringa nebularia* (270) L 32 cm

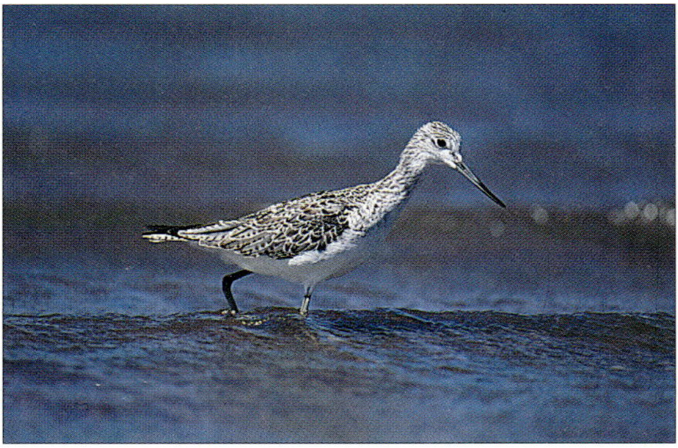

NIGEL J DENNIS

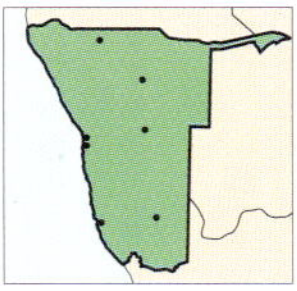

A *medium-sized, pale grey wader which has greyish olive legs*. The *upturned black bill with a grey base* differentiates it from other waders. In flight it shows a conspicuous white rump which extends up the back in a white wedge. Immatures are similar to adults. It has a loud, rasping 'chew-chew-chew' call. Often seen in the shallows chasing fish in a wide range of salt and freshwater wetlands, it is a common summer visitor with a few birds remaining throughout the year.

Red Knot *Calidris canutus* (271) L 25 cm

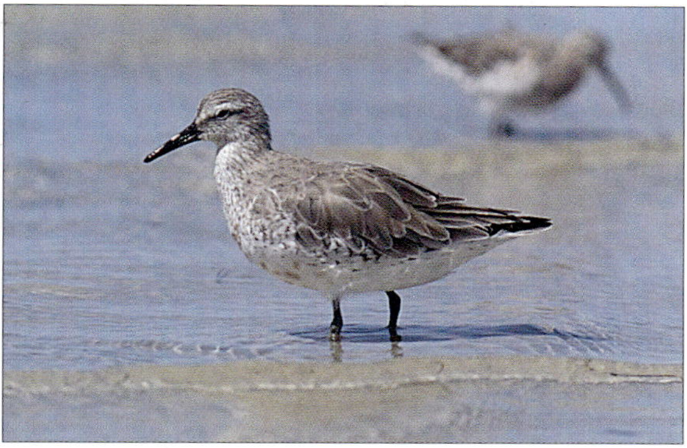

T D LONGRIGG

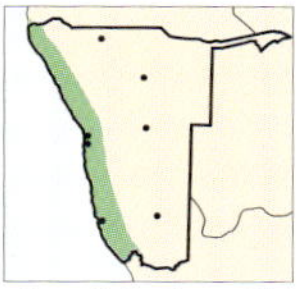

This short-legged, plain and dumpy wader differs from the similar Curlew Sandpiper by being larger and having a *straight bill and greenish legs*. In flight a pale wing bar is visible and the rump is flecked with grey. In breeding plumage the entire underparts, except for the underwing, are deep chestnut. The immature is slightly browner than the adult. Its call is a nondescript 'knut'. A gregarious wader of estuaries and bays, it is a common to abundant summer visitor.

Curlew Sandpiper *Calidris ferruginea* (272) L 19 cm

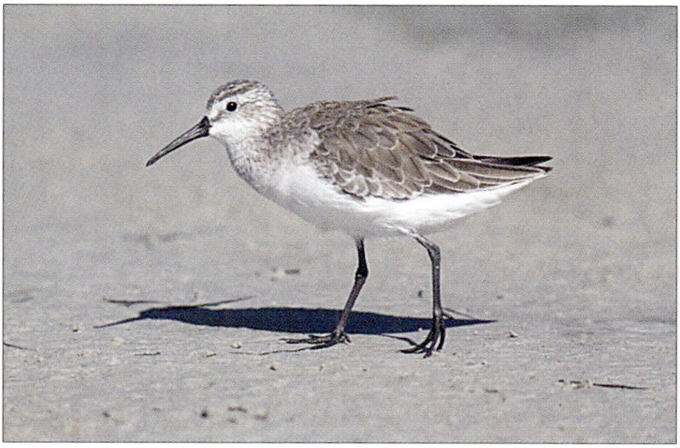

T D LONGRIGG

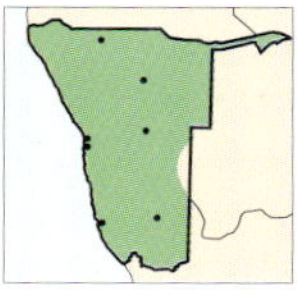

A *small, long-legged wader with a long, obviously decurved bill*. This bird appears grey with a squarish white rump variably scalloped with pale grey. In breeding plumage the underparts and face become rust coloured and the rump finely barred. The male is brighter than the female. The immature has buffy edges to the mantle feathers. The call is a short 'chirrup' trill. This common to abundant summer visitor feeds in a variety of inland wetlands and coastal estuaries.

Little Stint *Calidris minuta* (274) L 14 cm

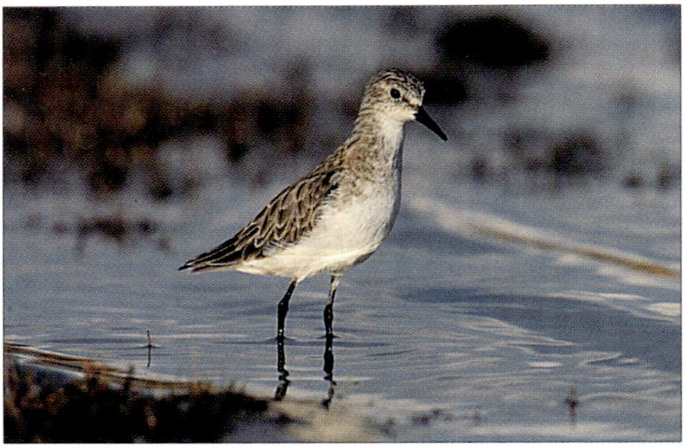

ABPL/NIGEL J DENNIS

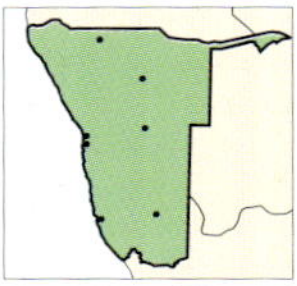

This tiny wader is easily identified by its *small size*; when seen foraging in a flock of shorebirds, this species is invariably the smallest. The feeding action of the bird is typically nervous and rapid. *The narrow white wing bar and white sides to the rump are obvious in flight.* In breeding plumage the head and neck become suffused with a rich russet colour. The call is a short, repeated 'teet'. It is a common summer visitor to inland and coastal wetlands in the region.

Sanderling *Caladris alba* (281) L 19 cm

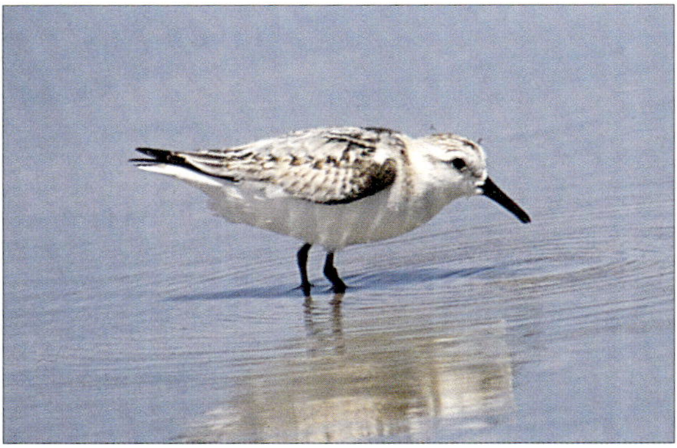

COLIN URQUHART

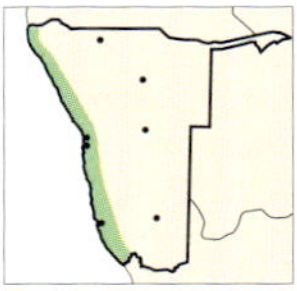

In non-breeding plumage this is the *palest sandpiper in the region. It has a short, stubby, black bill and a dark shoulder.* In breeding plumage the wing and back feathers are black with rufous centres and there is a broad, diffuse chestnut breast band streaked with black. In flight it shows a distinct white wing bar. The immature resembles the non-breeding adult. Its call is a single, decisive 'wick'. It is common on the coast, although sometimes individuals are found inland.

Ruff *Philomachus pugnax* (284) L m=30 cm, f=24 cm

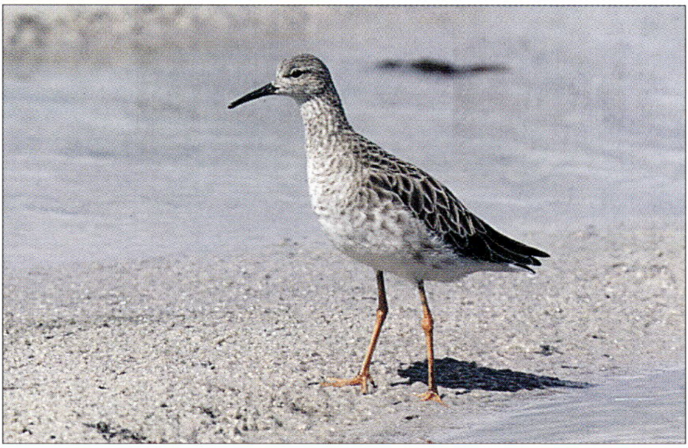

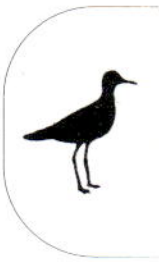

T D LONGRIGG

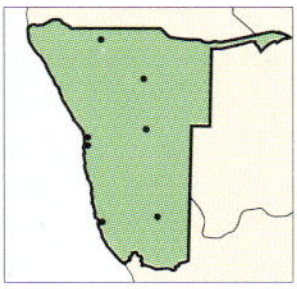

The *scaling on the upperparts* is conspicuous in this species. The colour of the legs is highly variable, often orange or reddish; the black bill may also show an orange or reddish base. In flight the white, oval patch on either side of the rump is diagnostic. During the non-breeding season the male may show a white head and neck. The immature resembles the non-breeding adult. It is mostly silent in Namibia. It is a common summer visitor to estuaries, bays and adjacent grassy areas.

Bartailed Godwit *Limosa lapponica* (288) L 38 cm

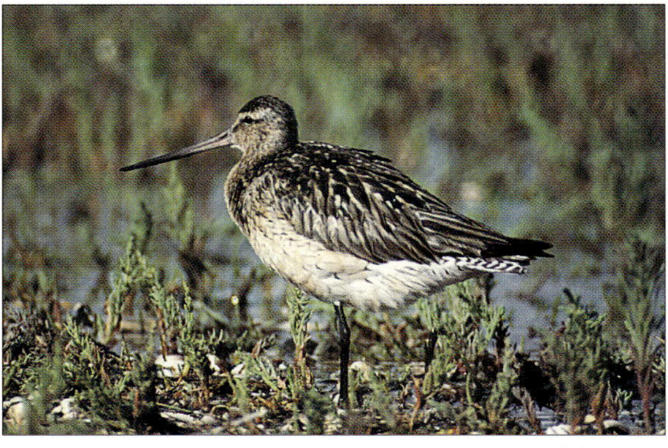

AQUILA/R GLOVER

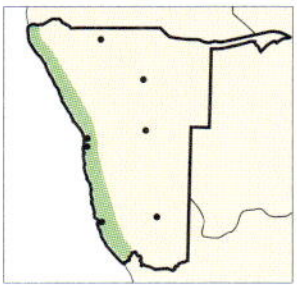

This *large wader has a very long, slightly upturned bill, the basal half of which is pink*. The *upperparts are mottled grey and brown*. In flight it shows a white rump and fine barring on the tail. In breeding plumage the head, neck and underparts are a rich chestnut. The immature resembles the non-breeding adult. It is usually silent but does utter a 'wik-wik' call. This common summer visitor frequents large estuaries, coastal lagoons and mud-edged lakes.

Eurasian Curlew *Numenius arquata* (289) L 55 cm

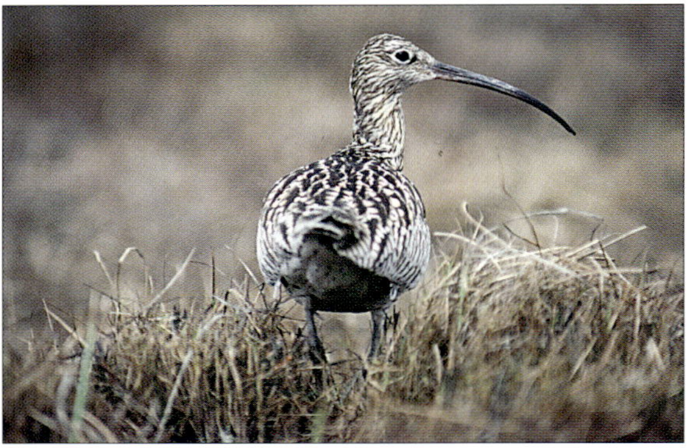

AQUILA/LARKING & POWELL

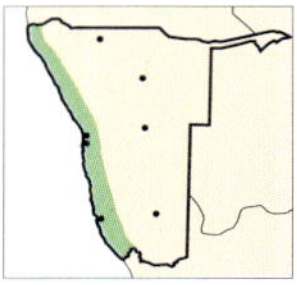

This is a very large wader with an *extremely long, decurved bill* which is proportionately longer than that of the Whimbrel. The Eurasian Curlew lacks the Whimbrel's head stripes and is also paler overall. In flight this bird shows a *white rump that extends up the back as a white triangle*. Immatures have a relatively short bill. The name derives from the loud 'cur-lew' call. It is found in large estuaries and lagoons, and is an uncommon summer visitor to coastal regions.

Whimbrel *Numenius phaeopus* (290) L 43 cm

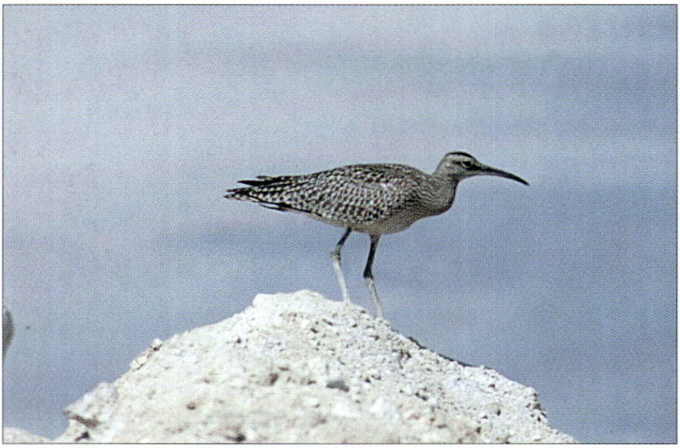

IAN SINCLAIR

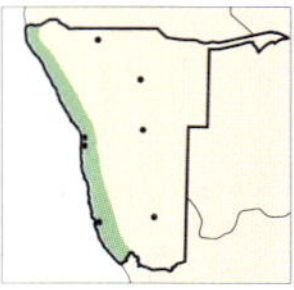

This species and the Eurasian Curlew are the only large waders in Namibia with *decurved bills*. The *parallel pale and dark stripes on the head, bisected by a pale stripe down the centre of the crown, and the pale eye-stripe* are diagnostic. In flight the tail is barred with dusky brown. Immatures resemble adults. It emits a staccato, whistled call when flushed. This common summer visitor is rarely seen outside estuaries and bays; it is rare during winter.

Rednecked Phalarope *Phalaropus lobatus* (292) L 16 cm

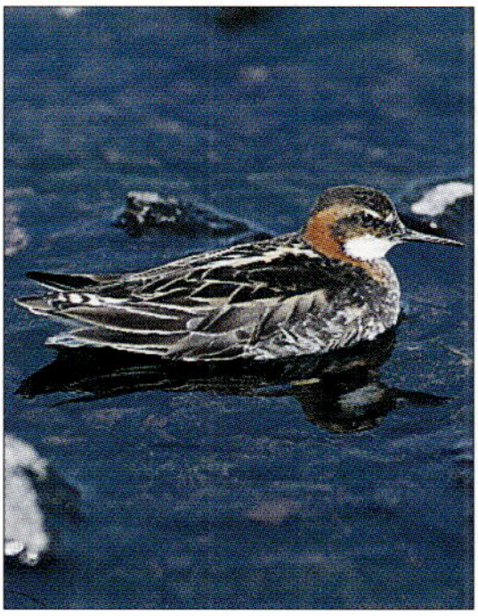
FLPA/ROGER WILMSHURST

Breeding plumage

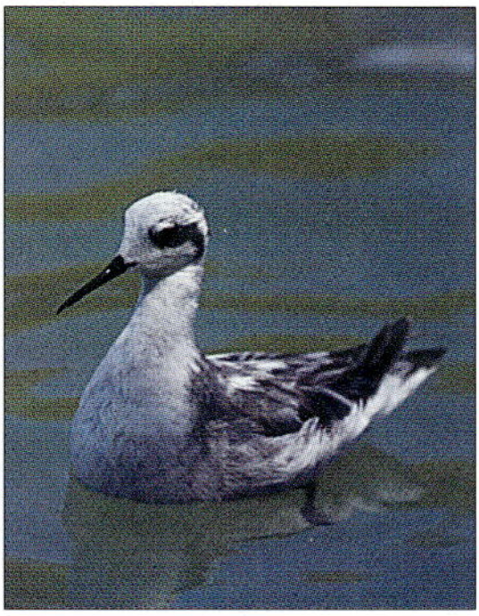
DR & MRS MANFRED REICHARDT

Non-breeding plumage

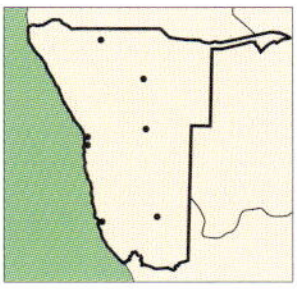

In breeding plumage this bird acquires a *small chestnut gorget on the upper neck and is darker overall*. It has a *dark grey back streaked with white and a thin, all-black bill*. The rump is black fringed with white. The immature is similar to the non-breeding adult. It emits a low 'tchick' when put to flight. Found on salt pans and on quiet water-bodies, this is an uncommon summer visitor to Namibian coastal regions; it is probably more common at sea.

Pied Avocet *Recurvirostra avosetta* (294) L 42 cm

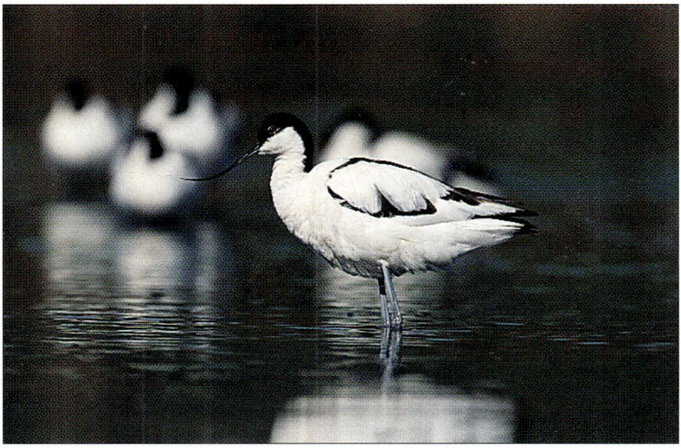
ABPL/NIGEL J DENNIS

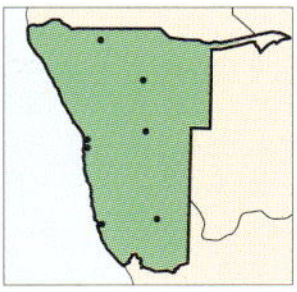

This is a *large, black and white wader with a long, very thin, upturned bill*. The *legs are long and pale blue* and the feet are partially webbed. In flight three black patches on each upperwing, forming a pied pattern, are visible. The immature has dusky brown, not black, wing patches. It emits a clear 'kooit' call and a 'kik-kik' alarm call. It is usually seen in flocks at lakes, estuaries, vleis and temporary pools of water, and is common in Namibia, with large flocks found on the coast.

Blackwinged Stilt *Himantopus himantopus* (295) L 38 cm

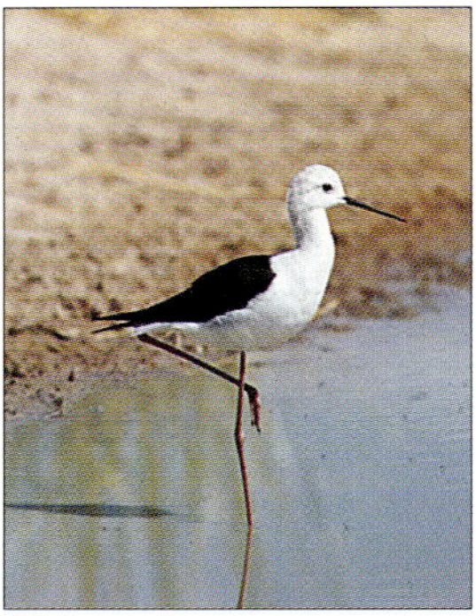
RAYMONDE JOHANNESSON

Adult

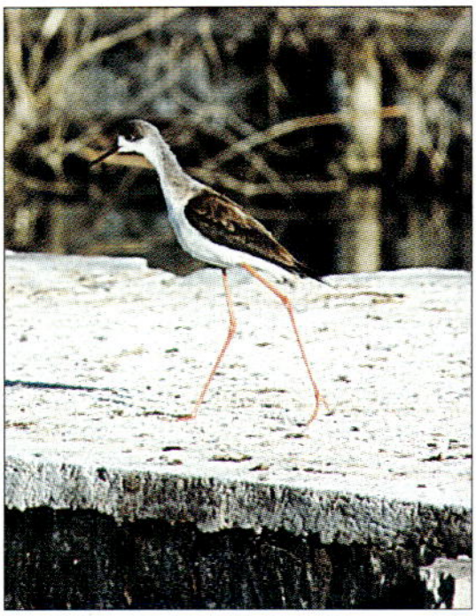
ALAN WEAVING

Immature

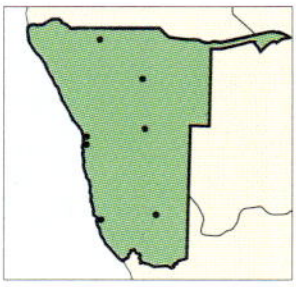

This large wader is distinguished by the combination of its *exceptionally long red legs and its long, very thin, black bill.* In flight the *black underwings contrast with the white underparts and white neck, and the long legs trail conspicuously.* The breeding male shows a black nape and crown. The immature has extensive brown markings on its hindneck and head. Its call is a short, harsh 'kik-kik'. It is common in suitable marshes, vleis, salt pans and flooded areas.

Spotted Dikkop *Burhinus capensis* (297) L 44 cm

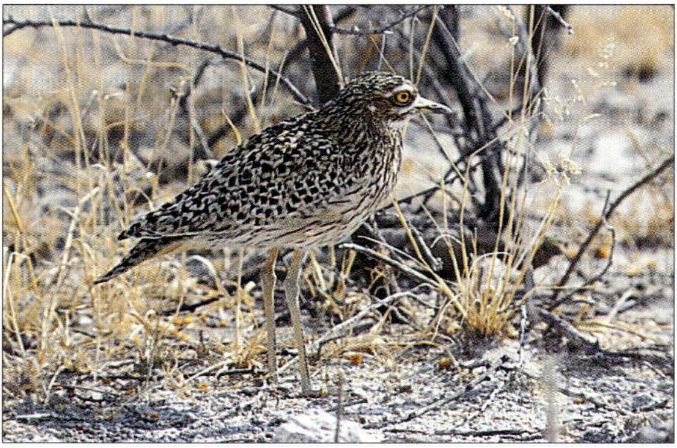
IAN DAVIDSON

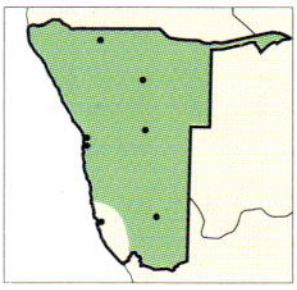

This wader has a *large head, big yellow eyes, a short bill with yellow at the base and greenish yellow legs.* The *spotted upperparts* are mottled brown, buff and black. In flight two small white patches are visible on each upperwing. Immatures resemble adults. A nocturnal bird, its 'whiw-whiw-whiw' call is heard at night; during the day it rests in the shade. It cccurs away from water and is common throughout Namibia except in extreme desert regions.

Burchell's Courser *Cursorius rufus* (299) L 23 cm

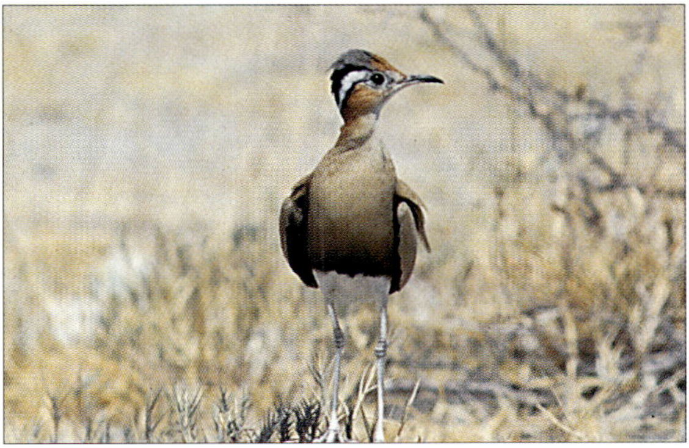

IAN DAVIDSON

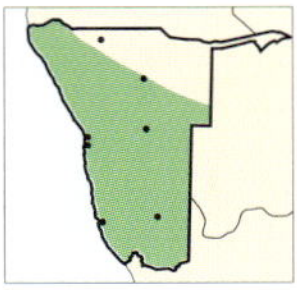

This is a plain, buff-grey courser with a black and white line extending back from the eye. It differs from Temminck's Courser by having a blue-grey, not rufous, crown and nape, and a black bar, not a patch, on the belly. A white bar on the secondaries and a white tip to the outertail can be seen in flight. The immature is mottled above and the lower breast markings are less well defined than in the adult. Its call is a harsh, repeated 'wark'. It is thinly distributed in dry, sparsely grassed areas.

Temminck's Courser *Cursorius temminckii* (300) L 20 cm

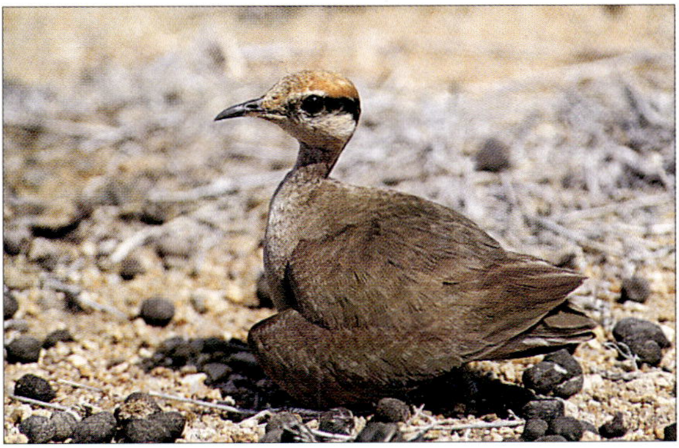

K BEGG

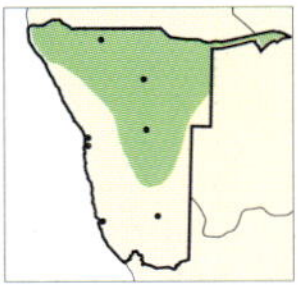

This courser is most likely to be confused with Burchell's Courser from which it differs by being *grey-brown above*, and having *a rufous, not grey, hindcrown and a black patch, not line, on its lower belly*. The immature is duller and has lightly speckled underparts. Its call is a piercing 'keer-keer'. This is a nomadic species which prefers dry, sparsely grassed or recently burned areas. It is fairly widespread in Namibia but uncommon in places in the north.

Doublebanded Courser *Rhinoptilus africanus* (301) L 22 cm

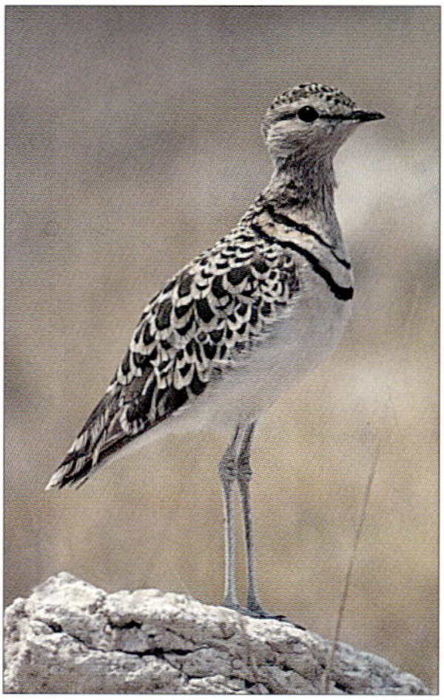

PETER CRAIG-COOPER

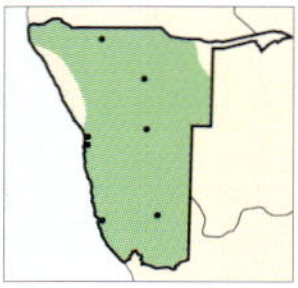

This species has the plainest head of all the local coursers, marked only with a creamy eyebrow stripe. The *two narrow black bands ringing the upper breast* are diagnostic. The wing and back feathers have dark centres with contrasting pale fringes. The white uppertail coverts are conspicuous in flight. Immatures have a chestnut breast band. Its call is a falling and rising whistle and repeated 'kee-kee' notes. It is a resident of desert edges and dry open areas.

Bronzewinged Courser *Rhinoptilus chalcopterus* (303) L 25 cm

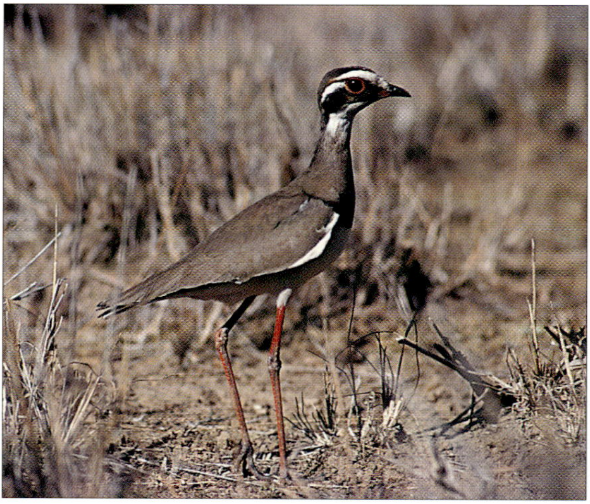

ALAN WEAVING

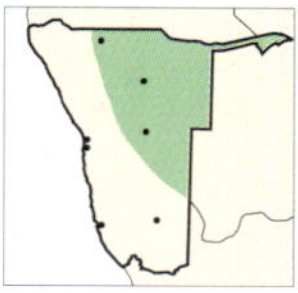

This *large, dark brown and white courser has a broad dusky band across the breast and lower neck, separated from the pale lower breast and belly by a black line. The belly is white and there is a white area on the upper neck*. In flight the white uppertail coverts and wing bars contrast with the dark upperparts. Immatures have rufous-tipped feathers. Its call is a ringing 'ki-kooi'. Active at night and easily overlooked, this species frequents woodlands and savanna in the northeast.

Arctic Skua *Stercorarius parasiticus* (307) L 46 cm

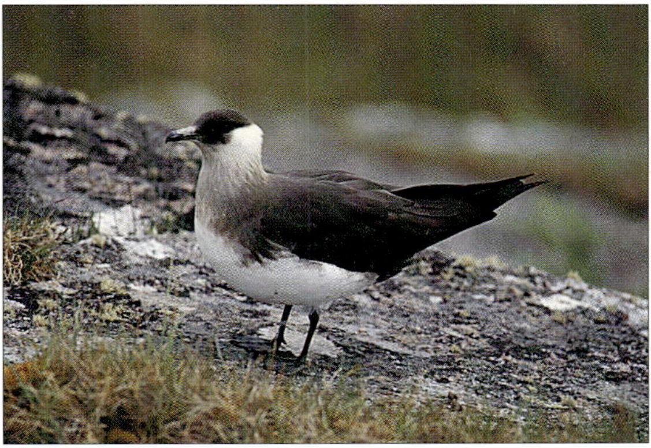

ABPL/BRENDAN RYAN

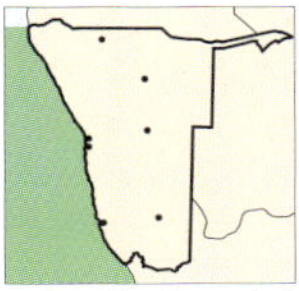

Plumage is variable, with light, dark and intermediate phases occurring. It differs from the Pomarine Skua by being less bulky, narrower winged, smaller billed and having the central tail feathers, if present, pointed, not spoon shaped. The immature is similar to the immature Pomarine Skua but is smaller, slighter in build and has longer, more angled and pointed wings. It is silent in Namibia. It is common on inshore waters during summer, entering Walvis Bay to chase terns which it parasitizes.

Pomarine Skua *Stercorarius pomarinus* (309) L 50 cm

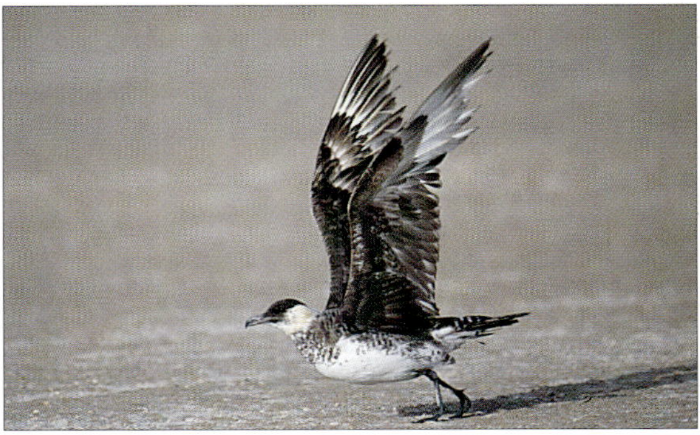

AQUILA/CONRAD GREAVES

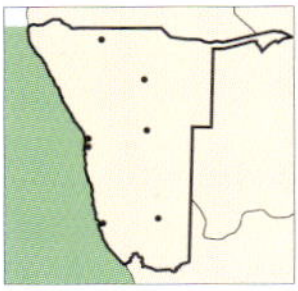

The Pomarine Skua may be confused with the smaller Arctic Skua from which it differs by having *long and blunt, not pointed, tail projections* and more white in the wing. The pale phase is more common than the all-dark phase in this species. The immature is more heavily barred on the upper- and undertail coverts than is the immature Arctic Skua and is larger and broader winged, and has a more gull-like flight. It is a common offshore visitor in the region during summer .

Kelp Gull *Larus dominicanus* (312) L 60 cm

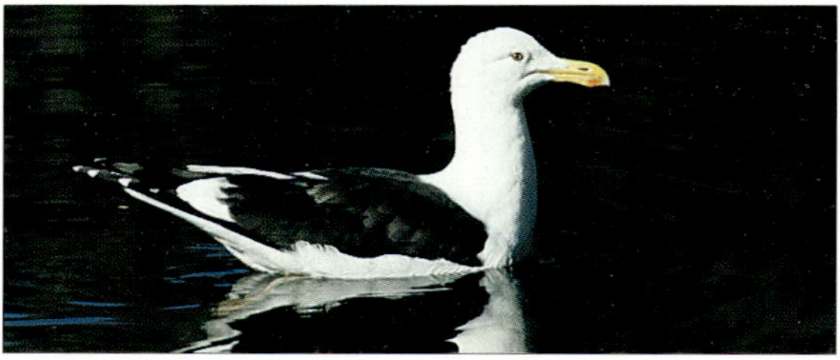

ZELDA WAHL

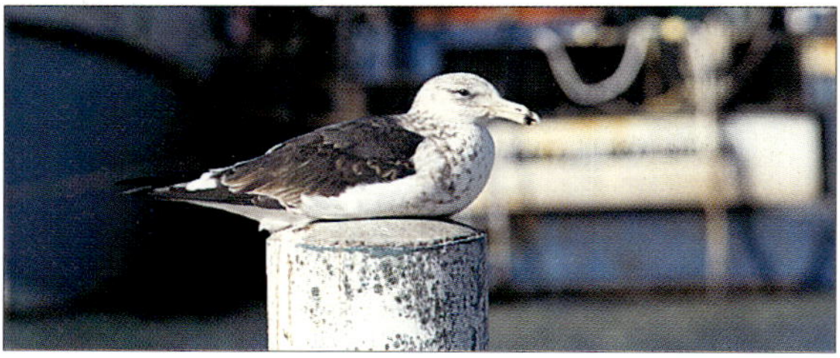

COLIN URQUHART

Above: adult. Below: immature

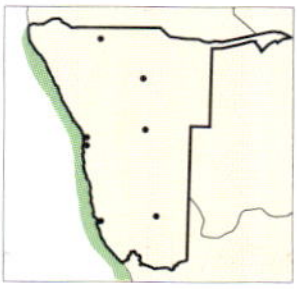

This gull, the largest in Namibia, is easy to identify with its *contrasting white body and jet-black back and upperwings, bright yellow, orange-tipped bill, and olive legs.* Immatures are very dark, becoming paler with age. It calls a loud 'ki-ok', and a short, repeated 'kwok' alarm. Common along the coastal strip, it forages along coastal and inland waters.

Greyheaded Gull *Larus cirrocephalus* (315) L 42 cm

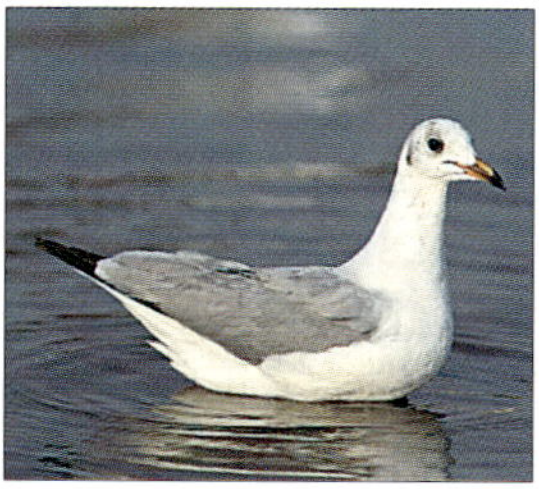

PETER CRAIG-COOPER

Immature

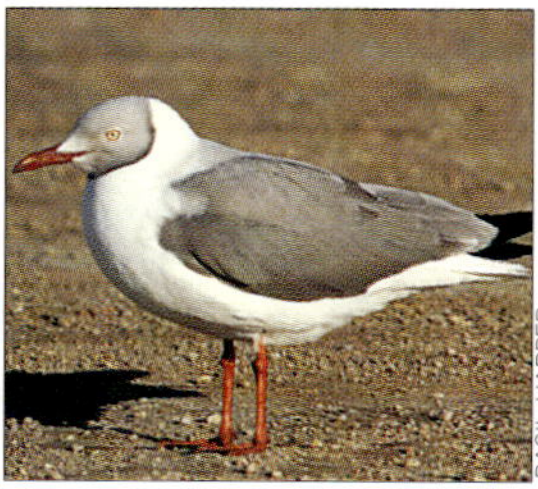

BASIL HARPER

Adult

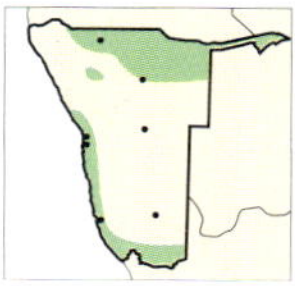

The breeding adult differs from the smaller Hartlaub's Gull by having a *more extensive grey hood, a pale yellow, not dark, eye and a brighter red bill, legs and feet.* The immature has darker, more extensive markings on the head, paler legs, a pinky orange bill and more black on the tip of the tail than the immature Hartlaub's Gull. A typical, small-gull 'kraah' is given. Although common in mixed flocks along the coast, at coastal and freshwater wetlands, it also occurs away from the sea.

Hartlaub's Gull *Larus hartlaubii* (316) L 38 cm

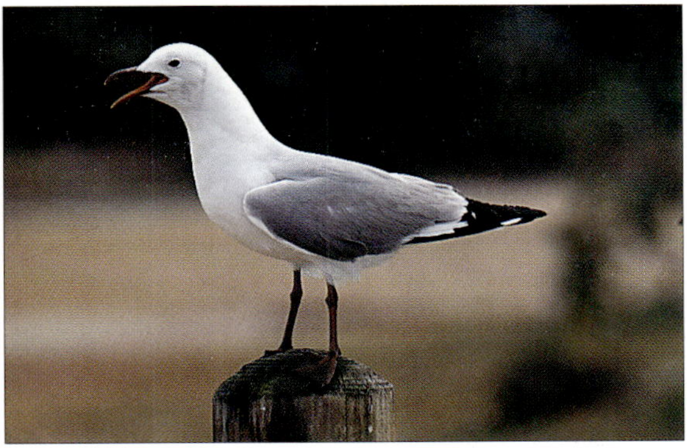

ALAN WEAVING

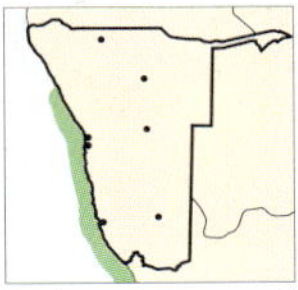

This gull is slightly *smaller than the Greyheaded Gull with a darker red bill, deeper red legs, and a dark eye*. In breeding plumage it shows a suggestion of a grey hood. In non-breeding plumage the head is plain white. The immature has faint brown markings on the head, a brown bill, and the black tip to the tail is either reduced or absent. Its call is a drawn-out, rattling 'karrh' and 'pok-pok'. This gull is common on the coast and on islands off Namibia.

Caspian Tern *Hydroprogne caspia* (322) L 50 cm

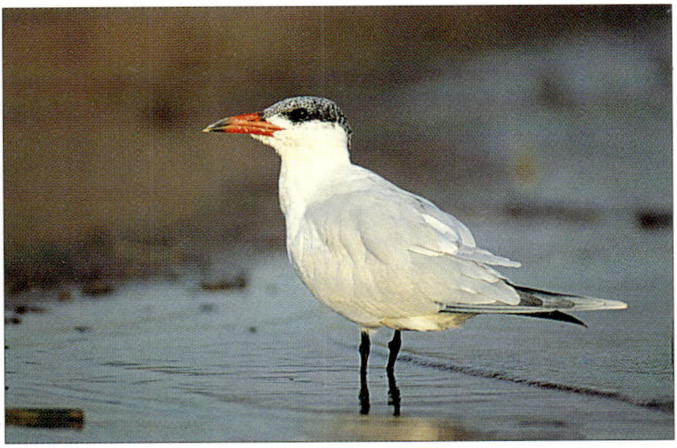

PETER CRAIG-COOPER

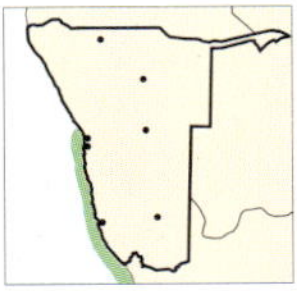

The largest tern in southern Africa, it is immediately recognized by its *orange-red bill, which is usually tipped with black*. In the breeding adult the cap is streaked black and white; the non-breeding adult has a totally black cap. The immature has an orange bill with a more extensive black tip, and dark-edged back feathers. The call is a loud, harsh 'kraaak'. Found in the vicinity of large rivers, lagoons, estuaries, bays, islands and inshore waters, it is uncommon on the coast.

Swift (Greater Crested) Tern *Sterna bergii* (324) L 46 cm

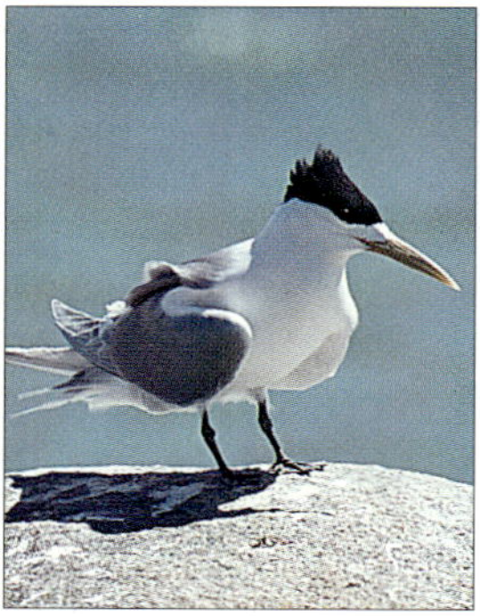

T D LONGRIGG

Breeding plumage

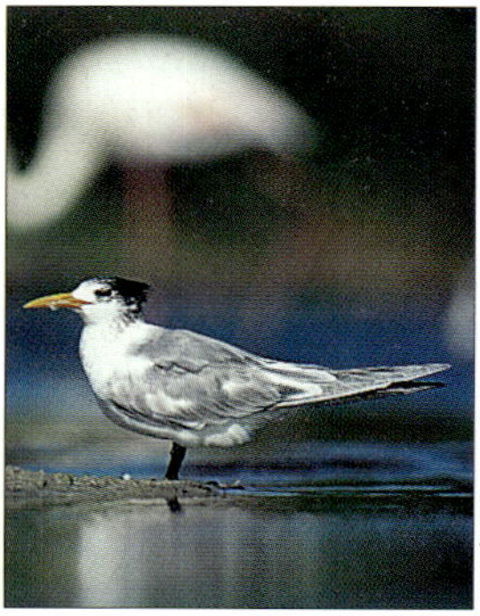

ABPL/NIGEL J DENNIS

Non-breeding plumage

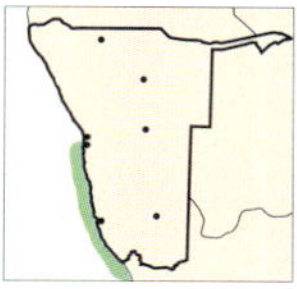

In *breeding plumage the black cap ends before the bill, showing a white forehead. In non-breeding plumage the forehead appears mostly white* and grizzled with variable amounts of black. It has a large yellow or greenish yellow bill. The immature is barred with blackish brown and has a dusky yellow-olive bill. The call is a 'kee-eck'; immatures give a thin, vibrating whistle. It occurs on inshore waters, larger bays and estuaries, and is common along the coastal strip.

Sandwich Tern *Sterna sandvicensis* (326) L 40 cm

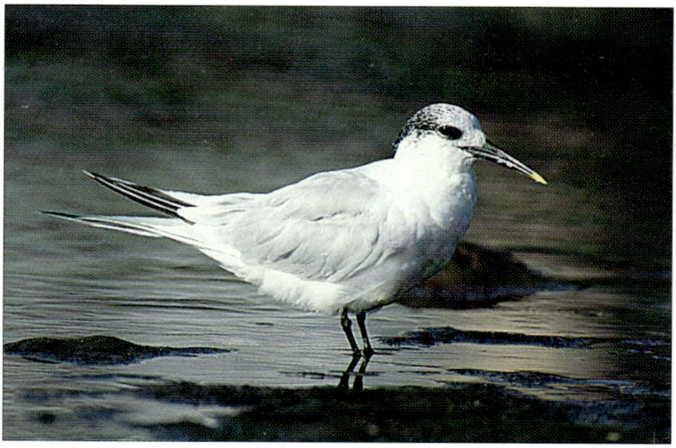

PETER CRAIG-COOPER

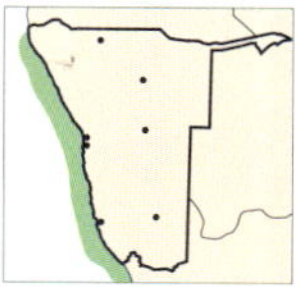

Smaller than the Swift Tern, this is a large, very pale tern with a *diagnostic slender black bill with a yellow tip*. It shows a white rump and a forked tail. The legs and feet are black. In breeding plumage the breast may show a faint rosy hue, and the cap is black. The immature resembles a non-breeding adult but the upperparts are mottled. The call is a loud, grating 'kirik'. This common summer visitor is found on inshore waters, estuaries and bays.

Common Tern *Sterna hirundo* (327) L 33 cm

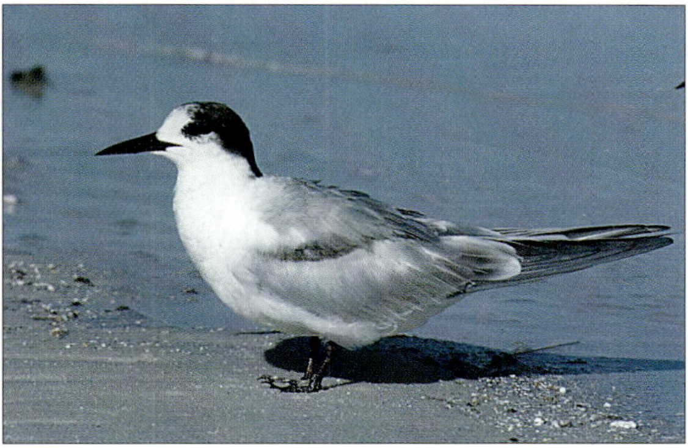

T D LONGRIGG

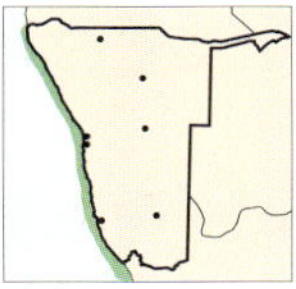

During summer this is the most abundant small tern on the Namibian coast. It has grey upperparts, white underparts, and a partially developed black cap, all features common to most small non-breeding terns. It has a *long, slightly decurved bill and uniform grey rump* which aid identification. In breeding plumage, it shows a black cap and pale grey underparts, a long, forked tail and a red, black-tipped bill. It is found on the open sea, coastal lakes and beaches.

Damara Tern *Sterna balaenarum* (334) L 23 cm

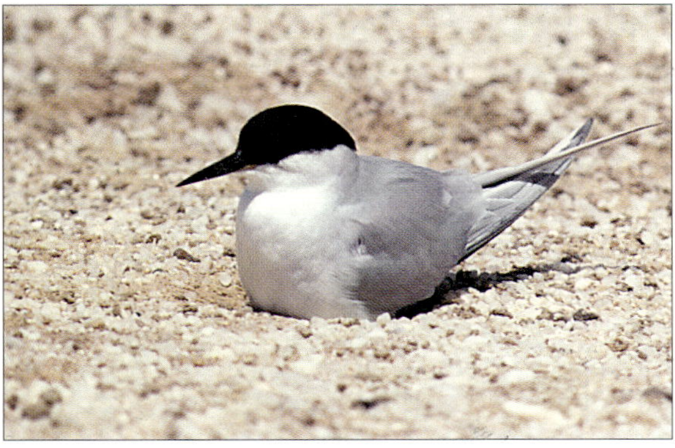

ABPL/CLEM HAAGNER

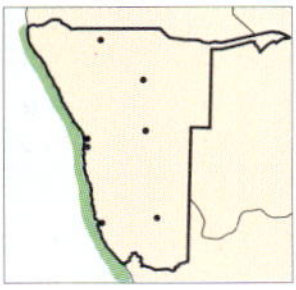

This small tern has a *long, slightly decurved bill and uniform pale grey upperparts, rump and uppertail*. In breeding plumage it shows a completely black cap, a black bill and black legs. The immature has brown barring on the upperparts. Its call is a high-pitched 'tsit-tsit' and a harsh, rapid 'kid-ick'. It frequents sandy coasts, and sheltered bays and lagoons. It is a common summer visitor to the coastal strip with a few birds remaining throughout the year.

Black Tern *Chlidonias niger* (337) L 22 cm

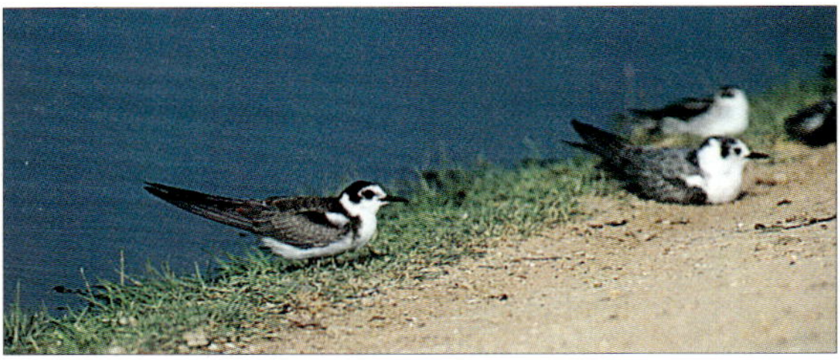

AQUILA/CONRAD GREAVES

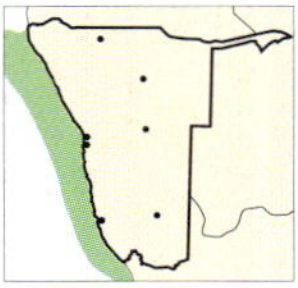

It is similar to the Whitewinged Tern but shows more black on the head. There is also no colour contrast between the back, rump and tail as in the Whitewinged Tern. The *dark shoulder smudge* is diagnostic. In breeding plumage it has a uniform, not pied, underwing, and upperwings which do not contrast with the back. Immatures resemble non-breeding adults. It is usually silent in this region. A common summer visitor along the Namibian coast, it is often seen foraging at sea.

Whitewinged Tern *Chlidonias leucopterus* (339) L 23 cm

ABPL/NIGEL J DENNIS

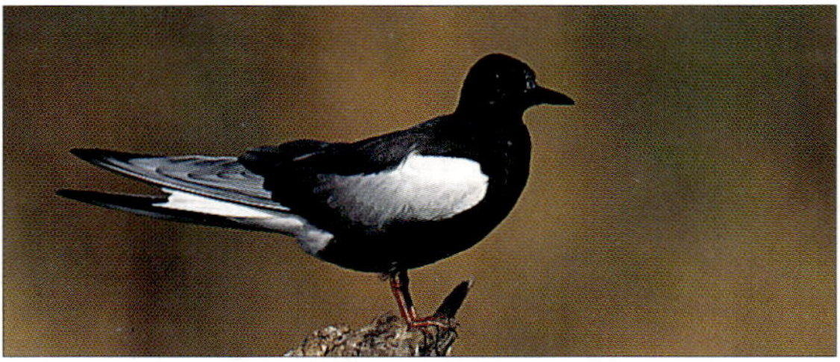

IAN SINCLAIR

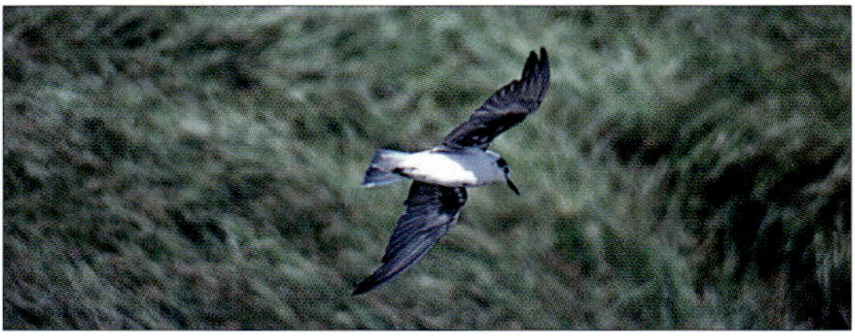

Top: breeding plumage. Bottom: non-breeding plumage

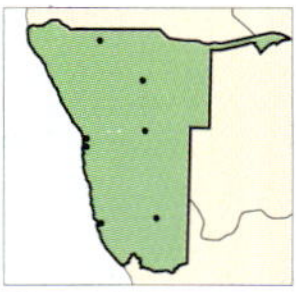

This is the most abundant small, freshwater tern in the area. In breeding plumage it resembles the Black Tern but has *black underwings, paler upperwings and a pale rump and tail.* In non-breeding plumage the adult is *pale grey and white, with small amounts of black* on the head and underwing. The immature is similar to the non-breeding adult. The call is a short 'kek-kek'. It occurs mostly in freshwater areas, but is also found on big estuaries.

Rock Pigeon *Columba guinea* (349) L 33 cm

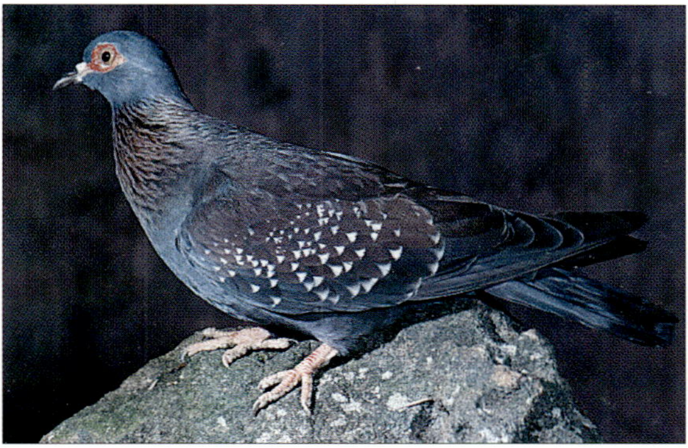

N BRICKELL

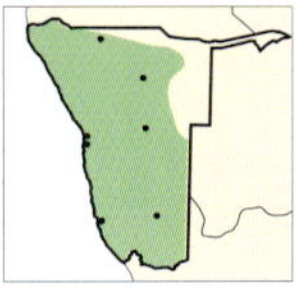

At close range the *white-speckled reddish back and wings, black bill, red legs and bare red skin around the eye* are diagnostic. The immature lacks red on the face. The call is a very owl-like, deep, resonant 'hoo-hoo'. It inhabits mountain ranges, rocky terrain and coastal cliffs. This pigeon has also adapted to urban life and is often seen on the ledges of buildings in cities. This bird is common throughout most of Namibia except in dense woodlands.

Cape Turtle Dove *Streptopelia capicola* (354) L 28 cm

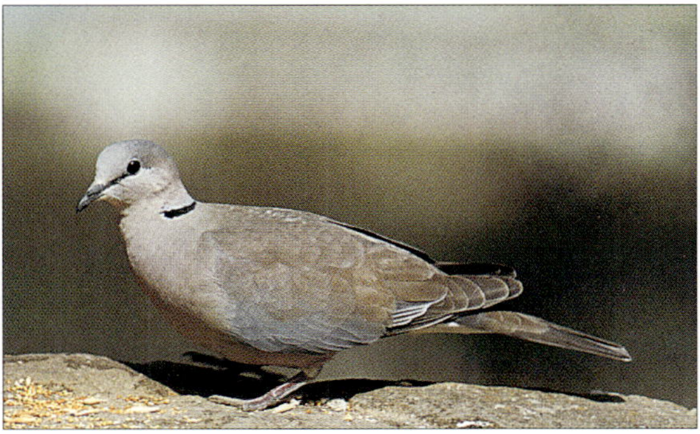

DR & MRS MANFRED REICHARDT

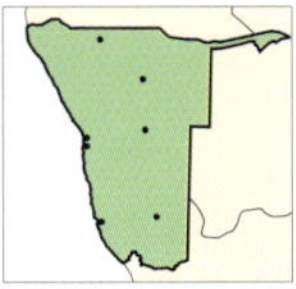

This is probably the most abundant dove in Namibia. It shows a diagnostic *white-tipped tail* which is conspicuous in flight. It has a pale head, a dark eye and a black hind collar. The immature resembles the adult, but is duller and lacks the hind collar. Its three-noted call, 'kuk-cooo-kuk', is a familiar background sound in the bushveld. This dove is found in virtually every habitat in this region but avoids extreme desert zones.

Laughing (Palm) Dove *Streptopelia senegalensis* (355) L 26 cm

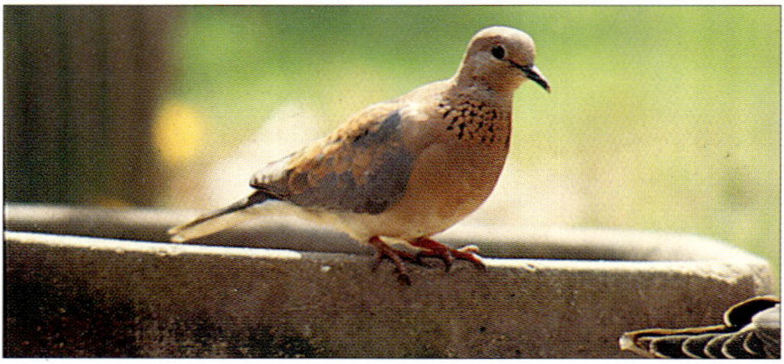

IAN SINCLAIR

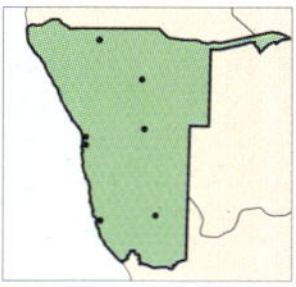

It is similar to the larger Cape Turtle Dove but lacks the black hind collar. It also differs by having a *black speckled necklace across its cinnamon breast*, and a cinnamon-coloured back. The blue-grey forewings and the white tip and sides of the tail are obvious in flight. Females are smaller and paler than males; immatures are duller than adults. Its name is derived from the chortled 'ooo-coooc-coooc-coo-coo' call. It frequents a wide range of habitats, avoiding extreme arid areas.

Namaqua Dove *Oena capensis* (356) L 28 cm

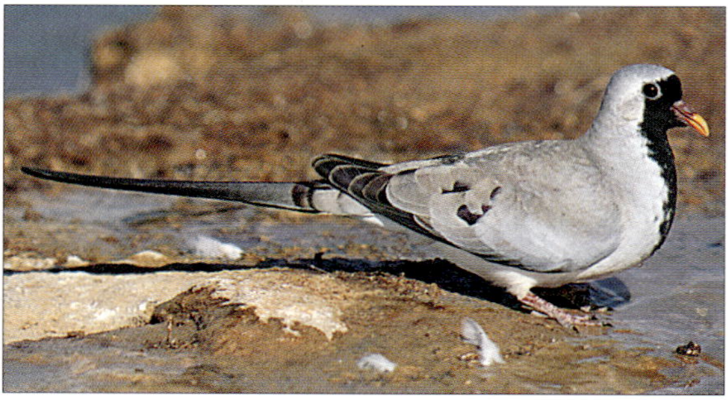

ABPL/TERRY CAREW

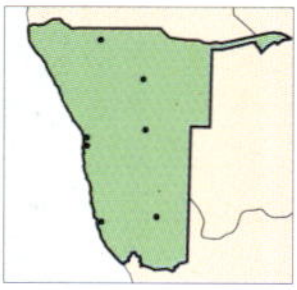

This, the smallest-bodied dove in Namibia, is the only one in southern Africa with a *long, pointed tail*. The male has a black face and throat. In flight the white underparts, chestnut flight feathers and long tail render this bird unmistakable. The immature and female lack the black face of the male and have a slightly shorter pointed tail. The call is a soft, low 'coooo-hoooo'. It prefers drier regions, such as thornveld, scrub and true desert, and is common in Namibia except in the moist northern regions.

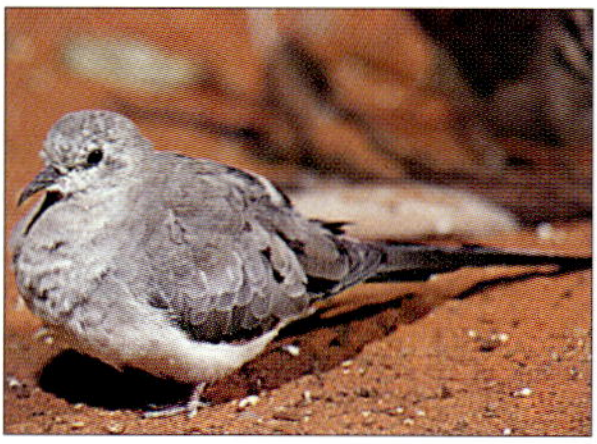

J VAN JAARSVELD

Top: male. Bottom: female

Rüppell's Parrot *Poicephalus rueppellii* (365) L 22 cm

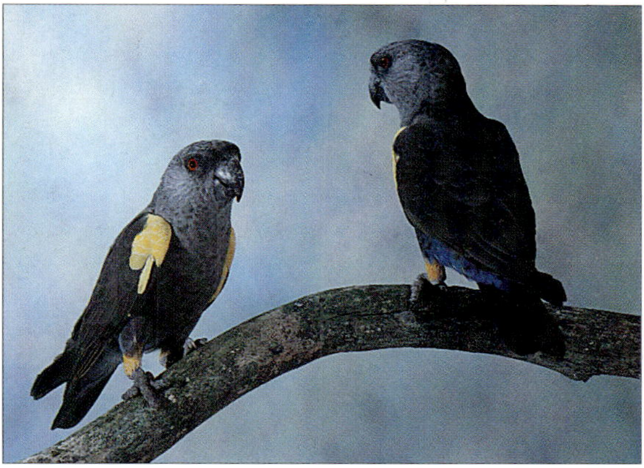

FLPA/E & D HOSKING

Male (left) and female (right)

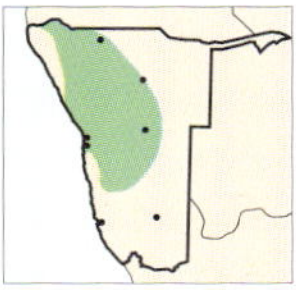

This small parrot has a *greyish throat and head, and a blue belly*. In flight the brown rump of the male is very obvious. The female is brighter than the male, with more extensive blue on the vent and a blue, not brown, rump. The immature resembles the adult but is duller. Its call is a loud screeching and squawking, accompanied by piercing whistles. Endemic to the region, it is thinly distributed through dry woodland, thornveld and dry river courses in northern Namibia.

Rosyfaced Lovebird *Agapornis roseicollis* (367) L 18 cm

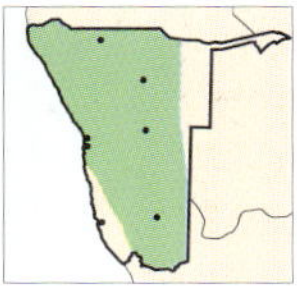

This small lovebird is extremely well camouflaged when sitting motionless among green foliage in a tree or bush; it can usually be detected only by its call, a series of typical parrot-like screeches and shrieks. Its flight is rapid with the *blue rump showing up clearly against the green back*. The immature is paler on the face and upper breast than the adult. This bird breeds colonially, utilizing natural cavities and crevices on cliff faces; it has also adapted to breeding under the eaves of houses. This common near-endemic occurs in mountainous terrain, dry broad-leafed woodland, and semi-desert regions.

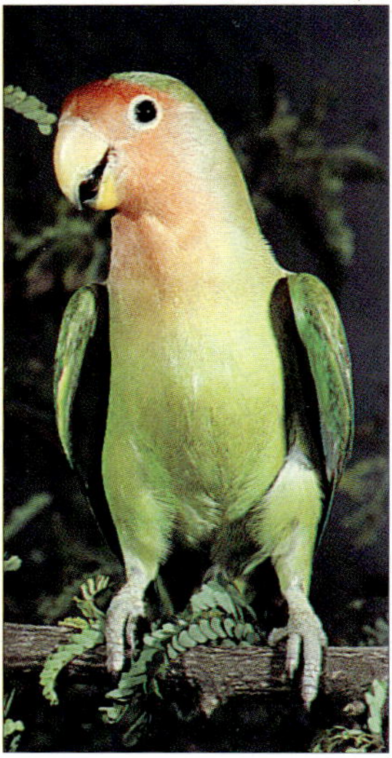

PETER CRAIG-COOPER

Grey Lourie *Corythaixoides concolor* (373) L 48 cm

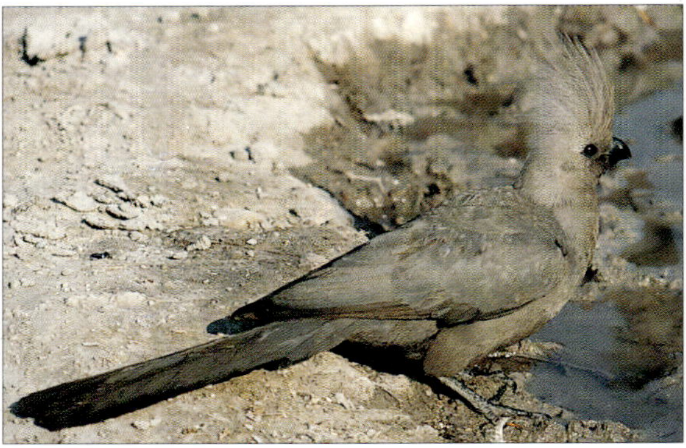

PETER CRAIG-COOPER

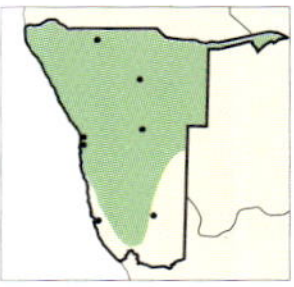

This conspicuous, *uniformly grey* bird resembles a giant mousebird *with its long tail and crest*, and is a common bird of the bushveld. The flight is strong, with flapping alternating with gliding. The immature is buffier than the adult and has a shorter crest. When uttering its harsh, nasal 'waaaay' or 'kay-waaaay' call, it raises its crest and flicks its tail. Occurring in thornveld and dry, open woodland, it is often seen in small groups perched on top of thorn trees.

Redfaced Mousebird *Colius indicus* (426) L 34 cm

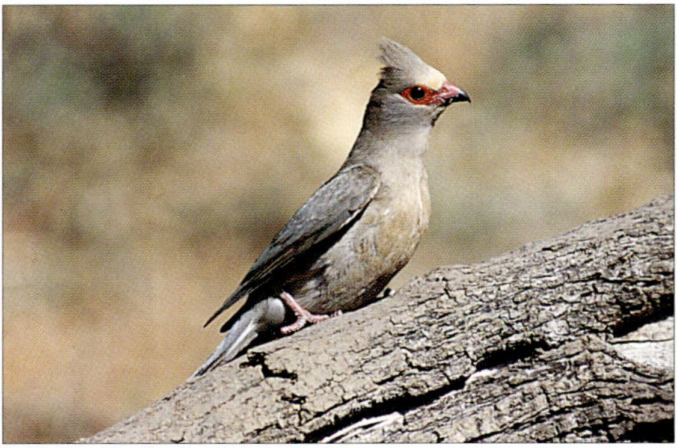

J J THERON

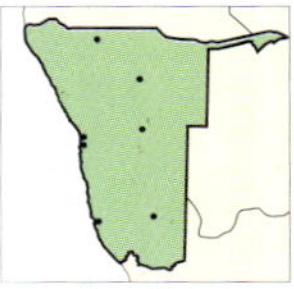

This mousebird is *pale grey, with the bill base and the naked skin around the eye bright red*. It usually flies in small parties, either in a group or in single file. The flight action is fast and direct. The immature has a yellowish green face. The call is a diagnostic, three- or four-noted whistle, 'whee-whe-whe'. Found in thornveld, open broad-leafed woodland and suburban gardens, this common mousebird occurs throughout Namibia except in totally arid regions.

Black Cuckoo *Cuculus clamosus* (378) L 30 cm

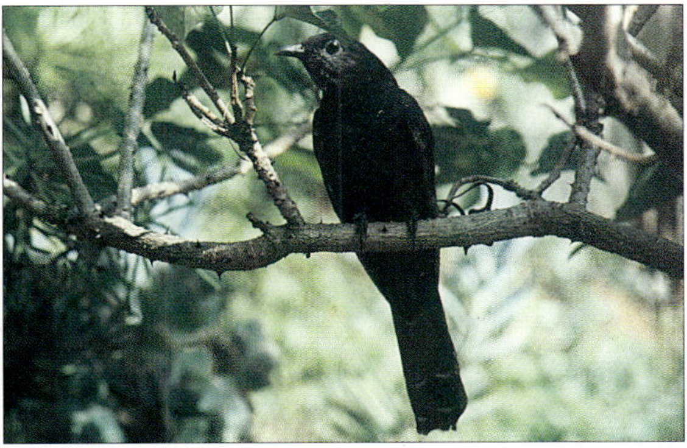

IAN SINCLAIR

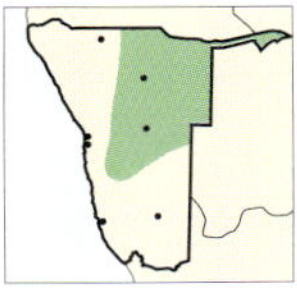

This, the *only all-black cuckoo* in southern Africa, is more often heard than seen. When observed in the canopy it might be confused with its host, the Forktailed Drongo, but it lacks the forked tail. The immature is a duller black than the adult and has a shorter tail. The frequently repeated call is a mournful, droning 'whooo-wheeee'. This bird is a common summer visitor to forest habitats, woodland, exotic plantations and suburban gardens.

Diederik Cuckoo *Chrysococcyx caprius* (386) L 18 cm

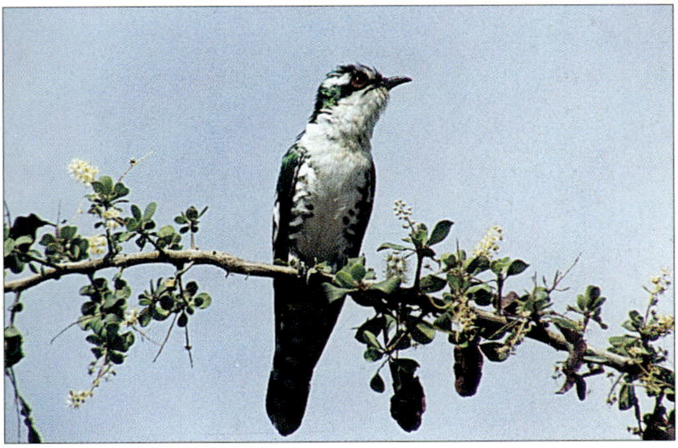

HELM THERON

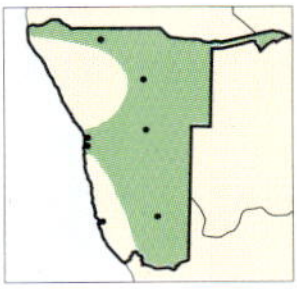

It can be distinguished by the *contrasting bottle-green and white plumage, broad white eye-stripe, white spots on the forewing and red eye*. The immature has a conspicuous red bill. During the summer the 'dee-dee-dee-deederic' call is heard around the colonies of the weavers and bishops that these birds parasitize. This common summer visitor occurs in open grasslands with stands of trees, in thornveld and exotic plantations, avoiding extreme arid regions.

African Scops Owl *Otus senegalensis* (396) L 20 cm

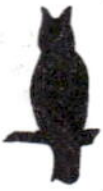

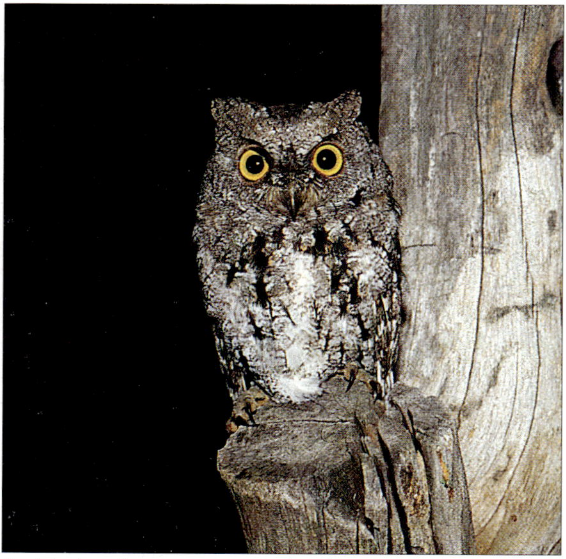

W T TARBOTON

At night the yellow eyes are extremely wide open

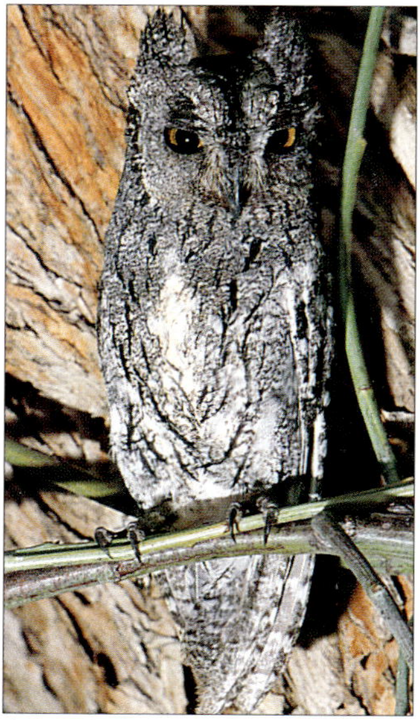

PETER CRAIG-COOPER

During the daytime the owl roosts

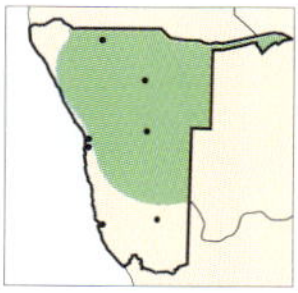

This is a *diminutive, inconspicuous* owl. It might be confused with the Whitefaced Owl because both have ear tufts. However, the *tiny size and grey, not white, face* should identify this bird. It has a greyish, bark-like plumage, *yellow eyes* and long ear tufts. Its soft, croaking, frog-like 'prrrup' is a frequently heard call at night in the bushveld, but the bird itself is not often seen. The immature resembles the adult. When roosting during the day, it compresses its body, huddles against a tree trunk and slits its eyes, making it almost impossible to detect. The African Scops Owl occurs in bushveld areas and dry, open woodland.

Whitefaced Owl *Otus leucotis* (397) L 28 cm

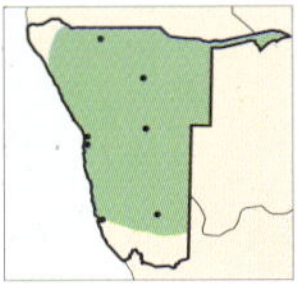

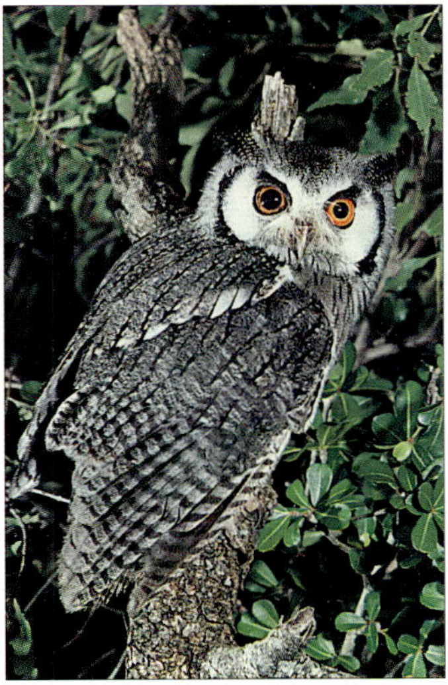

ABPL/J VAN JAARSVELD

This species differs from the similar, smaller African Scops Owl by having a *conspicuous white facial disc edged with black, paler grey plumage and by having bright orange, not yellow, eyes.* The Whitefaced Owl and the African Scops Owl are the only small owls to show ear tufts. The immature is buffier than the adult with a greyish face and yellow, not orange, eyes. Its call is a fast, hooting 'doo-doo-doo-doo-hohoo'. This owl occurs in thornveld and dry broad-leafed woodland, either singly or in pairs. It is less common and more thinly distributed in the region than is the African Scops Owl, but is generally less well concealed than that species.

Pearlspotted Owl *Glaucidium perlatum* (398) L 18 cm

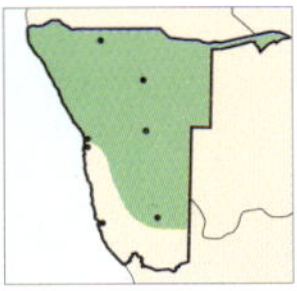

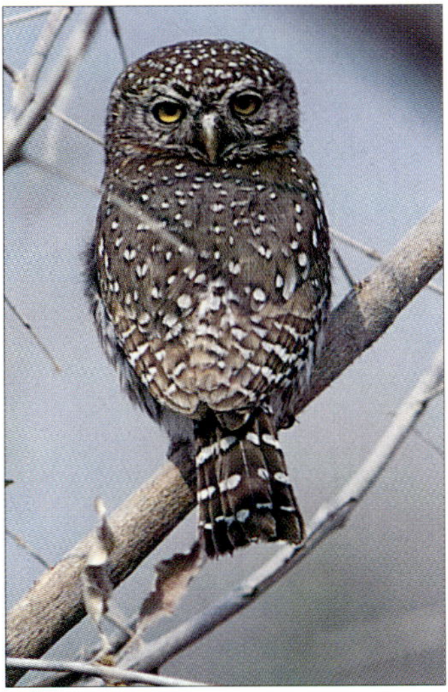

PETER CRAIG-COOPER

This owl, the smallest in the region, has a rounded head with no ear tufts. It further differs from the African Scops Owl and Whitefaced Owl by the *white spotting on its tail and back.* It shows *two black eye-like spots on the nape.* The immature resembles the adult. The call is a series of 'tu-tu-tu-tu' whistles, rising and descending in pitch, to which it responds during the day. It is common in dry thornveld and broad-leafed woodland, but may be found in suitable habitat throughout the region except in the south.

Spotted Eagle Owl *Bubo africanus* (401) L 43-50 cm

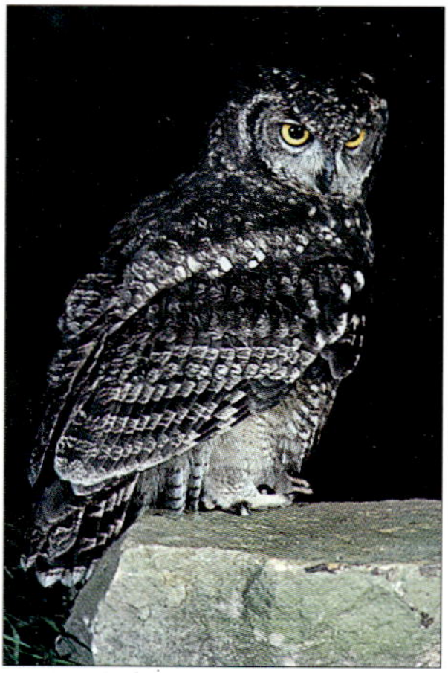

MAY CRAIG-COOPER

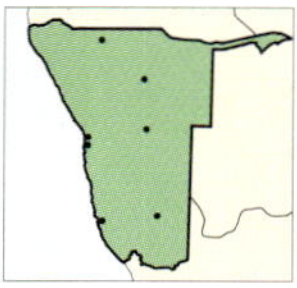

The Spotted Eagle Owl is definitely the most commonly seen large owl in Namibia. Both grey and rufous colour forms occur. It has *fine barring on the belly and flanks, ear tufts and yellow eyes*. Immatures resemble the adults. It occurs in a diverse range of habitats, from desert to mature woodland and savanna, but avoids dense forest. It has adapted well to suburbia and can be seen in the evening when its 'hu-hoo' call can be heard.

Rufouscheeked Nightjar *Caprimulgus rufigena* (406) L 24 cm

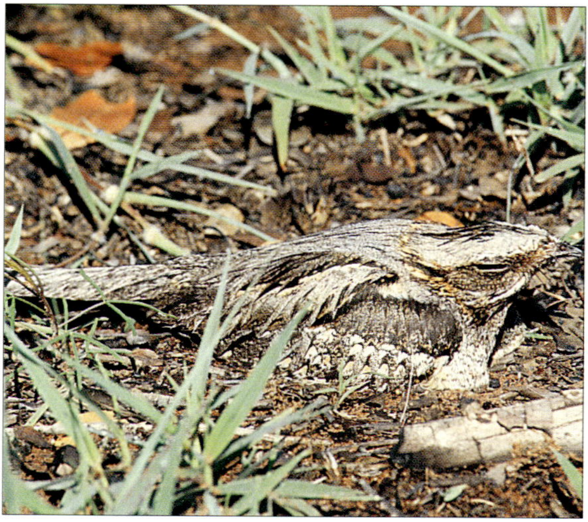

W R TARBOTON

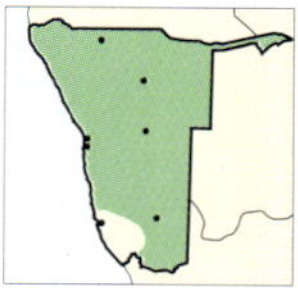

This is the nightjar which is most frequently encountered through most of Namibia. It is *smaller than the Freckled Nightjar and has a more slender appearance, longer and narrower wings* and a completely different call. The immature resembles the female. The call of this species is a prolonged 'churring', usually preceded by a choking 'chukoo-chukoo'. This nightjar is a common summer visitor and occurs widely, from arid and semi-arid areas to lightly wooded regions.

Freckled Nightjar *Caprimulgus tristigma* (408) L 28 cm

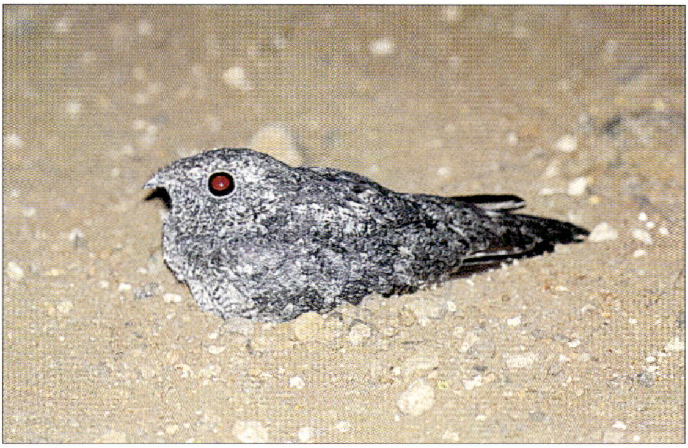

ABPL/BRENDAN RYAN

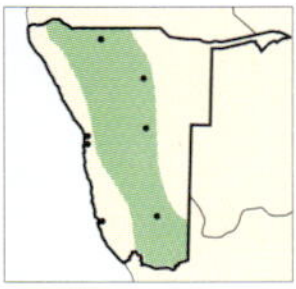

This species is similar in size to the Pennantwinged Nightjar but differs by having *freckled greyish upperparts* which camouflage it against the rocky terrain it frequents. In flight the white tips to the outertail feathers can be seen. The immature and female lack the white tail patches of the male. Its call is a yapping 'kow-kow-kow-kow'. It frequents rocky outcrops in woodlands and hilly terrain, and is common in rocky areas in central and southern Namibia.

Pennantwinged Nightjar *Macrodipteryx vexillaria* (410) L 28 cm

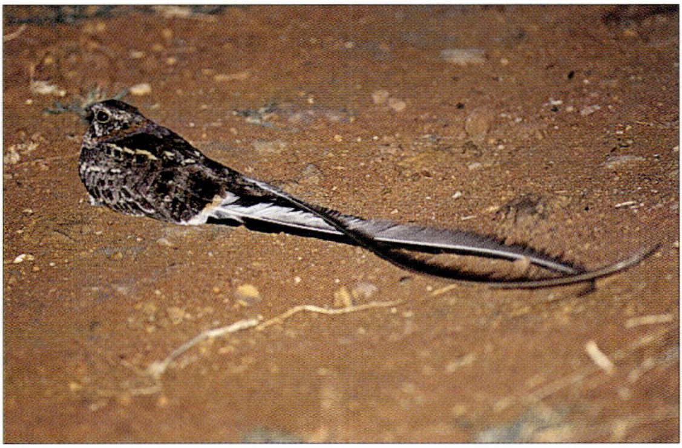

ABPL/BRENDAN RYAN

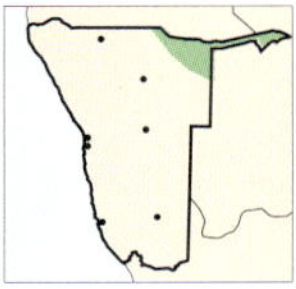

The breeding male of this species can easily be identified by the *broad white stripe across the primaries, and the white elongated inner primaries* which trail well behind the bird. The female is a nondescript, large, brown nightjar, lacking white on the wing or tail. The immature is similar to the female. The call is a bat-like, high-pitched twittering. It occurs in open woodland and bushveld, and is a common summer visitor to wooded areas of the north.

European (Eurasian) Swift *Apus apus* (411) L 17 cm

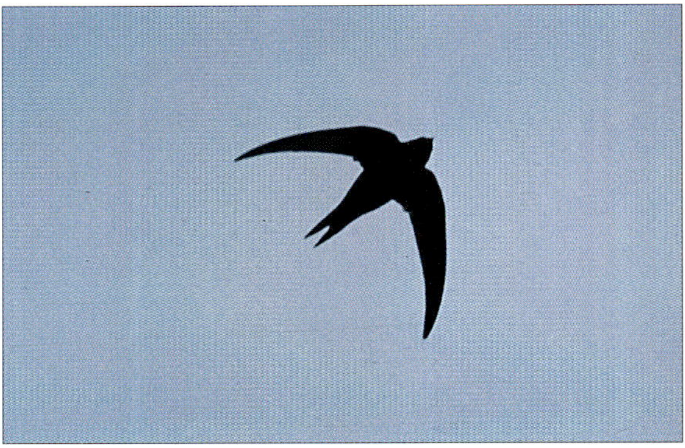

AQUILA/RA HUME

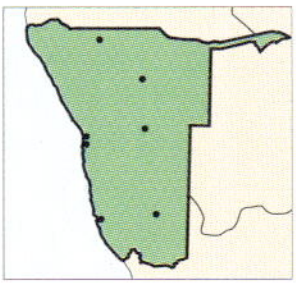

Large congregations of swifts foraging over the bushveld during summer are usually flocks of this species. The European Swift differs from the local Bradfield's Swift by being *much darker* and by having a *more contrasting, pale throat* and lacking scaling on the breast and belly. It is usually silent in the region but will give high-pitched 'screeee' notes, especially when breeding. The habitat is aerial and wide ranging. It is a common summer visitor to Namibia.

Bradfield's Swift *Apus bradfieldi* (413) L 18 cm

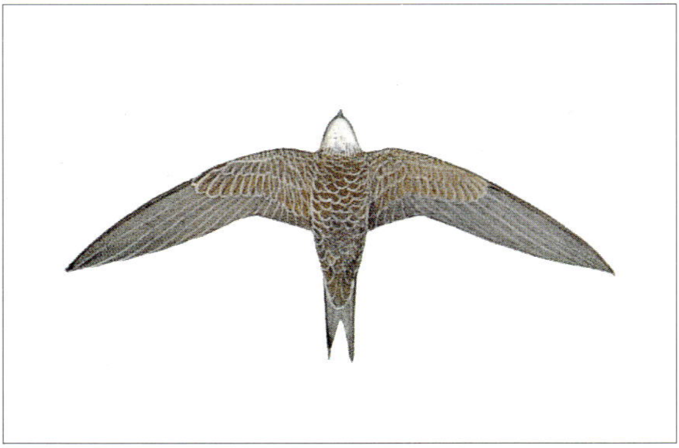

PETER HAYMAN

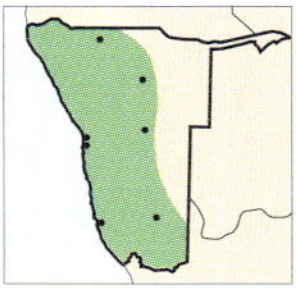

This species is very similar in outline to the European Swift but is paler overall and at close range it shows *scaling on the breast and belly*. The call is a loud and piercing 'screeee', heard at breeding sites. Very large swifts seen flying around palm trees could be members of this species; they also breed in crevices on cliffs. This common Namibian near-endemic could be encountered anywhere in the country; its habitat is aerial and wide ranging.

Whiterumped Swift *Apus caffer* (415) L 15 cm

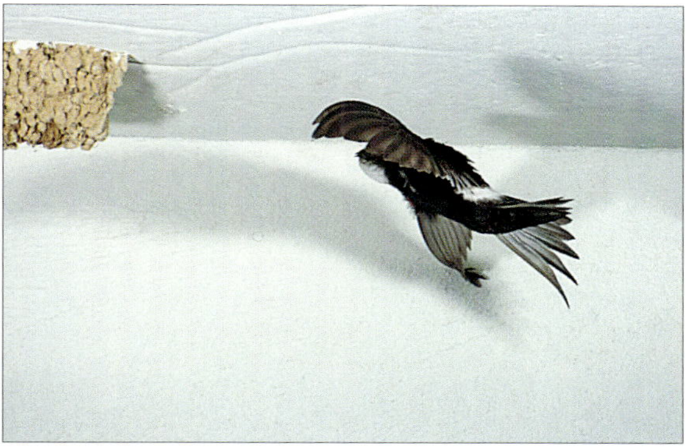

AQUILA/J J BROOKS

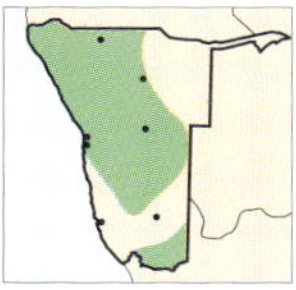

This swift has a white rump, and shows a diagnostic *long, deeply forked tail*. The tail usually appears long and pointed as the fork is frequently held closed. The thin, 'U'-shaped band across the rump is less obvious than in the Little Swift. A swift-like scream can be heard at breeding sites. It is a common summer visitor to the region, and is frequently seen over open country and in mountainous terrain. It commonly nests under roads in concrete culverts.

Little Swift *Apus affinis* (417) L 14 cm

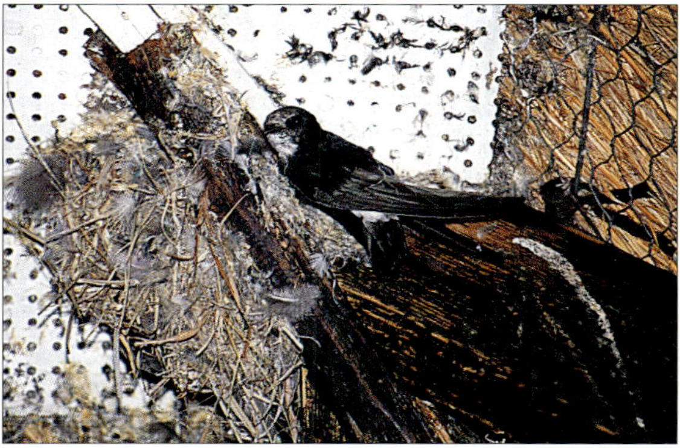

ABPL/BRENDAN RYAN

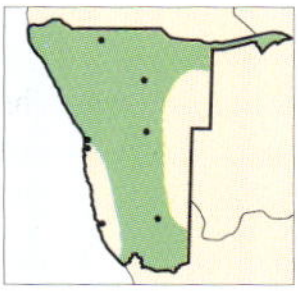

This small swift has a *large, square, white rump patch which wraps around the flanks, and a straight-ended, not forked, tail*. It is chunkier in body than the similar Whiterumped Swift, and shows a greater extent of white on the rump. In flight the wing tips appear rounded. The calls are a soft tittering and high-pitched screeching. It is commonly seen in tight flocks over cities and towns. It usually nests colonially under the eaves of buildings, bridges and rocky overhangs.

Pied Kingfisher *Ceryle rudis* (428) L 28 cm

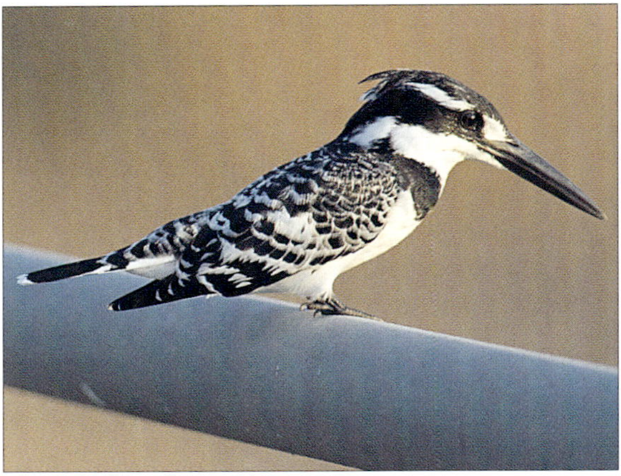

IAN SINCLAIR

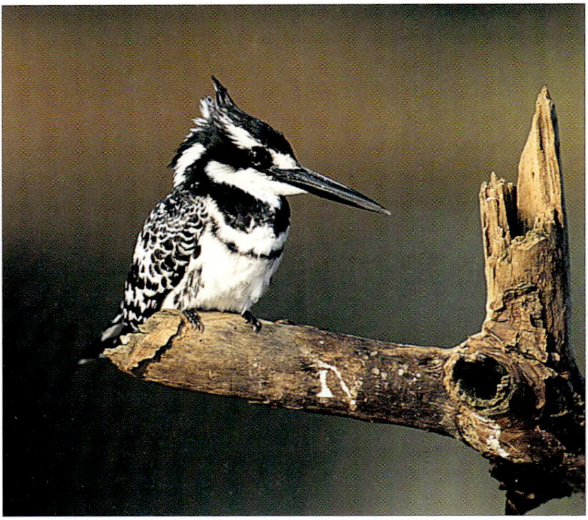

SIL/NIGEL J DENNIS

Top: female. Bottom: male

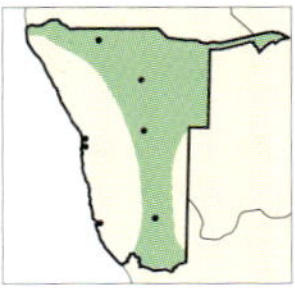

The *pied black and white plumage* renders this bird unmistakable; it is the only black and white kingfisher in the region. This species either perches on a branch overhanging water or it hovers over water before diving to seize a fish in its exceptionally long bill. The male has a double black breast band; the female has a single, incomplete breast band. The immature is like the female. Occasionally members in small groups interact excitedly, giving a twittering call and a sharp, high-pitched 'chik-chik'. It is found on any open stretch of freshwater, and also frequents coastal lagoons and wooded streams. It is more common in the moister north of Namibia.

European Bee-eater *Merops apiaster* (438) L 28 cm

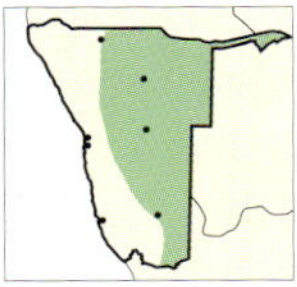

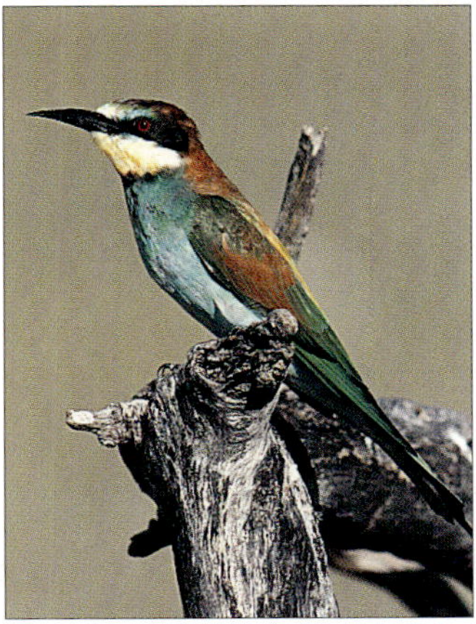

ABPL/CLEM HAAGNER

This is the only bee-eater in the region with a *chestnut crown and mantle*. In flight a dazzling array of colours can be seen; it has a *chestnut to golden back contrasting with torquoise-blue underparts and almost translucent rufous wings*. The immature differs from the adult by having a green back and pale blue underparts. Groups in flight utter a far-carrying, policeman's whistle-like, characteristic 'prrrup' call. This common summer visitor occurs in thornveld, open broad-leafed woodland and adjacent grassy areas.

Swallowtailed Bee-eater *Merops hirundineus* (455) L 22 cm

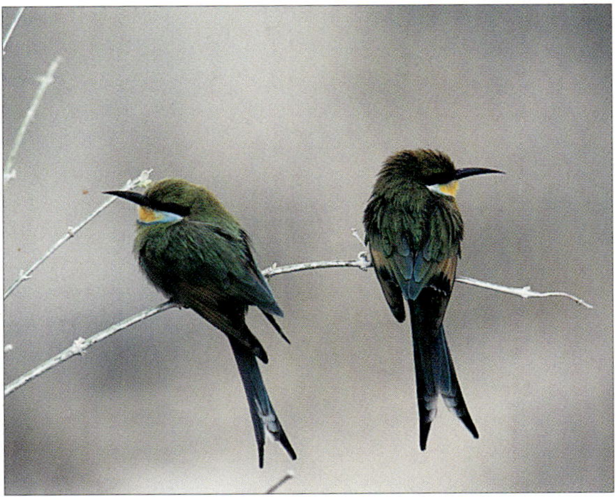

ABPL/NIGEL J DENNIS

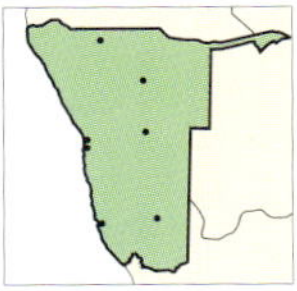

This is the only bee-eater in the region to have, as the name indicates, a *forked tail*. It is also identified by its *yellow throat, blue collar, blue-green underparts and blue tail*. The immature shows the diagnostic forked tail, but lacks the yellow throat and blue collar. It utters a soft twittering, and calls 'kwit-kwit'. A common resident of Namibia, this bird frequents a diverse range of habitats from semi-desert scrub to moist, evergreen forests.

Lilacbreasted Roller *Coracias caudata* (447) L 36 cm

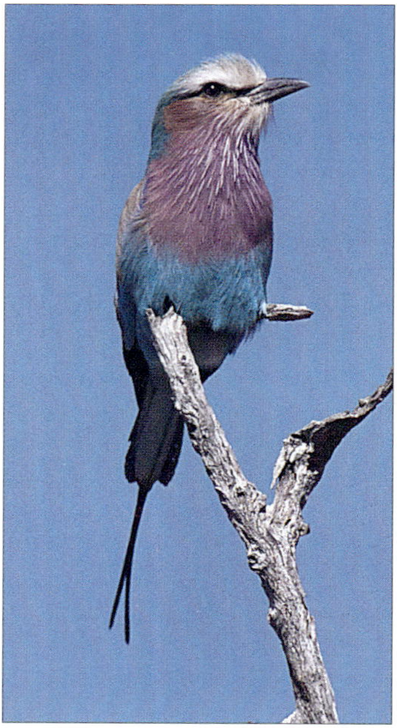

HELM THERON

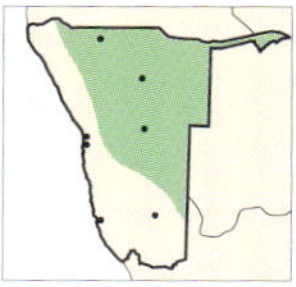

In flight this bird shows a range of *pale and dark blues in the wings*. The *lilac breast* and elongated, pointed outertail feathers can be seen at rest. The immature resembles the adult, but lacks the long outertail feathers. When displaying, the male utters harsh squawks and screams. It occurs in a range of habitats from thornveld to open broad-leafed woodland and is frequently seen on telephone wires and poles along roadsides. It is common in the more wooded and thornveld regions of Namibia.

Purple Roller *Coracias naevia* (449) L 38 cm

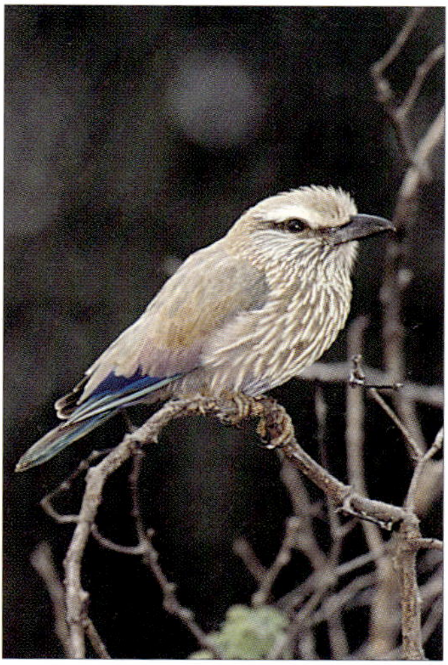

HELM THERON

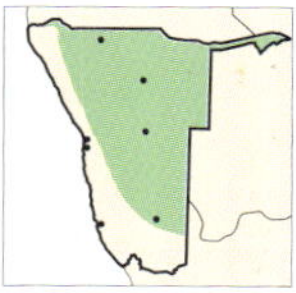

This is the largest roller in southern Africa and is easily identified by its *broad, pale eyebrow stripe and lilac-brown underparts streaked with white*. The immature is a duller version of the adult. In display flight this bird utters a harsh, repeated 'karaa-karaa' while flying with an exaggerated, side-to-side rocking motion. It is found in dry thornveld and open broad-leafed woodland. This roller is a common resident in Namibia, with some local movement in certain areas of the region.

African Hoopoe *Upupa africana* (451) L 28 cm

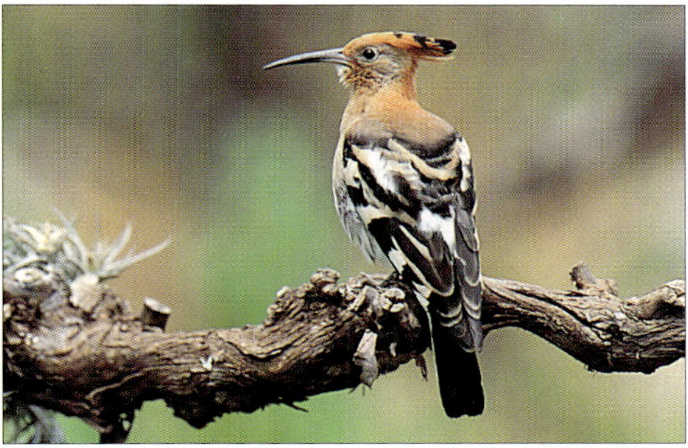

NIGEL J DENNIS

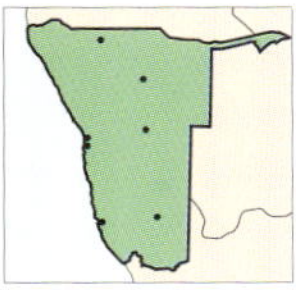

This species is easily identified by the combination of a *cinnamon-coloured body, black and white barred wings and tail, and long decurved bill.* The female is duller than the male with less white in the wings; the immature is duller than the female. The *black-tipped crest* is often kept closed but when the bird is alarmed it is held erect. Its call is a soft, frequently uttered 'hoop-hoop-hoop'. This common resident inhabits thornveld, open broadleafed woodland, parks and gardens.

Southern Violet Woodhoopoe *Phoeniculus damarensis* (453) L 40 cm

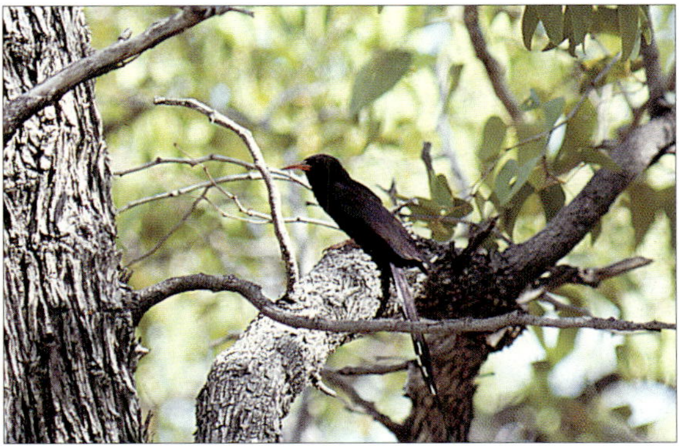

IAN DAVIDSON

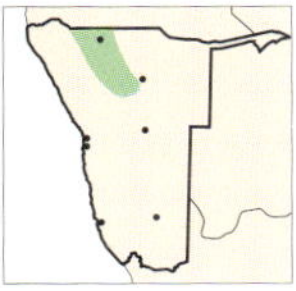

This large woodhoopoe has a *violet head, mantle and back,* but lacks the bottle-green sheen of the similar Redbilled Woodhoopoe. It is also larger and longer-tailed, with a more laboured and floppier flight action. The immature resembles the adult but is duller and has a black, not red, bill. Its call is a harsh cackling and chattering. This common endemic is found in the central and northern areas in tall thornveld, on dry river courses and in broad-leafed woodland.

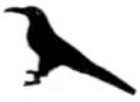

Redbilled Woodhoopoe *Phoeniculus purpureus* (452) L 36 cm

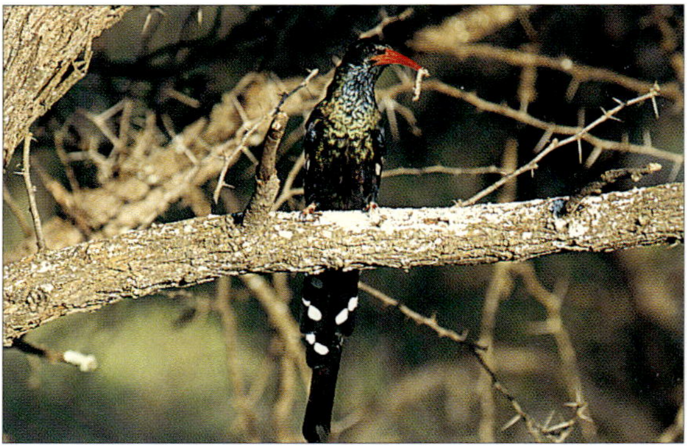

ABPL/CLEM HAAGNER

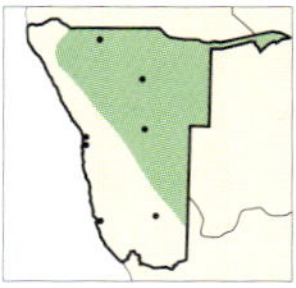

Larger than the Greater Scimitarbill, this species has a *long, decurved, red bill, red legs, white wing bars and a long, white-tipped tail.* The bottle-green head and back distinguish it from the similar Southern Violet Woodhoopoe. Females have a shorter, less decurved bill; immatures have a black, not red, and far less decurved bill. Its harsh, cackling call is slower than that of the Southern Violet Woodhoopoe. It is common in mixed woodland and thornveld, and replaces the Common Violet Woodhoopoe in the northeast of the region.

Greater Scimitarbill *Rhinopomastus cyanomelas* (454) L 26 cm

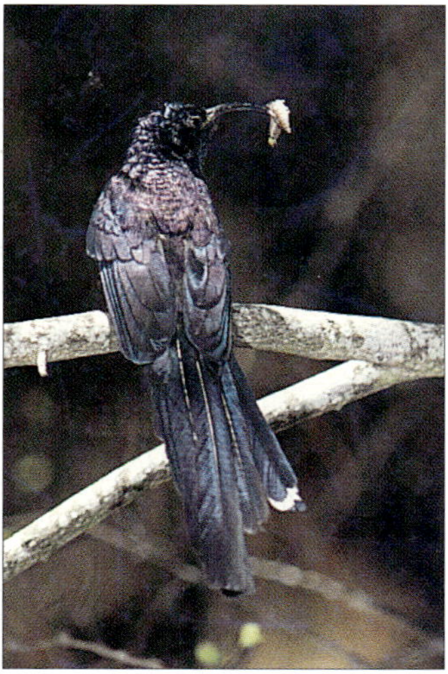

P J GINN

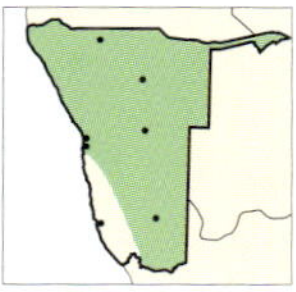

The *white bars on the primaries are visible in flight, as well as a long, graduated, white-tipped tail.* In the field it appears black, except in direct sunlight when a purple sheen is noticeable. It has a *thin, black, extremely decurved bill* and is smaller and more slender than the Southern Violet and Redbilled wood-hoopoes. The imm-ature has black, not red, legs and feet and a more decurved bill than the immature Redbilled Woodhoopoe. Its call is a high-pitched, whistling 'sweep-sweep-sweep', and harsh chattering. It frequents thornveld as well as dry broad-leafed woodland.

Grey Hornbill *Tockus nasutus* (457) L 46 cm

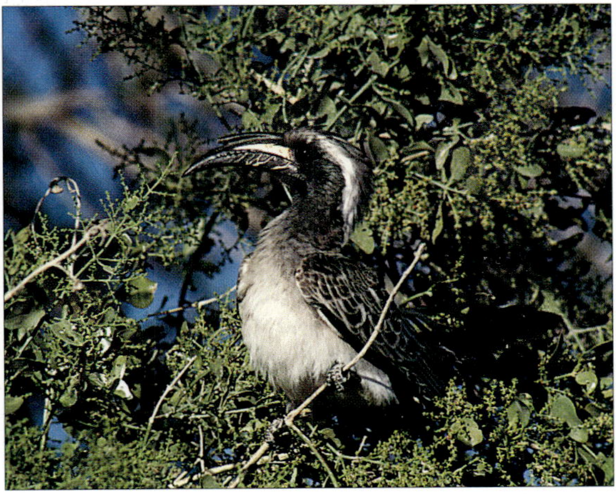

ABPL/NIGEL DENNIS

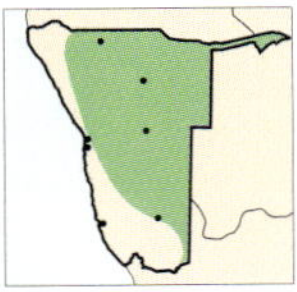

The male is the only small hornbill in the region with a dark bill. The female might be confused with the Southern Yellowbilled Hornbill as the upperparts of the bill are yellow. The *dark head and breast and conspicuous white eyebrow stripe* aid identification. Immatures are similar to males but lack the casque. It emits a series of piping, 'phee pheeoo phee pheeoo' notes. Occurring in thornveld and dry, broad-leafed woodland, it is common in the region except in true desert areas.

Southern Yellowbilled Hornbill *Tockus leucomelas* (459) L 55 cm

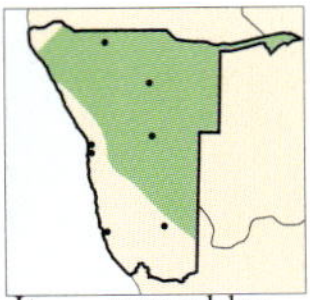

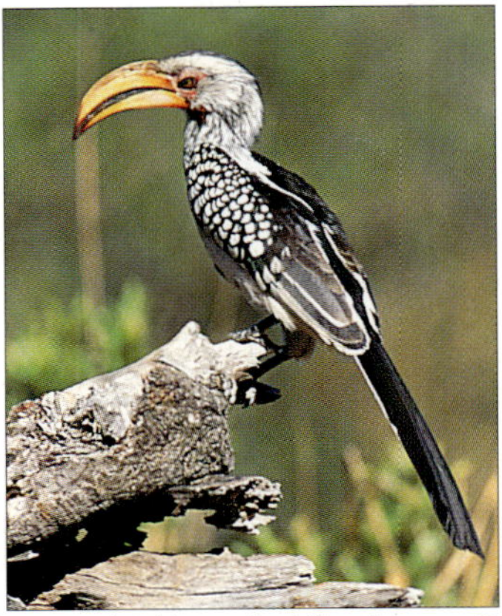

SIL/NIGEL J DENNIS

It resembles the Redbilled Hornbill in plumage coloration but has a diagnostic *large, long, yellow bill.* This species might be confused with the female Grey Hornbill, which has a shorter, part-yellow bill, but may be distinguished by its dark head and breast. Both immature and female have a noticeably smaller bill and casque. It spreads its wings while giving 'tok-tok-tork-tork' call notes. This bird frequents thornveld and broad-leafed woodland and is more widely but thinly distributed in the region than the Redbilled Hornbill.

Redbilled Hornbill *Tockus erythrorhynchus* (458) L 46 cm

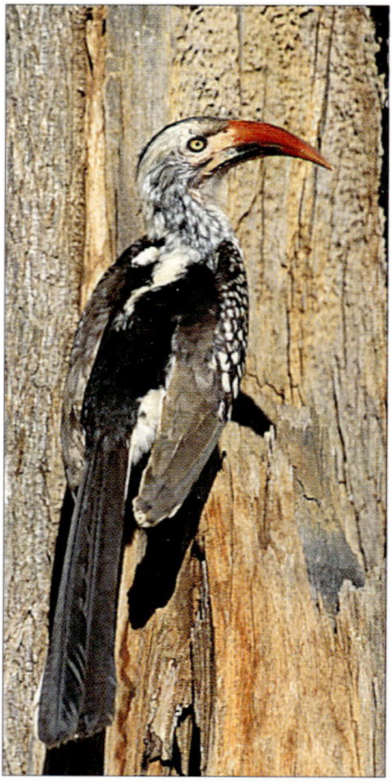

SIL/NIGEL J DENNIS

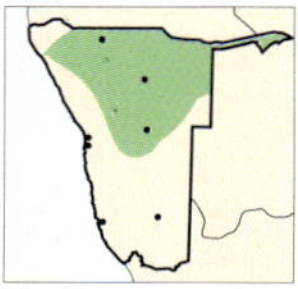

Similar to the Southern Yellowbilled Hornbill, this species has a shorter, more slender, all-red bill. The *pale head, broad white eyebrow stripe, and black and white speckled upperparts* with a *white stripe down the back* should rule out any confusion with other larger, red-billed hornbills. The male has a black patch at the base of the lower mandible. The immature has a duller, less well-developed bill, and buff, not white, spotting on the wings. The female has a smaller, all-red bill. The display call is a 'kokwe-kokwe-kokwe'; in calling display the head is lowered and the wings held closed. This bird usually occurs singly or in pairs in thornveld and mopane woodland and is the most common small hornbill in the central and northern areas.

Monteiro's Hornbill *Tockus monteiri* (462) L 56 cm

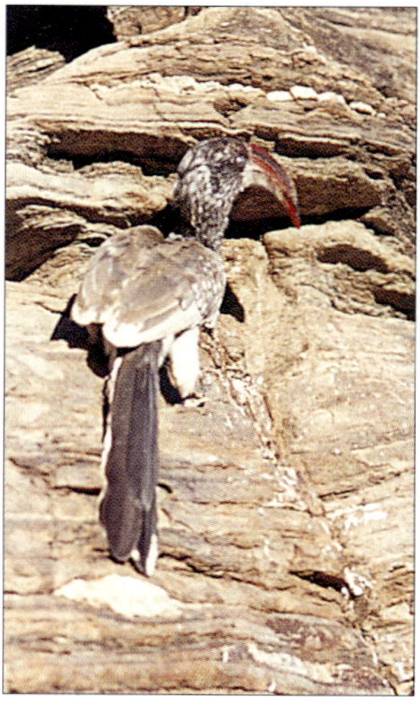

TRANSVAAL MUSEUM/A C KEMP

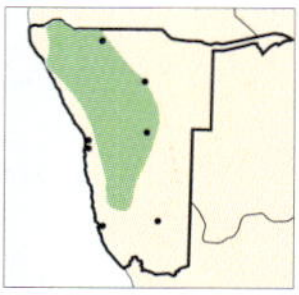

This large, red-billed bird has diagnostic *white patches on the secondaries* as well as a *large expanse of white on the outertail feathers*. Bradfield's Hornbill differs from this species by lacking white in the wings and having a white-tipped tail. The immature has a smaller bill. Its call is a hollow-sounding 'tooaaka tooaaka'. It is a common Namibian endemic, frequenting dry thornveld, well-treed, dry river beds and broad-leafed woodland.

Acacia Pied Barbet *Lybius leucomelas* (465) L 18 cm

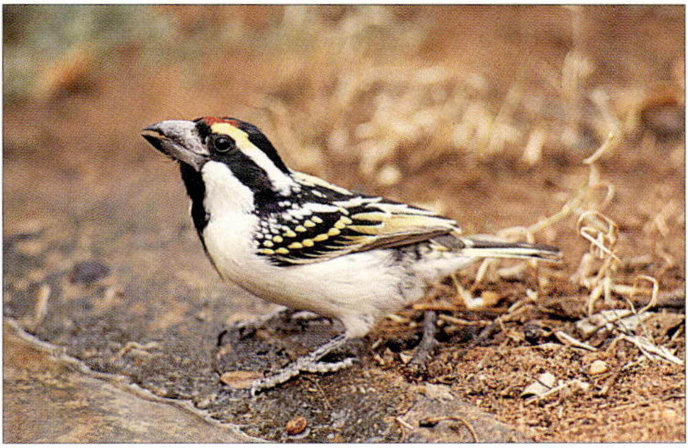

W R TARBOTON

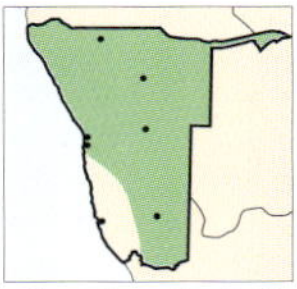

The combination of the *red forehead, bright yellow eyebrow and broad white stripe behind the eye* in this species is diagnostic. It has a black throat, white underparts and a black back with narrow yellow streaking. The immature has a black, not red, forehead. The call of this species is either a nasal 'nehh-nehh', repeated at intervals, or a hoopoe-like 'doo-doo-doo'. Found alone or in pairs in dry broad-leafed woodland, thornveld and scrub, this common resident avoids true desert.

Lesser Honeyguide *Indicator minor* (476) L 15 cm

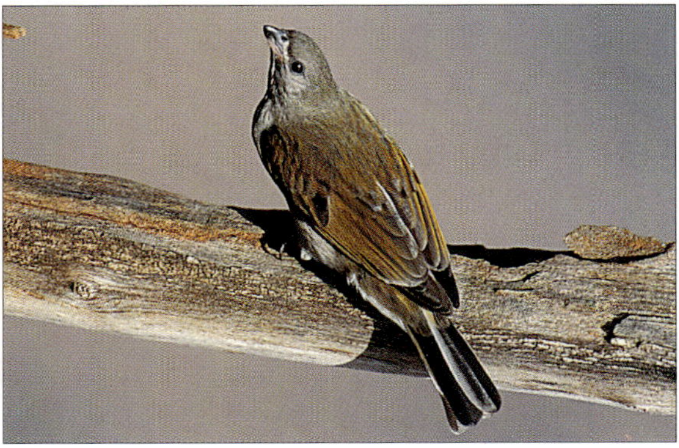

ABPL/NIGEL J DENNIS

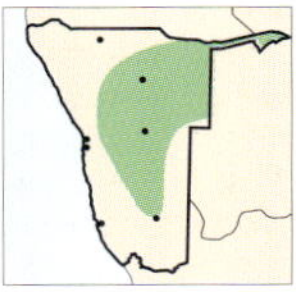

Overall a dull, greyish bird with an unmarked grey head, a *greenish wash on the wing coverts, dark moustachial stripes and conspicuous white outer-tail feathers*. The immature lacks the moustachial stripes of the adult. This bird is easily detected by its distinctive 'klew klew klew' call. It occurs in woodland, forests and thornveld, and has adapted to suburban gardens. This common resident is often seen interacting with its host, the Acacia Pied Barbet.

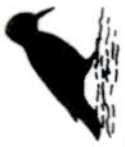

Cardinal Woodpecker *Dendropicos fuscescens* (486) L 15 cm

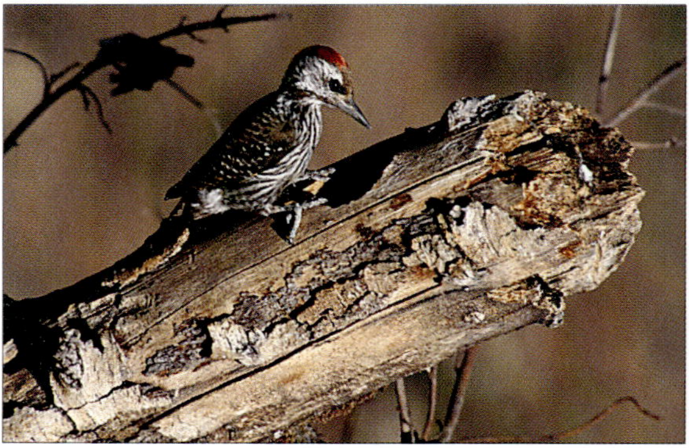

PHOTO ACCESS/G P L DU PLESSIS

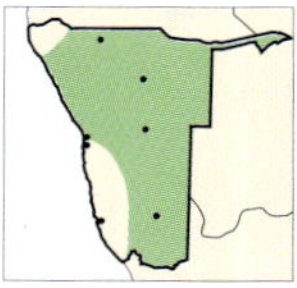

This is the smallest woodpecker in the region. It has *bold black moustachial stripes* and appears *black and white all over*. The male has a brown forehead and a red nape; the female lacks the red nape. The immature has a red crown and a black nape. This bird is sometimes difficult to locate, but its incessant soft tapping on wood and high-pitched 'krrrek-krrrek-krrrek' call reveal its position. It frequents a wide range of habitats from thornveld to thick forest.

Bearded Woodpecker *Thripias namaquus* (487) L 25 cm

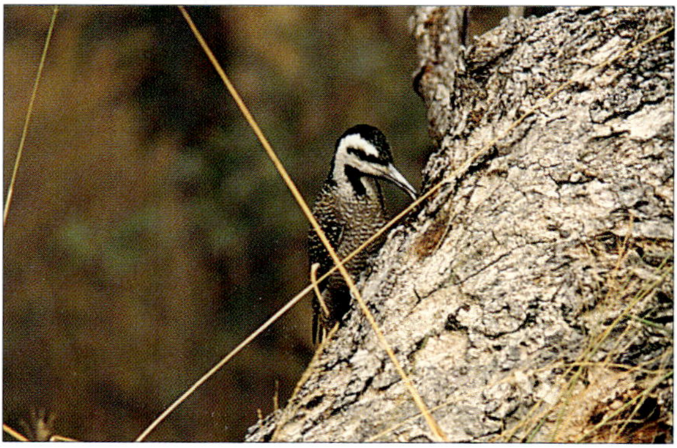

PHOTO ACCESS/DAVID STEELE

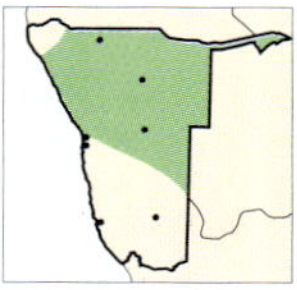

It is much bigger than the Cardinal Woodpecker. *The white face, bold black moustachial stripes and black stripe through and behind the eye are diagnostic*. The dark underparts are finely barred with black and white. The male's hind crown and nape are red; those of the female are black. The immature has a red crown and nape. It taps wood loudly and utters a loud 'kweek-eek-eek-eek'. This common resident is found in thornveld, riverine forests and broad-leafed woodland.

Monotonous Lark *Mirafra passerina* (493) L 14 cm

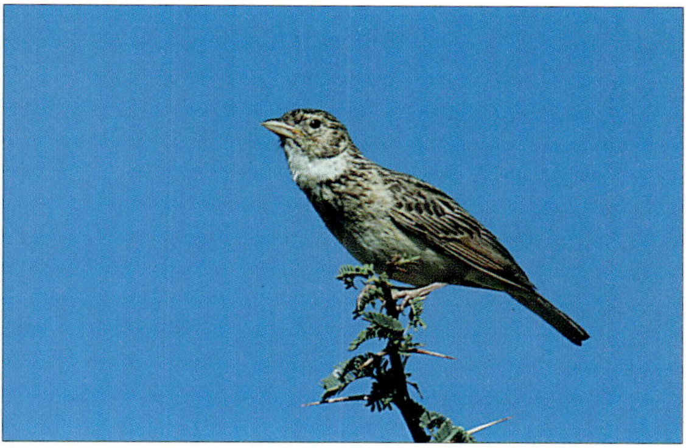

ABPL/CLEM HAAGNER

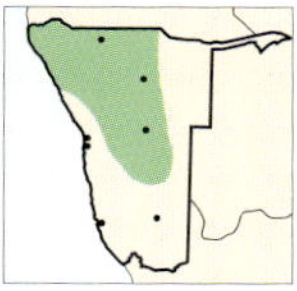

This bird is easily overlooked when it is not singing or displaying, but when it is observed it has an obvious *white throat contrasting with a dark streaked breast, rufous wings and white outertail feathers*. During the late summer and rainy season the bird displays conspicuously and calls from exposed perches. The call is a 'trrp-chup-chup-choop', repeated often during the day and at night. It is very common and evident in lightly wooded habitat during the rains.

Sabota Lark *Mirafra sabota* (498) L 15 cm

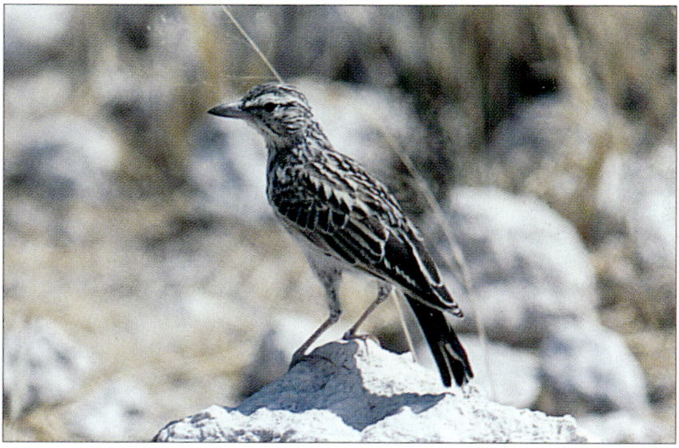

T H BUCHHOLZ

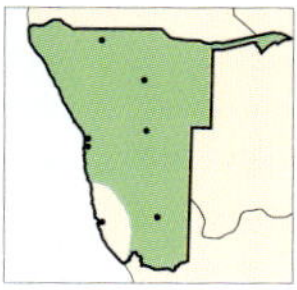

This small, nondescript lark has a *short, thick bill and a straight white eye-stripe, giving a capped appearance*. It lacks the chestnut in the outer wings seen in many similar larks. Immatures are tawnier than adults with mottled upperparts. It has a habit of sitting on small trees or telephone wires, mimicking other birds and producing its jumbled song. It is often found in rocky areas in dry thornveld and open broad-leafed woodland. It is common in Namibia, especially in Etosha.

Dune Lark *Certhilauda erythrochlamys* (503) L 17 cm

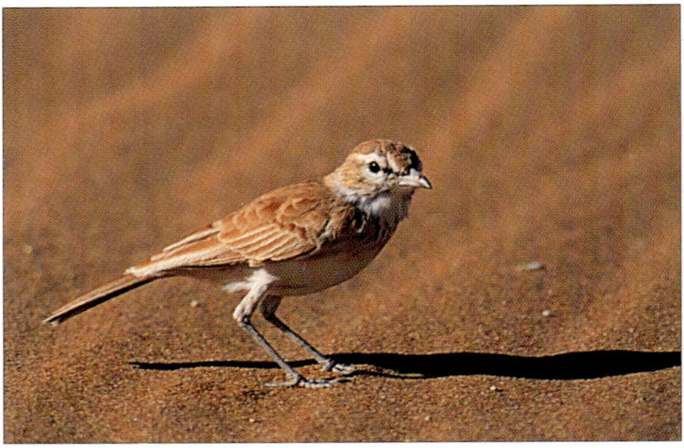

JOSEPH WILLIAMS

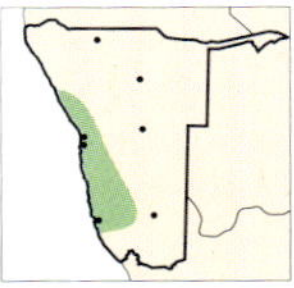

This sandy-coloured lark is endemic to Namibia. It has a *plain or slightly streaked sandy-brown back, and slightly streaked underparts*. The immature shows pale edgings to the feathers on the back. It is usually silent but a short, clipped song is sometimes given. This species, although locally common, is thinly distributed in the region. It occurs in scant scrub in dry river beds or gravel valleys between the sand dunes of the Namib Desert.

Dusky Lark *Pinarocorys nigricans* (505) L 19 cm

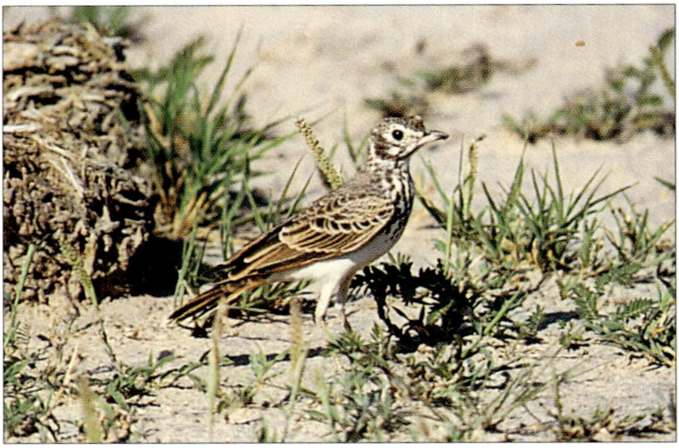

W R TARBOTON

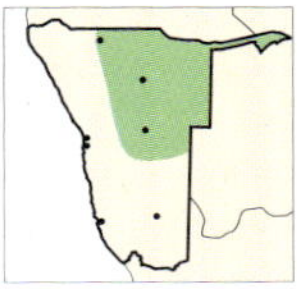

This large, thrush-like lark shows a *bold black and white facial pattern*. When perched in trees, the heavy spotting on the underparts is visible. It *characteristically raises its wings slightly above its body when walking*. Immatures have heavily mottled underparts. It utters a soft 'chrrp, chrrp' call when flushed. It occurs in open grassy areas in thornveld and broad-leafed woodland, especially recently burnt areas. A regular summer visitor, it is neither common nor predictable.

Spikeheeled Lark *Chersomanes albofasciata* (506) L 15 cm

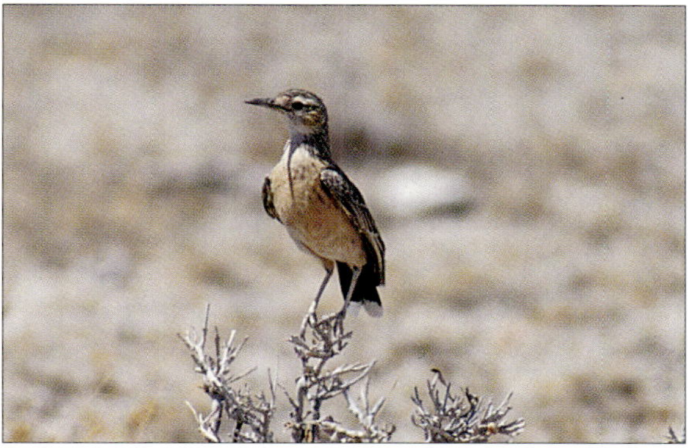

ALAN WEAVING

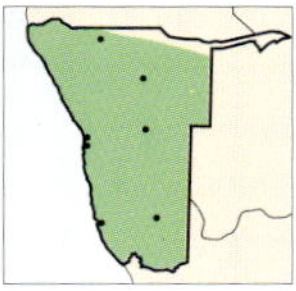

This long-legged lark has a very upright stance. The combination of a *long, slightly decurved bill, white throat patch contrasting strongly with the darker underparts and the remarkably short, dark, white-tipped tail* is diagnostic. The male is larger than the female. The immature has white mottling above and below. It can be heard giving its trilling 'trrrep, trrrep' call in flight. This lark is a common resident and occurs in sparse grassland and scrub desert, and on gravel plains.

Stark's Lark *Calandrella starki* (511) L 14 cm

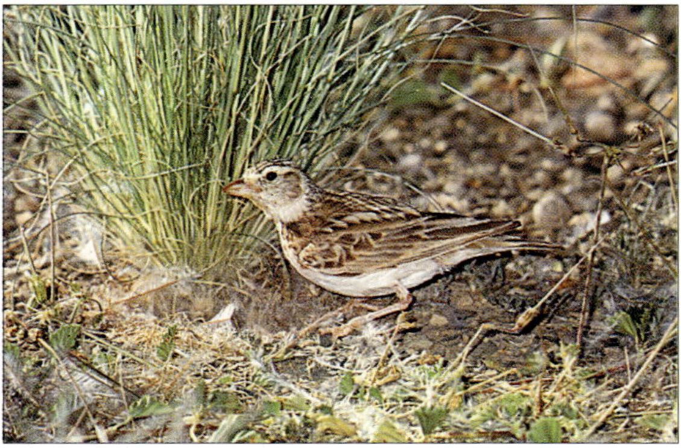

PHOTO ACCESS/PETER STEYN

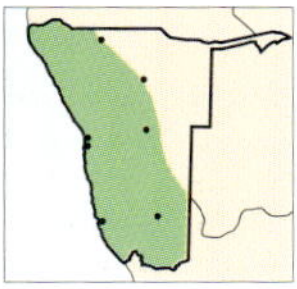

This small, pale-coloured lark sometimes occurs singly but is most likely to be seen in small flocks. At rest it shows a *pale pink bill* and *a streaked necklace on the breast.* When startled it raises its *long, pointed, erectile crest* which is diagnostic. The immature is spotted white on the upperparts. In display flight it dangles its long, flesh-coloured legs. Its song is a short, jumbled mixture of notes. Common but nomadic, it occurs on stony desert and in grassy semi-desert areas.

Gray's Lark *Ammomanes grayi* (514) L 14 cm

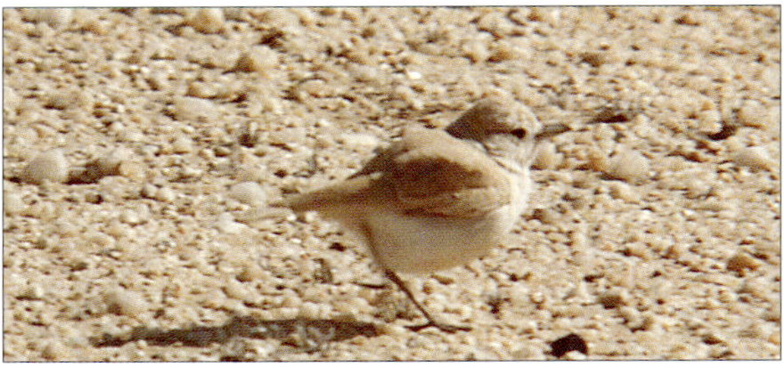

TRANSVAAL MUSEUM

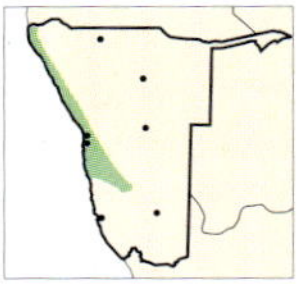

This small, endemic lark is the palest and least marked in the region. The *plumage is very plain, lacking streaking and barring*, which renders it unlikely to be confused with any other lark species. The immature is mottled above. It has a short 'tseet' flight call and a ringing, metallic 'ping-ping' call. This lark frequents gravel plains along the coastal desert and desert edge of Namibia, and is common but thinly distributed in the region.

Greybacked Finchlark *Eremopterix verticalis* (516) L 13 cm

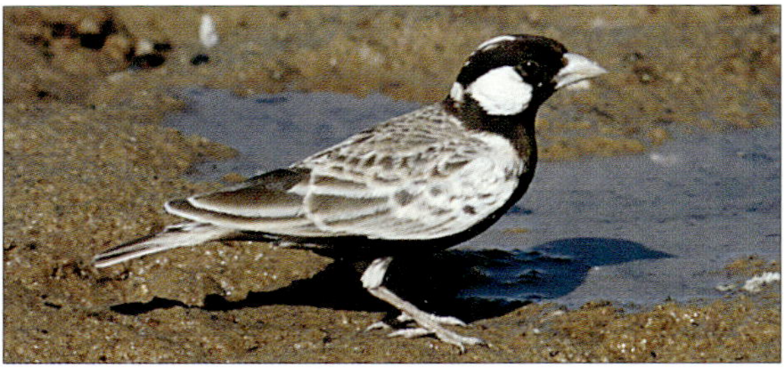

PETER CRAIG-COOPER

Above: male. Below: female

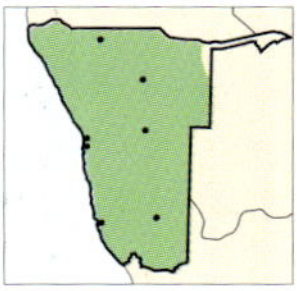

When this species is observed on the ground its diagnostic *totally black underparts, greyish upperparts and wings, and black and white patterned head* are clearly visible. The male has a white patch on the hind crown. The female has a pale conical bill and greyish upperparts, but has only a patch of black down the centre of her belly. The immature is more mottled than the female. In flight it utters a sharp 'chruk, chruk' note. Occurring mostly in small flocks in scrub, true desert and cultivated lands, this common resident is nomadic in some areas.

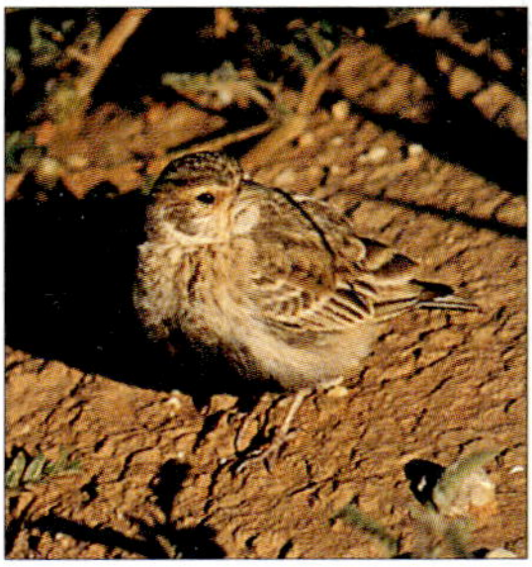

ABPL/BRENDAN RYAN

European (Barn) Swallow *Hirundo rustica* (518) L 18 cm

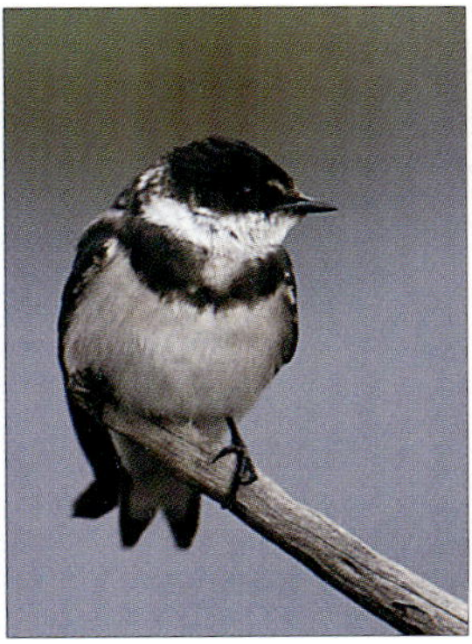
DR & MRS MANFRED REICHARDT

Immature

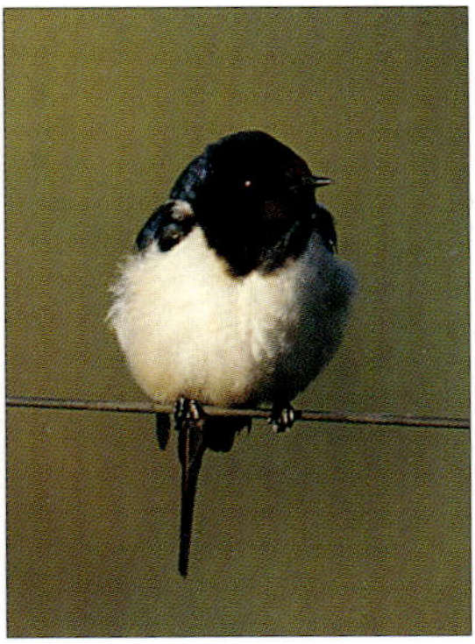
W R TARBOTON

Adult

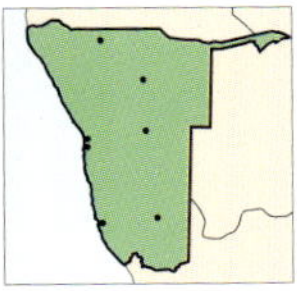

This species can be identified by the *diagnostic brick-red face and throat, black breast band and deeply forked tail.* Its underparts are off-white to buffish in colour. The tail has long streamers and white spots on the tail base; the male has a longer tail than the female. The immature is browner and has shorter outertail feathers. It has a soft, high-pitched, twittering call. A common summer visitor, it is found in virtually every habitat in the region.

Pearlbreasted Swallow *Hirundo dimidiata* (523) L 14 cm

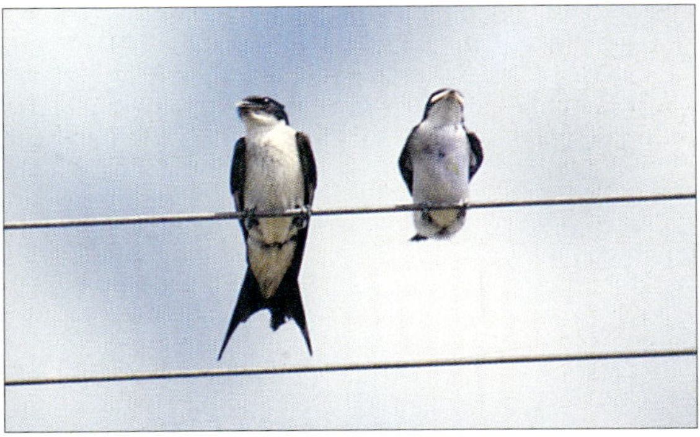
IAN SINCLAIR

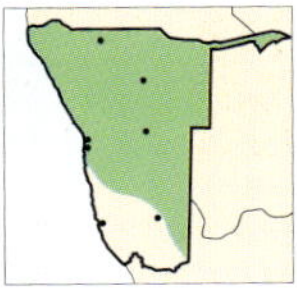

This small swallow has *off-white to white underparts and completely blue-black upperparts.* In flight the contrasting black and white plumage rules out confusion with other swallows in the region. The call is a subdued, chipping note, given mostly in flight. It is most often seen perched on telephone or fence wires along roadsides, especially near road culverts where it breeds. It is a common but thinly distributed resident with local movements in parts of its range.

Redbreasted Swallow *Hirundo semirufa* (524) L 24 cm

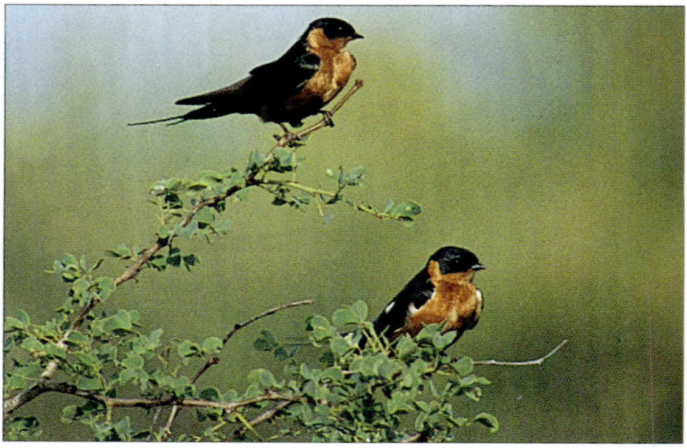

IAN SINCLAIR

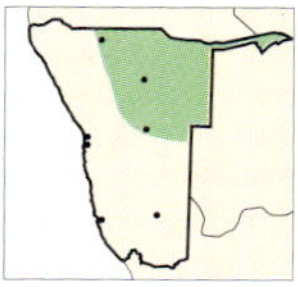

This very large, dark swallow is easily identified by its diagnostic *red throat and breast*. In flight the dark, buffy underwing coverts can be seen. The remaining plumage is a dark, glossy blue-black. The immature has a creamy white throat and breast. It has a soft, warbling song with harsh, twittering notes uttered in flight. This common summer visitor to the more northerly regions is usually encountered in pairs along the roadside in grassland and savanna areas.

Greater Striped Swallow *Hirundo cucullata* (526) L 20 cm

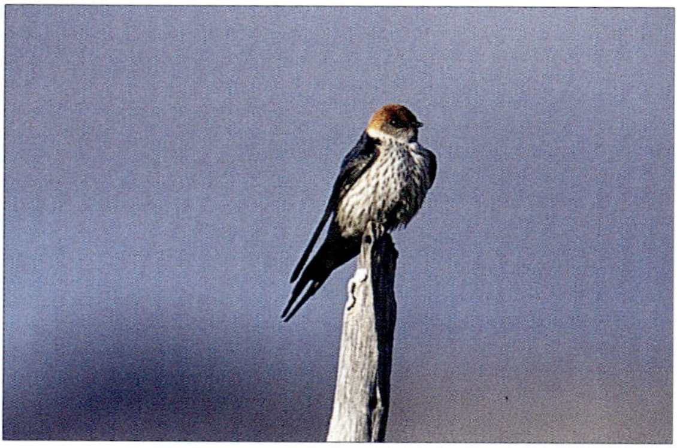

DR & MRS MANFRED REICHARDT

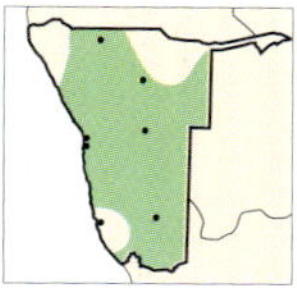

The *crown and rump are pale orange and the ear coverts are white*. Only at close range is the faint striping on the white underparts noticeable. The immature has a small amount of blue-black gloss above; the crown is reddish brown, and the breast has a partial brown band. The call is a twittering 'chissick' and a discordant 'zzrreeeoo'. It is a common summer visitor to the region, and is found in open grassland and near vleis as well as along roadsides, especially near culverts.

South African Cliff Swallow *Hirundo spilodera* (528) L 15 cm

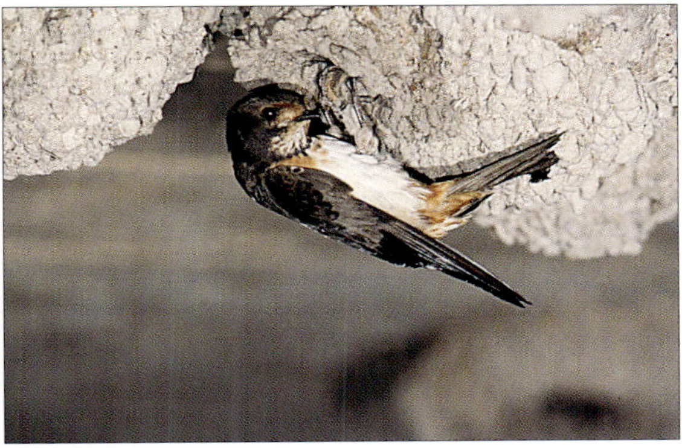

PETER GINN

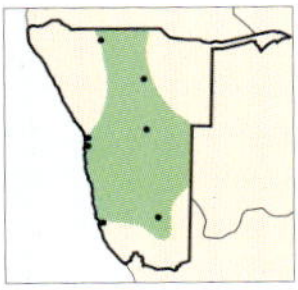

It differs from the similar Greater Striped Swallow by having only a *slight notch in the square-ended tail, a distinct breast band, and by being more rufous below with much reduced streaking*. The immature lacks the blue-black gloss above. Its call, an indistinct 'chooerp-chooerp', is uttered near nesting colonies. It occurs in upland grasslands, usually in the vicinity of road bridges under which it frequently builds its nest. It is a common but unevenly distributed summer visitor.

Rock Martin *Hirundo fuligula* (529) L 15 cm

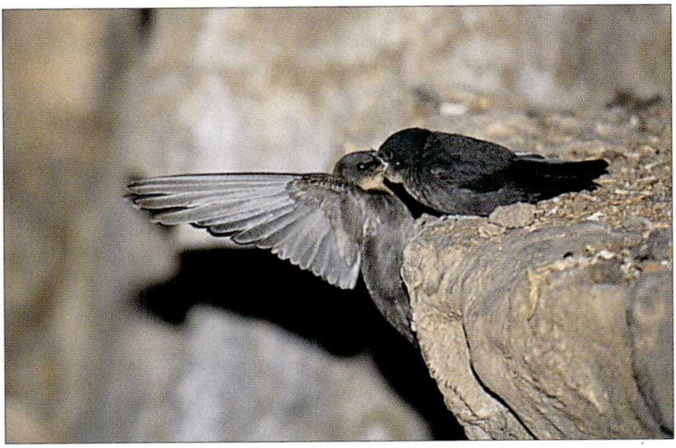

ABPL/BRENDAN RYAN

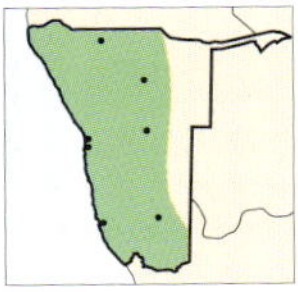

This is a *medium-sized martin with all-brown plumage*. It could be confused with the dark form of the Brownthroated Martin, a smaller species. The Rock Martin has slightly paler underparts and, when in flight, white spots are visible on the tail. The immature has pale edges on the upperwing coverts and secondaries. The call is a series of soft indistinct twitterings. This common resident prefers rocky, mountainous terrain but has adapted to towns and cities.

Brownthroated Martin *Riparia paludicola* (533) L 12 cm

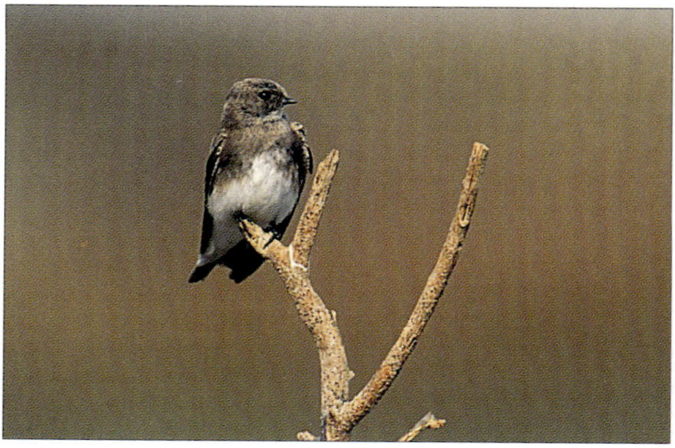

ABPL/NIGEL J DENNIS

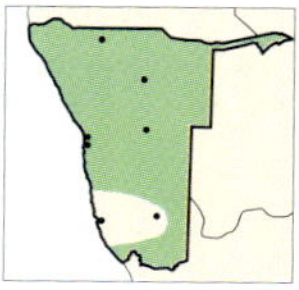

This species occurs in two colour forms: *one is dark brown and shows a small amount of white on the vent, while the other paler form has a brown throat and breast with the remainder of the underparts white*. The dark brown form is often confused with the Rock Martin but is smaller, darker brown below and lacks the white tail spots. The immature has pale fringes on the secondaries. The call is a soft twittering. A common resident, it occurs over sand banks near rivers.

Black Cuckooshrike *Campephaga flava* (538) L 22 cm

P J GINN

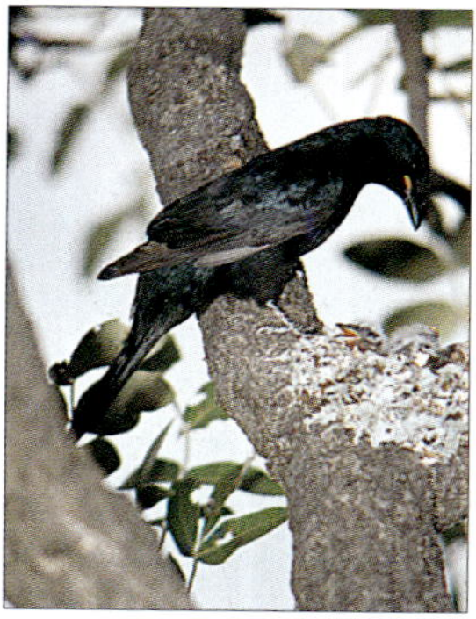

Male

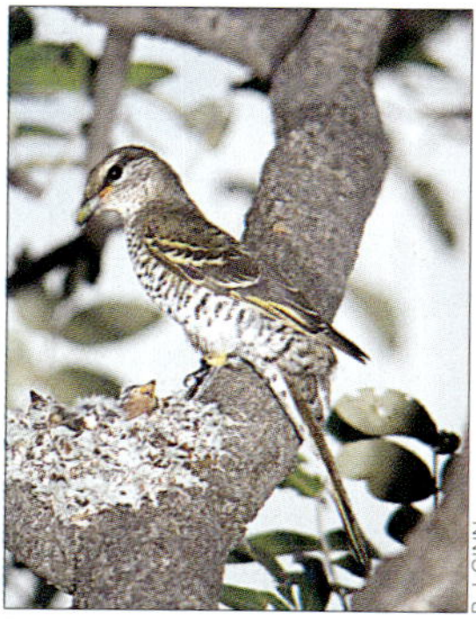

Female

P J GINN

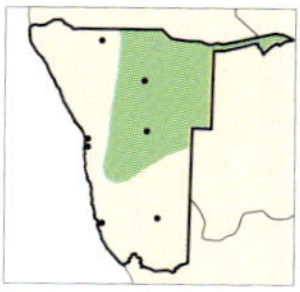

The male is distinguished by its *slightly glossy, all-black plumage, and yellow gape*. It often shows a yellow shoulder. The female of the species has a *green and yellow barred plumage with bright yellow outertail feathers*. The immature resembles the female. Its call is a high-pitched, prolonged 'trrrrrrr'. This common resident avoids desert areas and can be seen creeping through the foliage in a variety of woodlands, from thornveld to broad-leafed and riverine habitats.

Forktailed Drongo *Dicrurus adsimilis* (541) L 25 cm

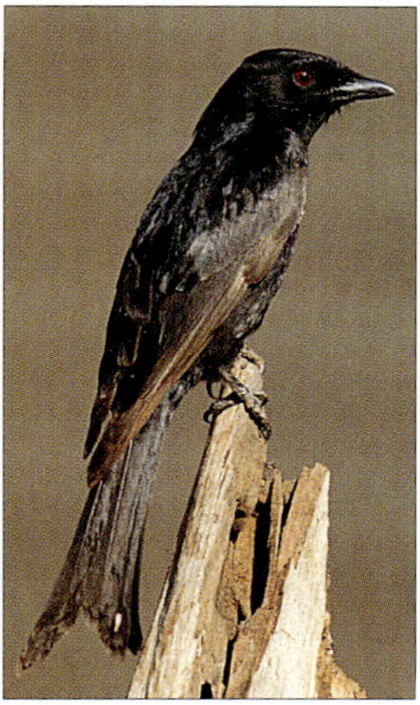

J J THERON

Adult

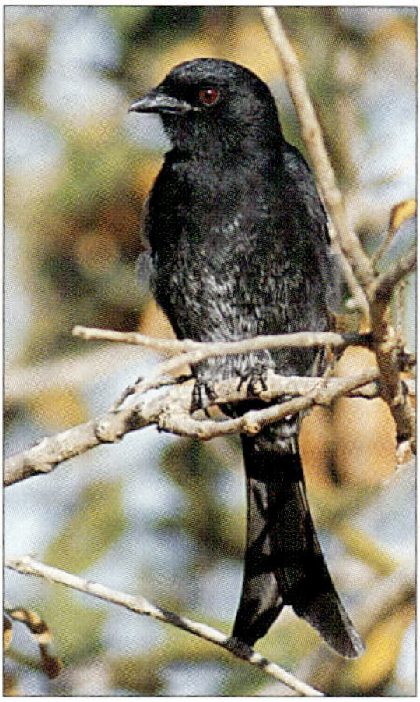

J J THERON

Immature

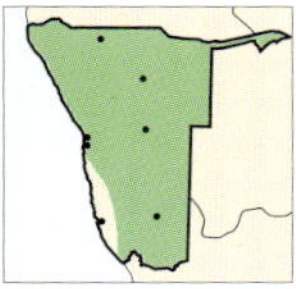

This is a noisy, *all-black bird with a deeply forked tail*. It perches freely in the open, from where it hawks insects in flight or drops to the ground to retrieve food. The immature has buff-tipped feathers on the underparts and forewing, and shows a yellow gape. It sometimes mimics the calls of birds of prey, especially that of the Pearlspotted Owl, and produces a variety of grating or shrill 'tchwaak tchweeek' notes. This common resident inhabits a diverse range of habitats.

African Golden Oriole *Oriolus auratus* (544) L 24 cm

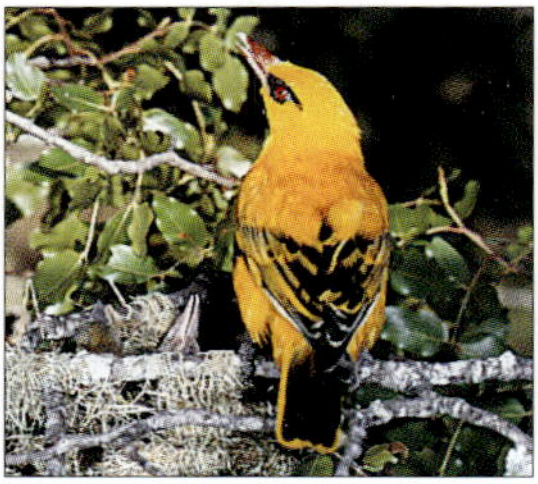

P GINN

Male

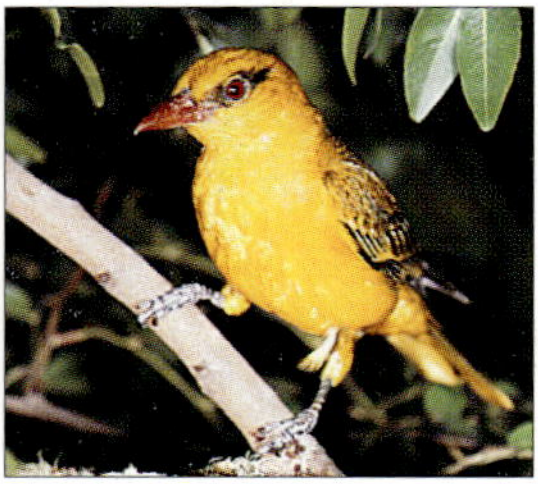

P GINN

Female

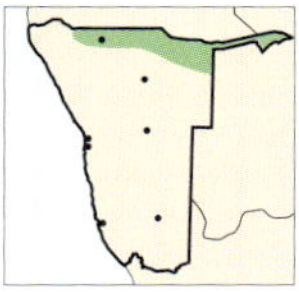

This is a bright golden yellow bird, showing yellow wing coverts and the *diagnostic lozenge-shaped black area around the eyes*. The female is similar to the male, but has duller streaking on the breast and belly, and yellowish green wing coverts. The immature resembles the female. Its call is a liquid, whistled 'fee-yoo, fee-yoo'. It is a fairly common summer visitor to the wooded northern regions of Namibia, including miombo woodland, riverine forest and thornveld.

Black Crow *Corvus capensis* (547) L 50 cm

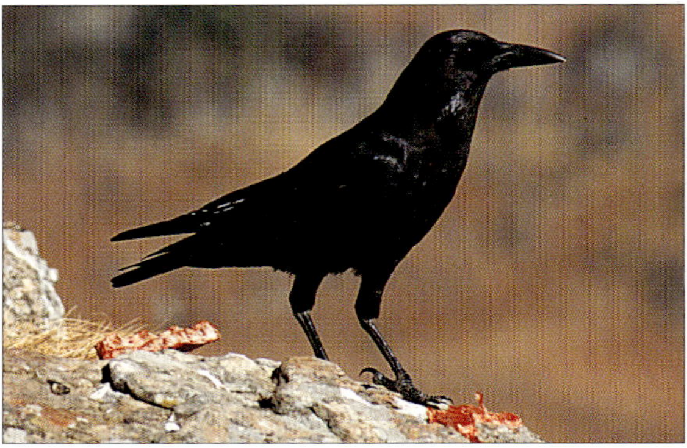

PETER CRAIG-COOPER

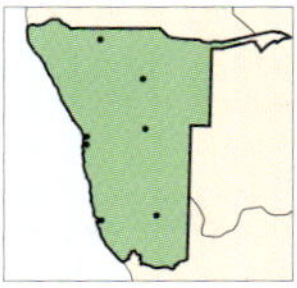

This is a *glossy black* crow with a *long, slender, slightly decurved bill*. It is the only all-black crow likely to be seen in the veld away from human habitation. The immature is duller and lacks the glossy black plumage of the adult. Its call is a loud, crow-like 'kah-kah' and other deep, bubbling notes. This crow occurs in open country and cultivated fields as well as in arid regions, and is often seen on roadsides through the desert. It is a common resident.

Pied Crow *Corvus albus* (548) L 50 cm

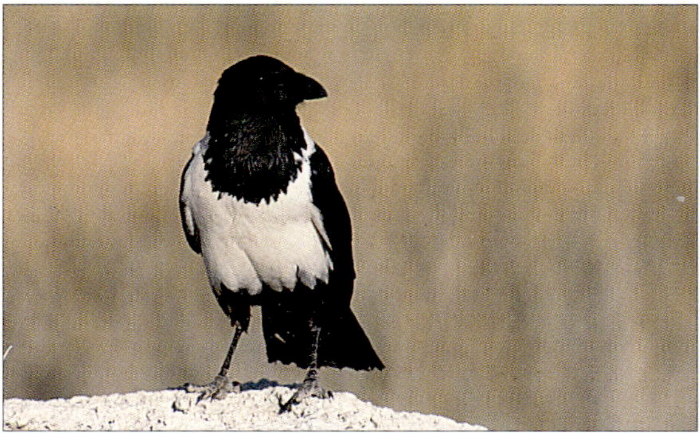

ALAN WEAVING

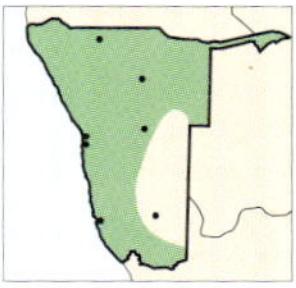

This species is very easy to identify as it is the only crow in the region with a *white belly* contrasting sharply with the otherwise black plumage. The black and white plumage of the immature resembles that of the adult but is less contrasting. Its call is a loud 'kwaaa' or 'kwooork' cawing. A common resident, this crow often occurs in flocks, and is found in virtually every habitat. It is also a common city dweller, roosting in trees and regularly visiting rubbish dumps.

Ashy Tit *Parus cinerascens* (552) L 13 cm

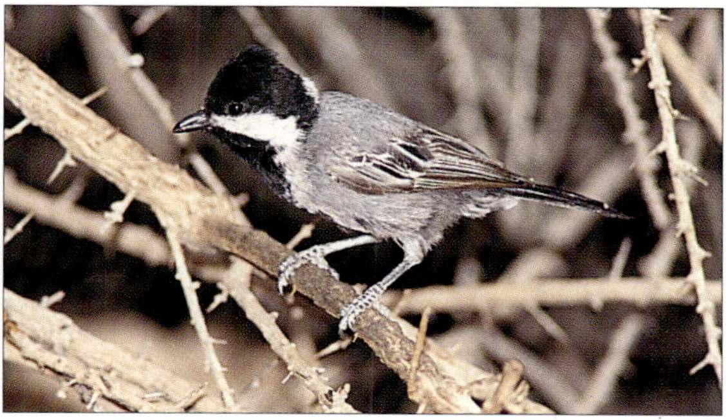

ABPL/BRENDAN RYAN

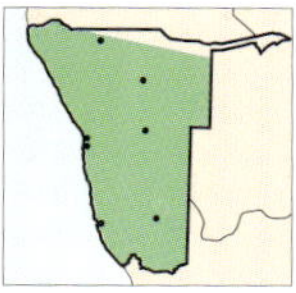

A *slate-grey body, white-fringed wings, a black cap, white cheeks, and a black throat and bib*, extending as a black line down the belly, identify this small bird. The immature is a duller version of the adult. It travels in pairs or parties, keeping in contact with others in the party using a variety of ringing whistles and harsher calls. This very active bird is constantly on the move and occurs in thornveld, broad-leafed woodland and riverine scrub. It is a common resident.

Southern Black Tit *Parus niger* (554) L 16 cm

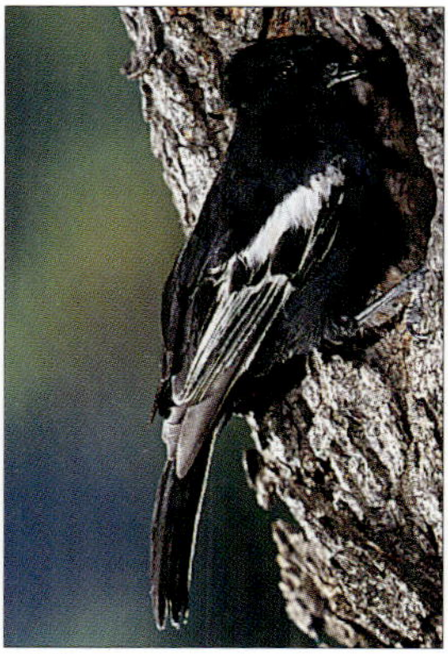

ABPL/HEIN VON HÖRSTEN

Male

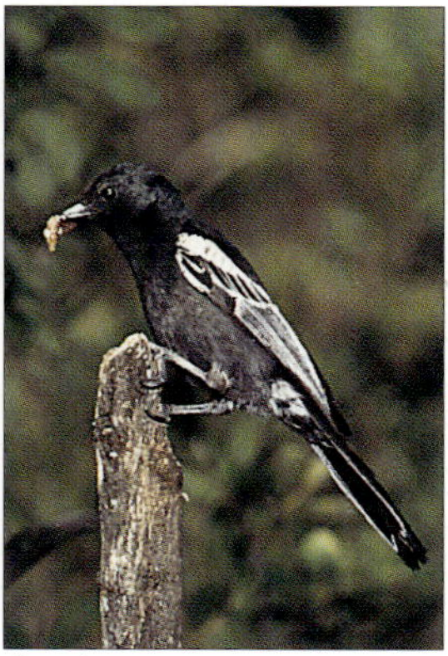

P J GINN

Female

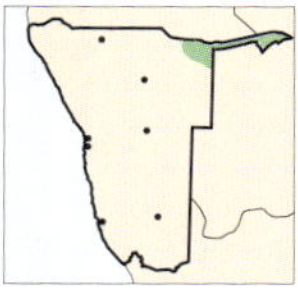

In this species the male and female are similar but the male is *darker*, and has a large area of white in the wings and *white-tipped undertail coverts*; the female is greyer than the male. A typical tit in both behaviour and calls, its harsh, chattering 'chrr-chrr-chrr' notes and musical 'phee-cher, phee-cher' call are often the first indication that a bird feeding party is in the area. It is distributed more in the northern sector of the region, in common and teak woodland.

Cape Penduline Tit *Anthoscopus minutus* (557) L 8 cm

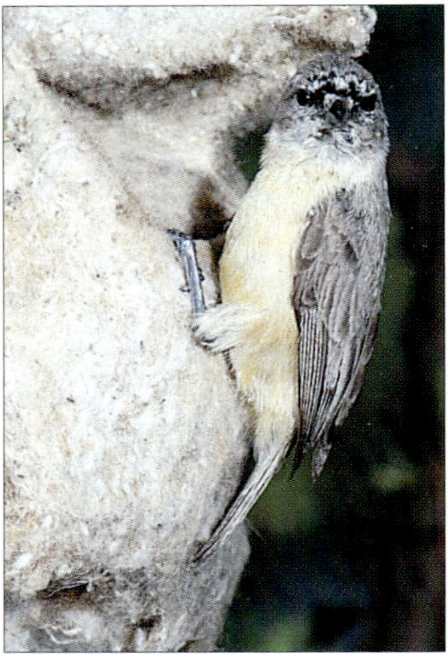

ABPL/CLEM HAAGNER

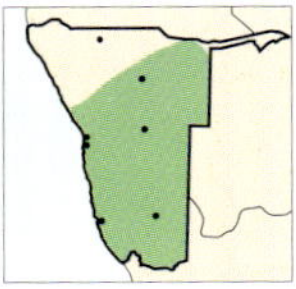

This bird's most distinguishing feature is its diagnostic *black forehead extending as an eye-stripe*. The *yellowish belly and flanks, and speckled throat* are also diagnostic. The immature has paler yellow underparts than the adult. This bird can be distinguished from the eremomelas by its tiny size, short, more conical bill, rotund body and very short tail. The call is a soft 'tseep'. It occurs in scrub, semi-desert and dry thornveld and is thinly distributed in the drier scrub regions of Namibia.

Blackfaced Babbler *Turdoides melanops* (561) L 28 cm

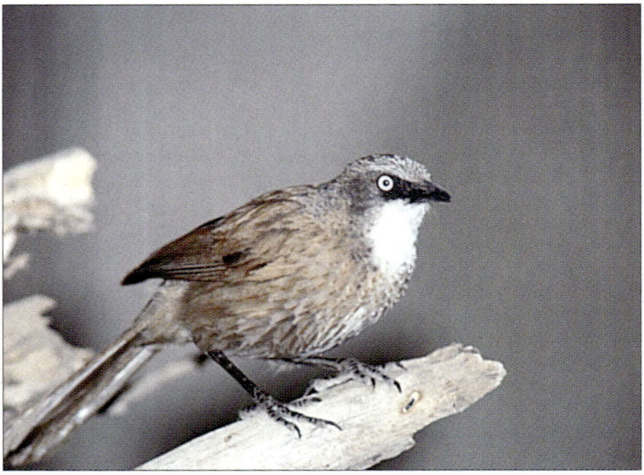

ABPL/BRENDAN RYAN

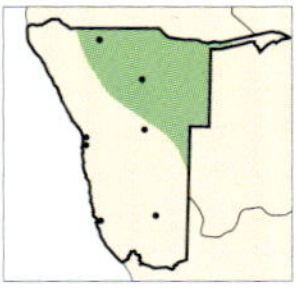

This is the most furtive of all the babblers. A *faint white streaking on the head, a small black patch at the base of the bill and a bright yellow eye* are diagnostic features of this species. The immature is similar to the adult but it has a brown, not yellow, eye. The call is a nasal 'wha-wha-wha' sound. It is locally common but unevenly distributed in the northern region. This shy babbler tends to forage in scattered groups among the leaf litter in broad-leafed woodland.

Hartlaub's Babbler *Turdoides hartlaubii* (562) L 26 cm

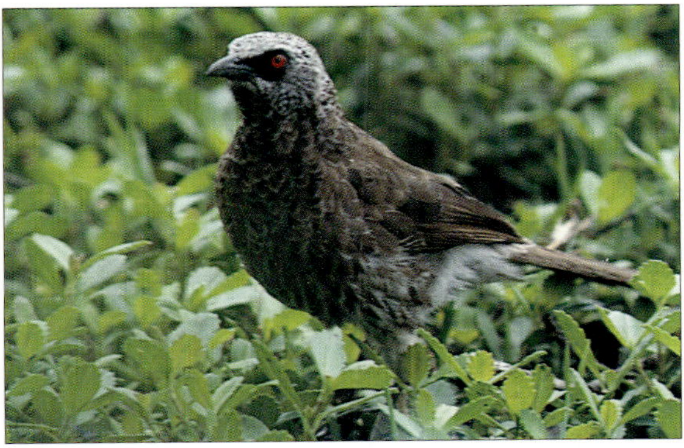

PHOTO ACCESS/C F BARTLETT

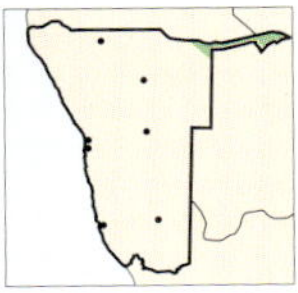

The *white rump*, a diagnostic feature in this species, can be seen in flight. When at rest it may be told from the Blackfaced Babbler by its *red, not yellow, eye* and its paler head with white scalloping, not streaking. The noisy 'whaaa-whaa-whaa' call is typical of babblers, with several birds often calling simultaneously. It occurs in thick tangles near water and sometimes frequents papyrus reed beds. This bird is locally common in the northern sector of the region.

Southern Pied Babbler *Turdoides bicolor* (563) L 26 cm

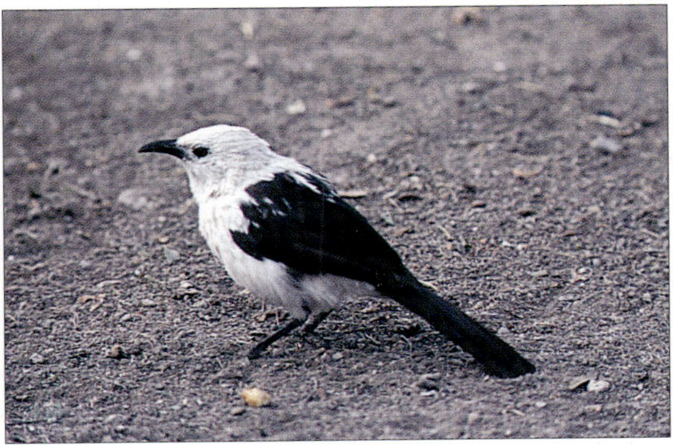

PETER CRAIG-COOPER

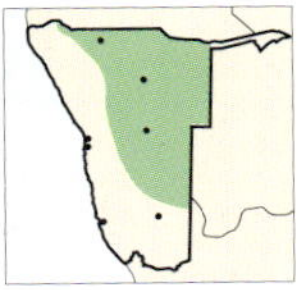

This is an easily identified babbler as it is the only one in the region to have an *all-white head, back and underparts*. The wings and tail are black. The immature is initially pale brown all over but lightens with age. The typical 'kwee kwee kwee kweer' babbling call is pitched higher than that of other babblers. Conspicuous small groups fly in loose formation from bush to bush in thornveld and arid savanna. This is a common resident in Namibia.

Barecheeked Babbler *Turdoides gymnogenys* (564) L 24 cm

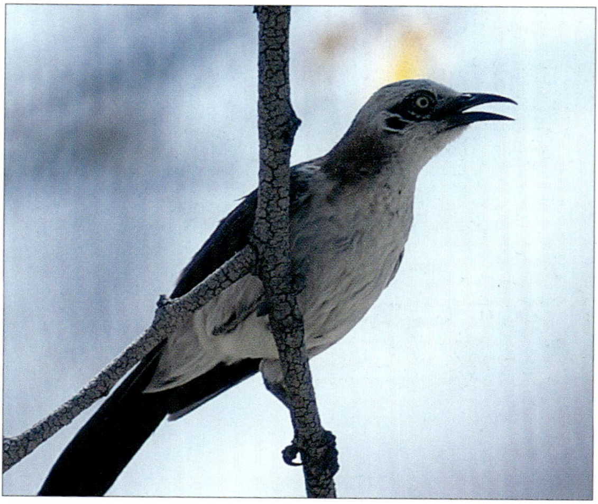

THEO BUCHHOLZ

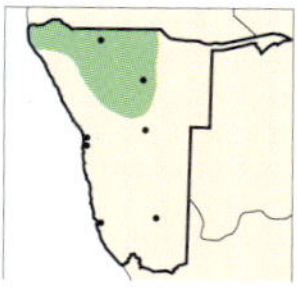

The small area of *bare black skin below and behind the eye* is diagnostic. It is unlikely to be confused with the Southern Pied Babbler as it has a dark back and lacks white on the wing coverts. The immature is much darker than the immature Southern Pied Babbler, especially on the back and nape. It gives a typical babbler 'kwee kwee kwee kweer' call. A locally common species, endemic to Namibia, it lives in groups frequenting river courses and wooded koppies in broad-leafed woodland.

Redeyed Bulbul *Pycnonotus nigricans* (567) L 21 cm

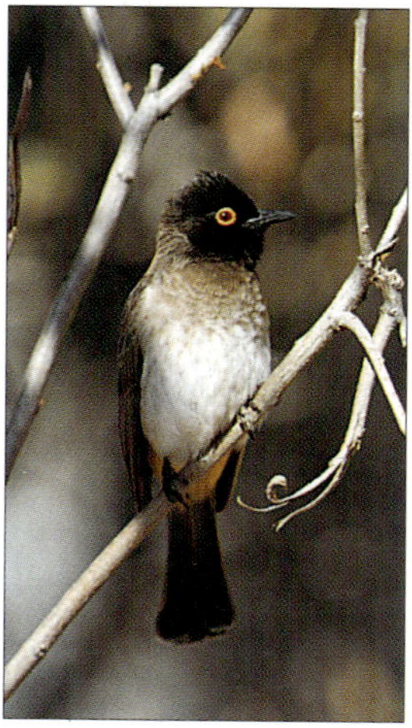

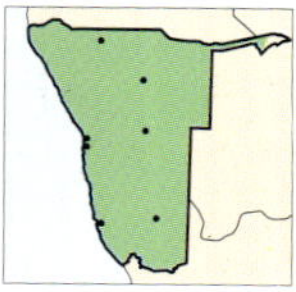

As its name implies, the Redeyed Bulbul has a diagnostic *red eye and eye-ring*. Its dark head contrasts with the greyish buff collar and breast. The immature differs from the adult by having a pale pink eye-ring. It utters a chirpy, liquid 'cheloop chreep choop' call, as well as a shorter 'kwit-kwit' call given as an alarm note. It is the most common bulbul in Namibia and is found in a variety of habitats, including thornveld and riverine bush, and in the more arid regions, especially around water holes. It is also commonly seen in suburban gardens.

Groundscraper Thrush *Turdus litsitsirupa* (580) L 22 cm

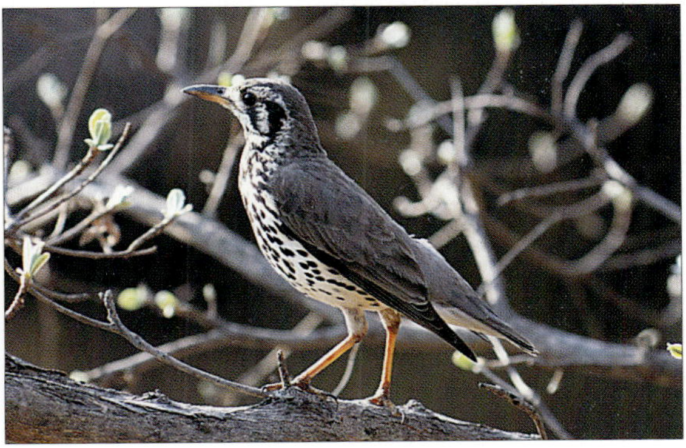

W R TARBOTON

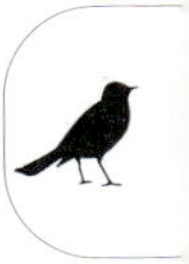

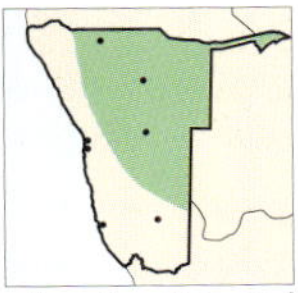

This bird is identified by the *bold, contrasting, black facial markings and heavy spotting on the breast*. A chestnut panel in the wing is visible. The immature has speckled, off-white underparts with conspicuous white-tipped wing coverts. The song is a clearly whistled phrase resembling its specific name. This common resident is much bolder than other thrushes and is frequently seen hopping around in parks and gardens; it also frequents thornveld and open broad-leafed woodland.

Short-toed Rock Thrush *Monticola brevipes* (583) L 18 cm

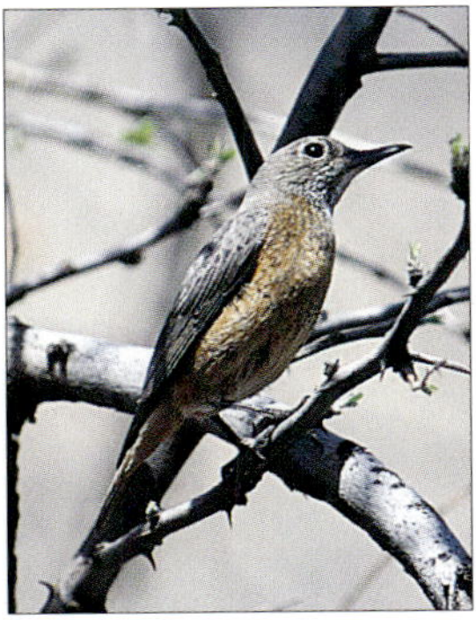

THEO BUCHHOLZ

Female

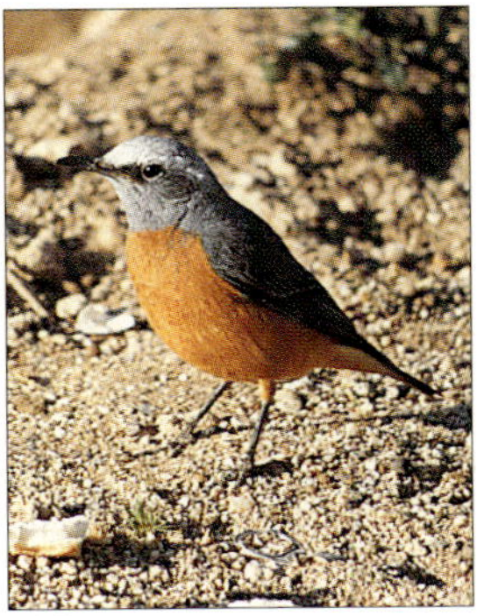

PETER CRAIG-CCOPER

Male

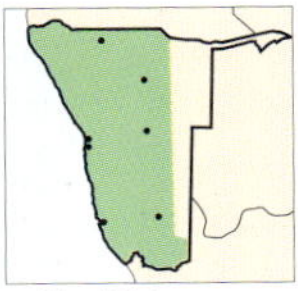

The male of this species has a diagnostic *blue-grey crown, forehead and nape*. The crown colour can be so pale as to appear almost white in some individuals. The female has an *extensively striped throat and breast*. The immature is spotted with buff on the upperparts, with black streaking below. Its thin, whistled song includes some mimicry of other bird calls. This common resident occurs on thickly wooded koppies and rocky slopes and is sometimes conspicuous on telephone poles.

Mountain Chat *Oenanthe monticola* (586) L 20 cm

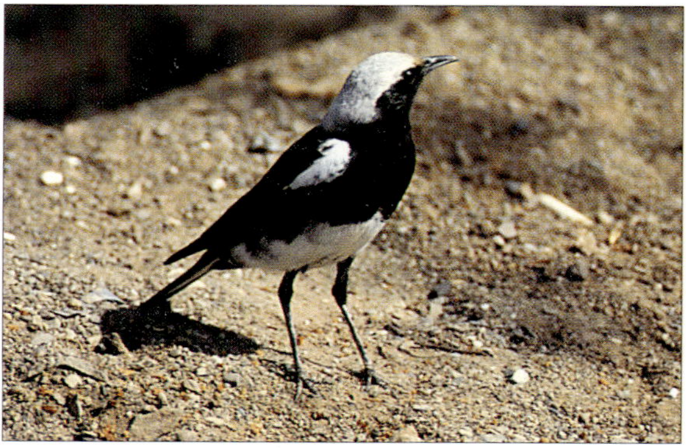

ALAN WEAVING

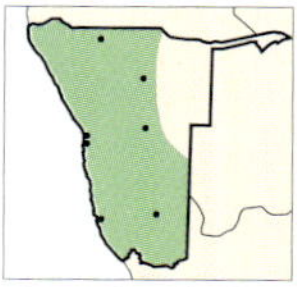

The *black and white pied plumage* should render this nervous and flighty bird unmistakable. The male shows variable plumage coloration but always maintains a white rump, white sides to the tail and a *white shoulder patch*. The greyish brown, nondescript female also shows a white shoulder patch. The immature is similar to the female. Its clear, thrush-like, whistling song is interspersed with harsh chatters. This common resident inhabits mountainous and rocky terrain.

Capped Wheatear *Oenanthe pileata* (587) L 18 cm

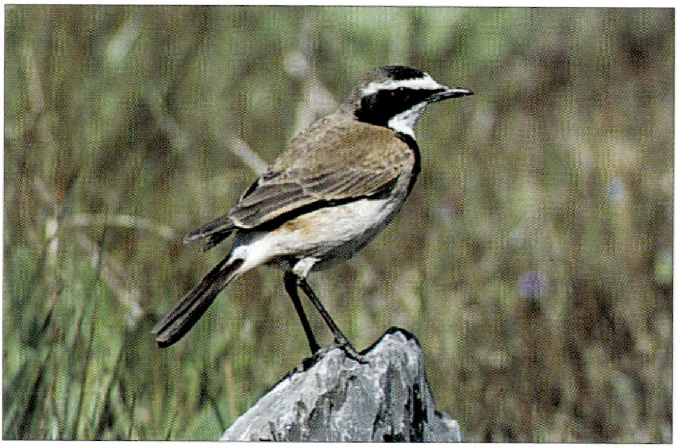

ROY JOHANNESSON

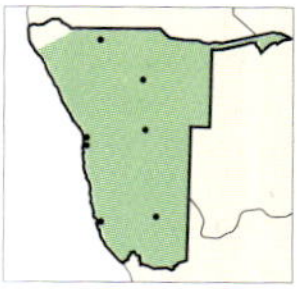

In the adult the *white eyebrow stripe and forehead contrasting with the black cap and black collar* are diagnostic. It can run very rapidly. When in flight, the white rump and sides of the tail are conspicuous. The immature has a paler head and collar markings. Its song is a loud warbling with slurred chattering; it is given during the hovering display flight, from the ground or a raised perch. This common resident frequents open, level veld with little grass cover.

Tractrac Chat *Cercomela tractrac* (590) L 15 cm

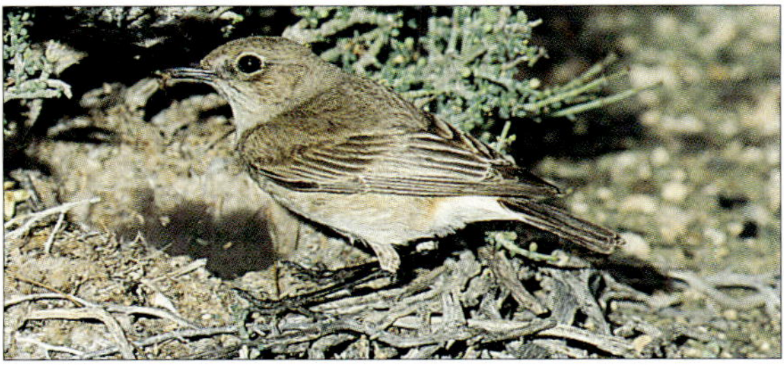

PHOTO ACCESS/P STEYN

Dark form

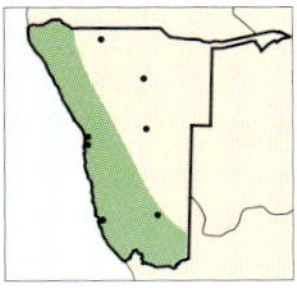

The Namib coastal form of this bird has a very upright posture, and is *almost white with darker wings* and a *darker tail*; it is larger than the inland form. The inland form is *darker above with a darker head but still shows a white rump and sides of the tail.* Its call is a soft and fast 'tactac' and the song is a quiet musical bubbling. It occurs on gravel plains and scrub desert, and is a common resident in the region.

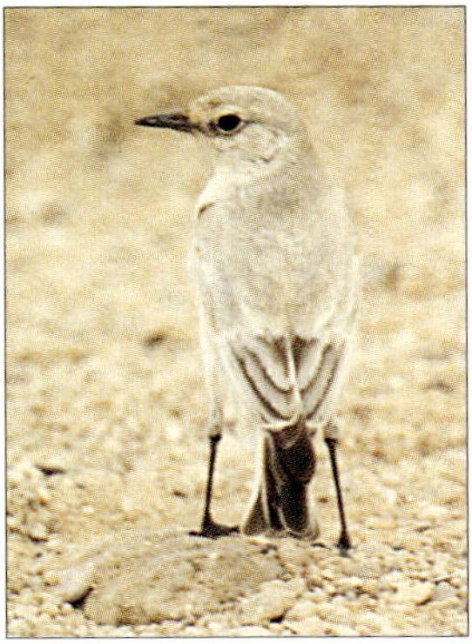

IAN DAVIDSON

Pale form

Karoo Chat *Cercomela schlegelii* (592) L 18 cm

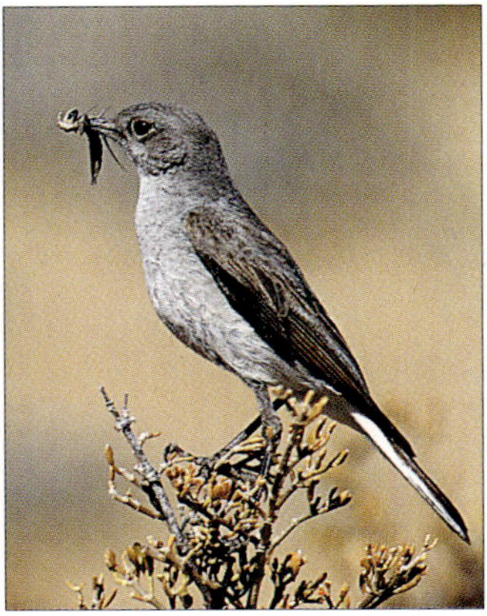

NICO MYBURGH

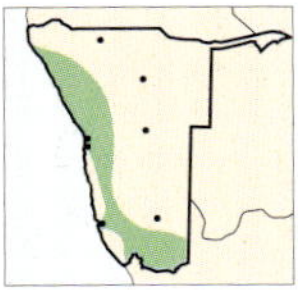

This is a *large grey chat* with an upright stance. In flight it shows all-white outertail feathers and a *grey, not white, rump* which differentiates it from the female Mountain Chat and Tractrac Chat. The large size also eliminates confusion with the Tractrac Chat. Immatures are buff-spotted above and scaled below. The call is a typical chat-like 'chak-chak'. This species is found in desert scrub with scattered bushes, and is locally common and thinly distributed along the desert edge in the region.

Southern Anteating Chat *Myrmecocichla formicivora* (595) L 18 cm

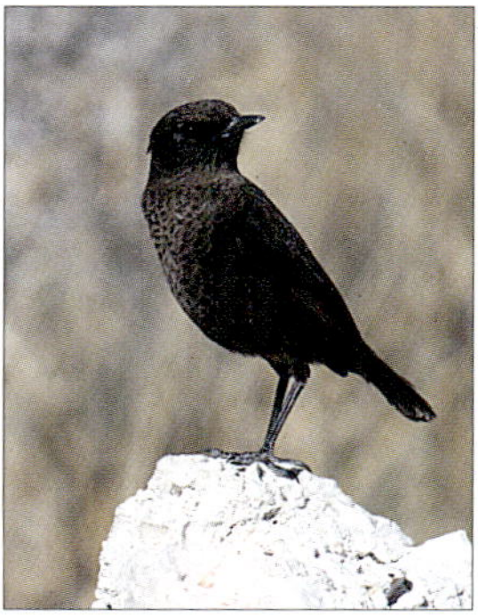

PETER CRAIG-COOPER

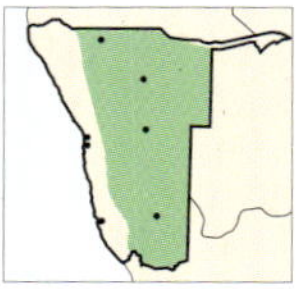

This chat is easily distinguished from other species in flight as it shows *white window-like patches on the wing tips*. At rest it has an upright posture and appears short tailed and plump. Its variable plumage can range from dark brown to mottled black. The male is very dark brown; the female is a paler brown. The immature is paler brown like the female and more mottled than the adult. Its call is a short, sharp 'peek' or 'piek'. This bird is associated with the open veld and termite mounds on which it perches to scan its territory. It is a common resident in Namibia.

Kalahari Robin *Erythropygia paena* (615) L 17 cm

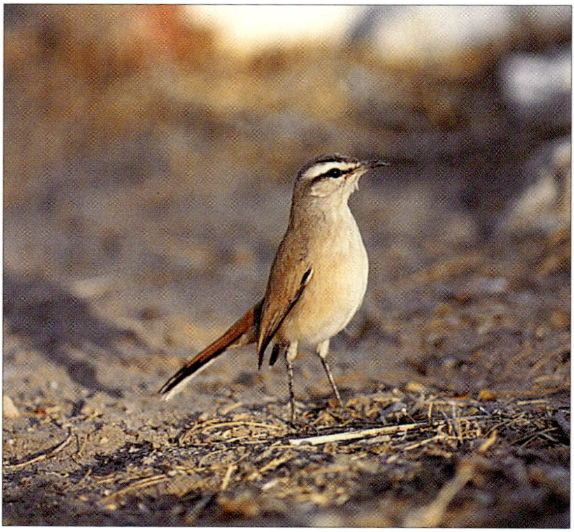

ABPL/BRENDAN RYAN

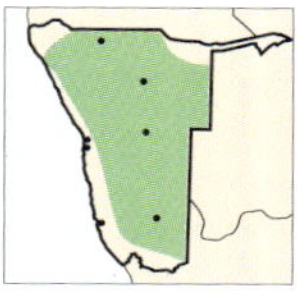

This sandy brown robin has a pale eyebrow and a rufous rump and uppertail. It is easily recognized by the conspicuous *white sides to the tip of the tail contrasting with the broad black subterminal tail bar*. The plumage of the immature is mottled with sooty black and buff. Its musical whistled song is varied and interspersed with harsher notes. This robin is a common resident and inhabits dry thornveld, thicket and the tangled growth around water holes and dry river beds.

Herero Chat *Namibornis herero* (618) L 17 cm

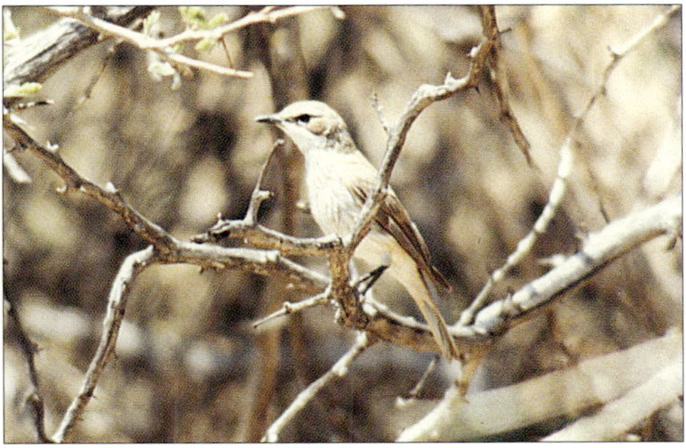

IAN SINCLAIR

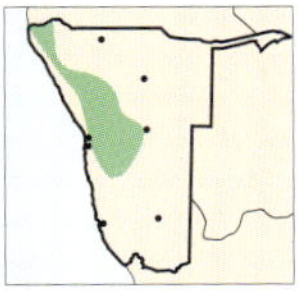

In this bird the *black line that runs through the eye contrasts with a clear white eyebrow stripe.* The outertail feathers and rump are rust coloured and at close range a faint streaking on the breast can be seen. The immature resembles the female but is more mottled. Usually silent, it gives a melodious, warbling song during the breeding season. It is found at the base of hills and in boulder-strewn country, in dry scrub and thornveld. This is an uncommon and thinly distributed endemic.

Chestnutvented Titbabbler *Parisoma subcaeruleum* (621) L 15 cm

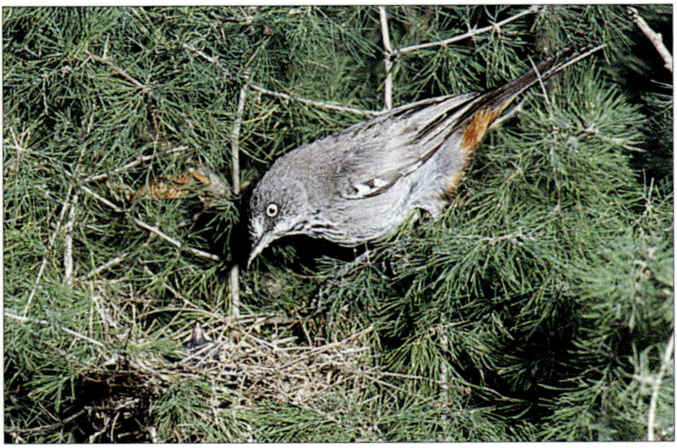

S M BLOOMFIELD

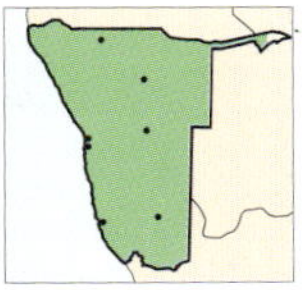

This grey bird has a *white-tipped, longish tail and a pale eye.* It has extensive black streaking on the throat. This bird differs from the very similar Layard's Titbabbler by being darker grey and having a diagnostic *chestnut vent.* The immature lacks the black streaking on the throat. This common resident is most often seen as it creeps through thick thorn bush delivering its loud, explosive 'cheruuup-chee-chee' song. It inhabits dry thornveld and dry scrub in arid regions.

Layard's Titbabbler *Parisoma layardi* (622) L 15 cm

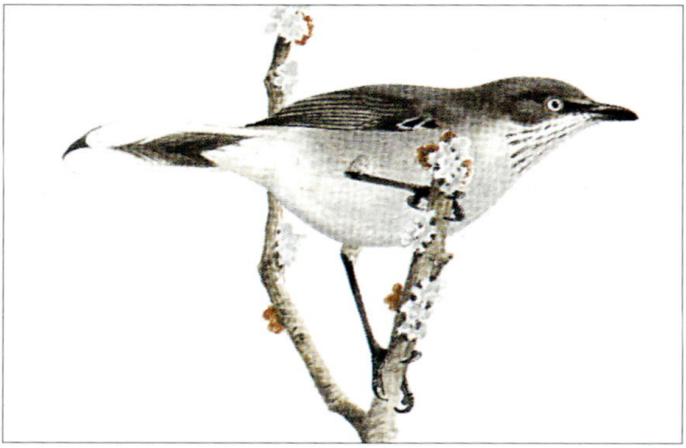

NORMAN ARLOTT

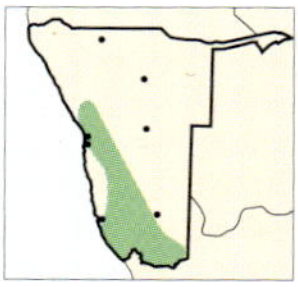

This bird differs from the Chestnutvented Titbabbler by being paler and having a *white, not chestnut, vent*. The silvery white eye contrasts with the *dark head*, and the throat streaking is less pronounced than in the Chestnutvented Titbabbler. Immatures lack any streaking on the throat. It has a clear 'pee-pee-cheeri-cheeri' call. This bird is uncommon and thinly distributed in Namibia. It may be found in rocky, hilly areas in thornveld and in desert scrub along dry watercourses.

Icterine Warbler *Hippolais icterina* (625) L 13 cm

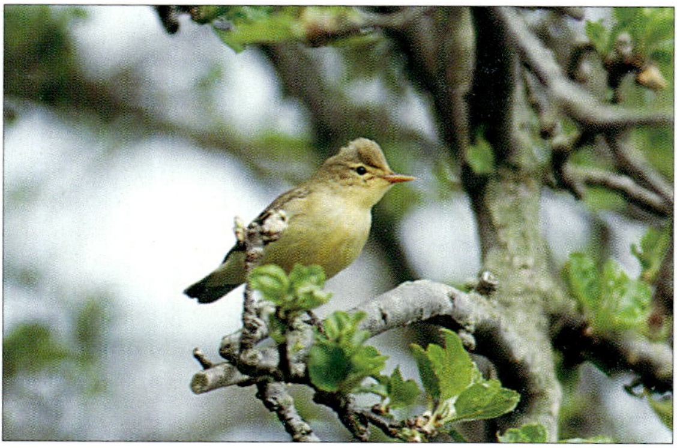

AQUILA/J DE MEESTER

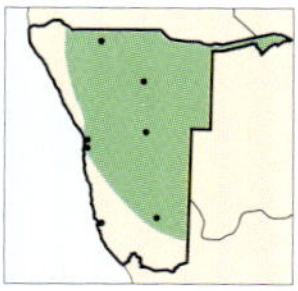

The plumage of this bird varies. Normally a brightish yellow below, it can also be whitish below and greyish brown above. It is best identified by the *large bill and head, bluish legs and yellow eye-stripe*. The immature appears much greyer with paler yellow underparts. It produces a jumbled song, comprised of harsh and melodious notes. This warbler frequents thornveld, dry broad-leafed woodland and riverine thickets. It is a common summer visitor.

African Marsh Warbler *Acrocephalus baeticatus* (631) L 13 cm

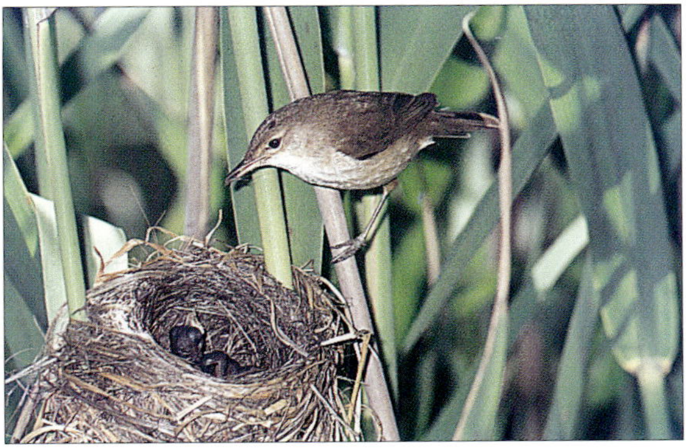

T D LONGRIGG

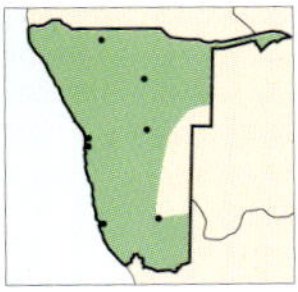

This is a small obscure warbler with *brown upperparts, off-white underparts, and warm buffy flanks*. It also has a *pale eyebrow stripe* and dark legs. When the African Marsh Warbler is compared with other similar-looking warblers it is not easy to identify, but it is the most common inhabitant of reed beds in Namibia. The call is a harsh 'tchak' and the song a jumbled mixture of harsh grating notes and melodious whistles; it is also known to mimic phrases of other birds.

Cape Reed Warbler *Acrocephalus gracilirostis* (635) L 17 cm

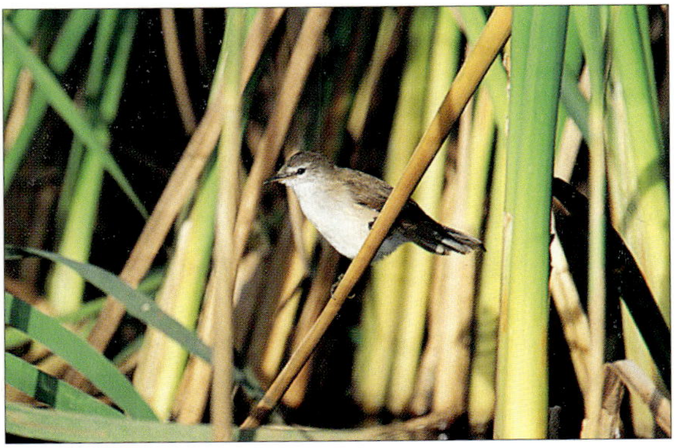

ABPL/NIGEL J DENNIS

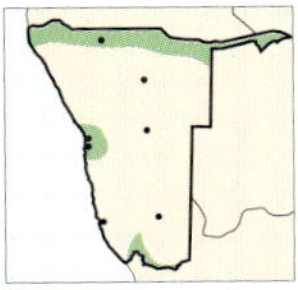

Although similar to any other drab warbler in the region, this species is fairly large with *brownish upperparts and a clearer white throat and breast* than have similar warblers. It has a *long heavy bill, a white eyebrow stripe and dark brown legs*. The immature resembles the adult. It has a liquid, melodious 'cheerup-chee-trrrree' call. A common resident in Namibia, it is often seen low down, close to the water on the edge of reed beds adjoining wetlands.

Willow Warbler *Phylloscopus trochilus* (643) L 11 cm

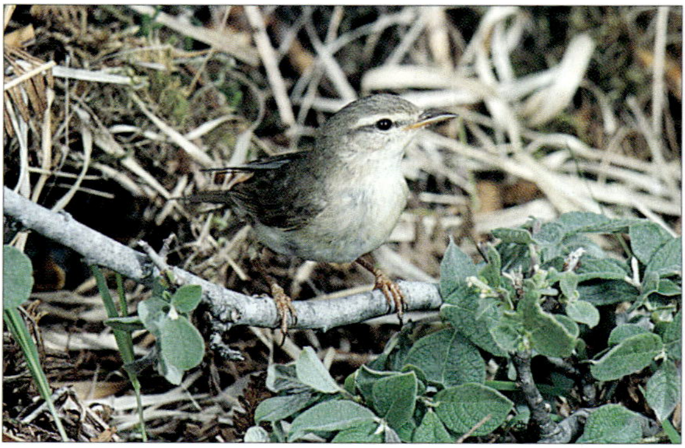

AQUILA/G G & I M BATES

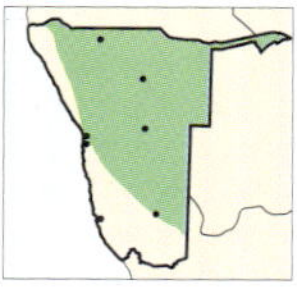

This warbler differs from the Icterine Warbler by its smaller size, much *lighter yellow underparts* and its *thinner, weaker bill*. The distinct yellow on the underparts is restricted to the throat and breast, with the belly mainly dull white. The immature has a much brighter yellow eyebrow stripe and face. It has a short, melodious song descending in scale. This is a common summer visitor that occurs in a wide range of habitats, from dry thornveld to broad-leafed woodland.

Yellowbreasted Apalis *Apalis flavida* (648) L 13 cm

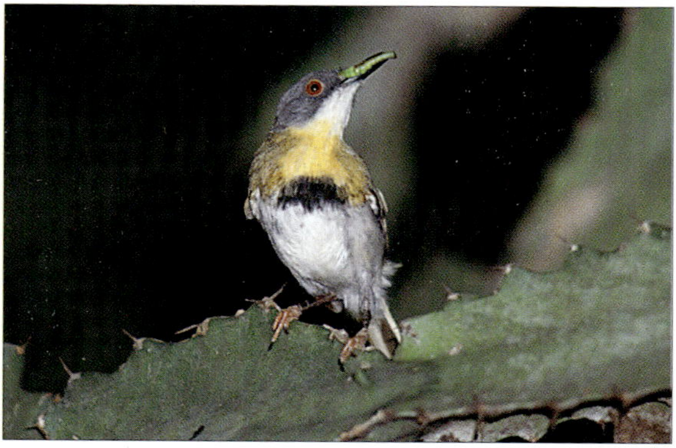

ALAN WEAVING

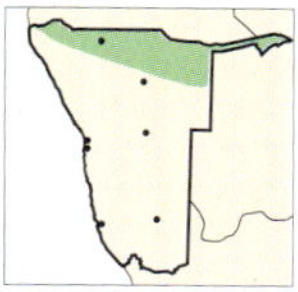

This bird can be identified by its *diagnostic grey head, white throat, yellow breast and white belly*. The male can further be distinguished by the small black bar on the lower breast. Immatures are paler yellow on the breast. Its call is a rapid, buzzy 'chizzick-chizzick-chizzick'. Apalises are lively and always on the move in the forest or the bush. Although many prefer to remain high up in the canopy, this species prefers the lower or mid stratum. It is a common resident in Namibia.

Longbilled Crombec *Sylvietta rufescens* (651) L 12 cm

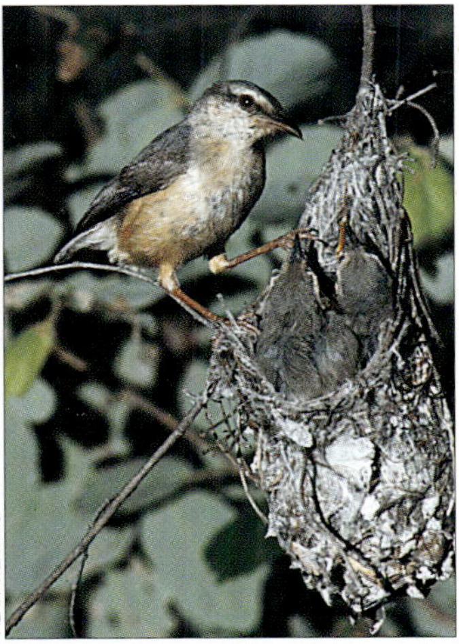

ALAN WEAVING

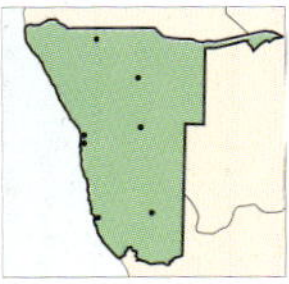

This small, plump, *greyish bird with its buffy cinnamon underparts appears to be almost tailless.* It is easily differentiated from other similar warblers as its bill is *long and slightly decurved.* When feeding it gleans insects from branches and leaves, and probes crevices with its long bill. The call of this bird is a frequently repeated 'tree-trriit'. This is a common resident and occurs in a wide range of habitats, from woodlands to semi-arid scrub; it avoids extremely arid regions.

Burntnecked Eremomela *Eremomela usticollis* (656) L 10 cm

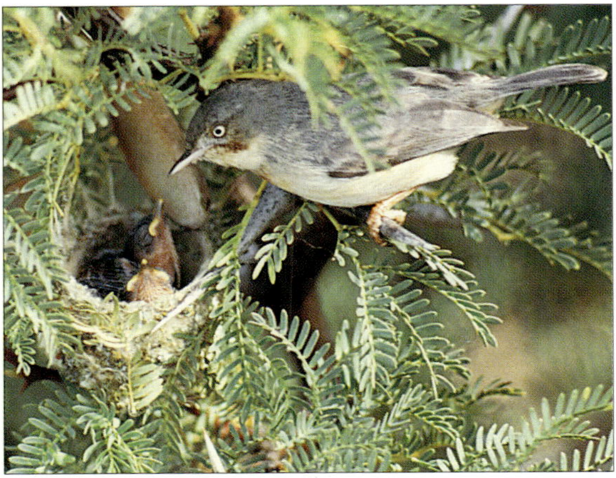

W R TARBOTON

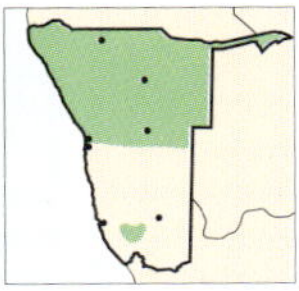

This is a small *bluish grey warbler with pale buff underparts. The pale yellow eye, and rufous cheeks and ear coverts* also aid identification. A *small rusty throat bar*, often inconspicuous or absent, is diagnostic. The immature lacks the throat bar and rufous cheeks. The call is a high-pitched 'chii-cheee-cheee'. This is primarily a thornveld species but it is also found in mixed, dry broad-leafed woodland and along dry river courses. It is a common but thinly distributed resident of Namibia.

Greybacked Bleating Warbler *Camaroptera brevicaudata* (657b) L 12 cm

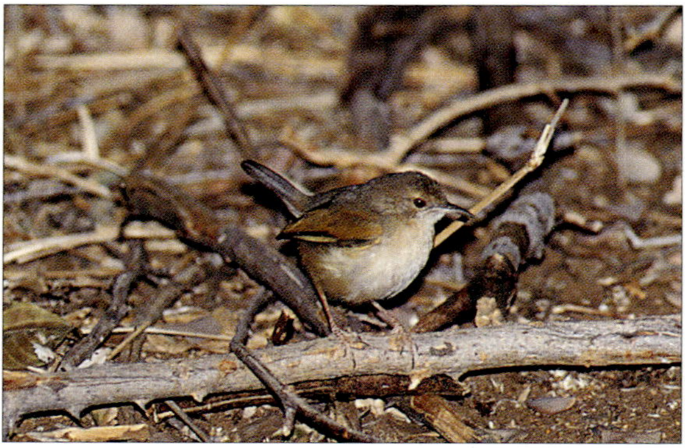

ABPL/BRENDAN RYAN

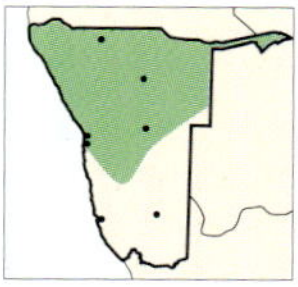

This species is recognized by its *off-white to greyish underparts and olive-green upperparts with a greyish nape and mantle*. The immature is lightly streaked below. It keeps a low profile in thick vegetation and habitually cocks its tail. When excited or disturbed it will emit a metallic, clicking sound but its normal call is a loud, snapping 'bidup-bidup-bidup' and a nasal 'neeeehh'. A common resident in Namibia, it occurs in thornveld, thickets in broad-leafed woodland and scrub.

African Barred Warbler *Camaroptera fasciolata* (658) L 14 cm

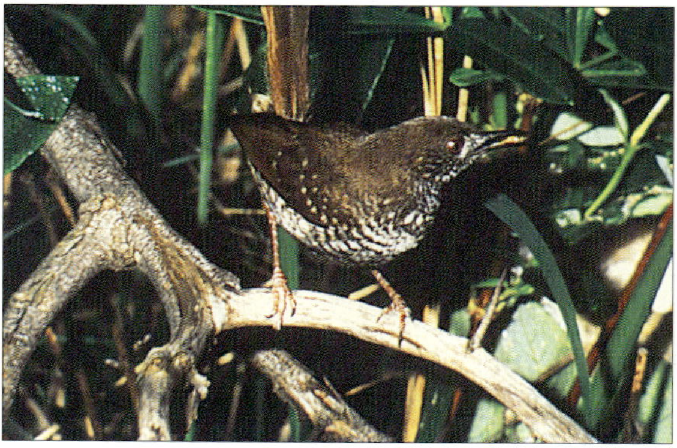

W R TARBOTON

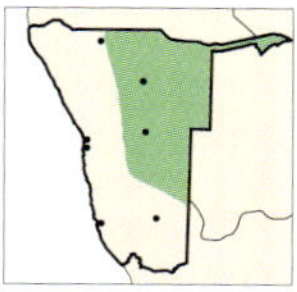

This is a medium-sized warbler with *barring from chin to belly, and brown eyes and legs*. The long tail is often held cocked or fanned over its back. The breeding male has a plain brown throat and breast. The immature is more rufous than the adult and shows a yellowish wash on the breast. An inconspicuous bird, it is best located by its call: a thin 'trrrreee' and a repeated 'pleelip-pleelip'. This is a common resident, occurring in dry thornveld and broad-leafed woodland.

Rockrunner *Achaetops pycnopygius* (662) L 17 cm

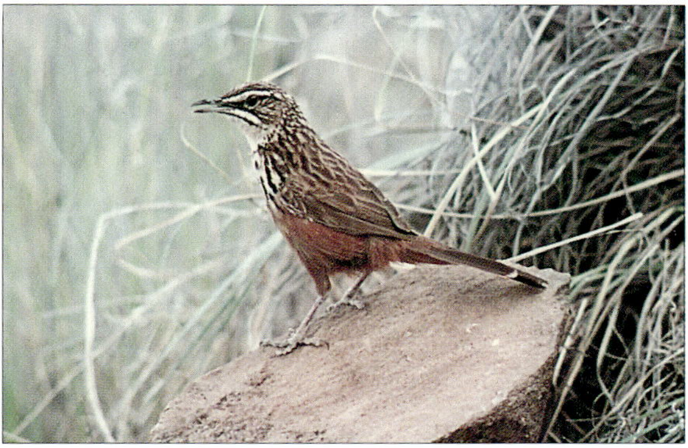

W R TARBOTON

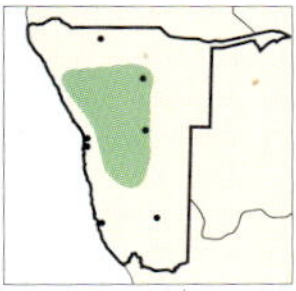

The Rockrunner can be identified by its *heavily streaked dark back, white breast spotted with black at the sides, and bright rufous belly and undertail.* By comparison, the immature is lightly streaked. It utters a hollow, melodious, warbling 'rooodle-trrooodlee' call. This bird is most often seen on the ground in thick grass or as it scrambles over rocks on boulder-strewn, grassy hillsides and at the base of small hills. It is a common endemic of Namibia.

Desert Cisticola *Cisticola aridula* (665) L 10 cm

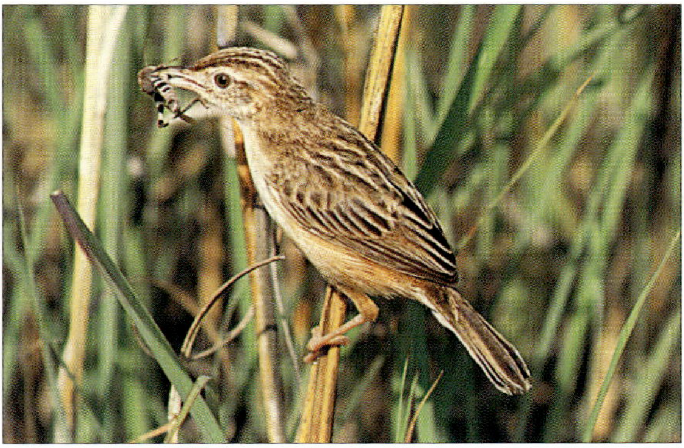

W R TARBOTON

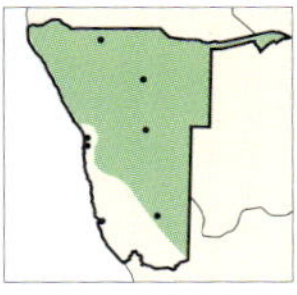

Cisticolas are notoriously difficult to identify and the Desert Cisticola is no exception, unless it is observed calling or displaying. It is a tiny bird with a *finely streaked forehead and a well-marked buffy back.* The sexes are alike, but the female has a shorter tail than the male. The immature is slightly paler below than the adult. The 'zink zink zink' song can be heard during the low-level display flight. This bird is a common resident and inhabits grasslands in dry areas.

Greybacked Cisticola *Cisticola subruficapilla* (669) L 13 cm

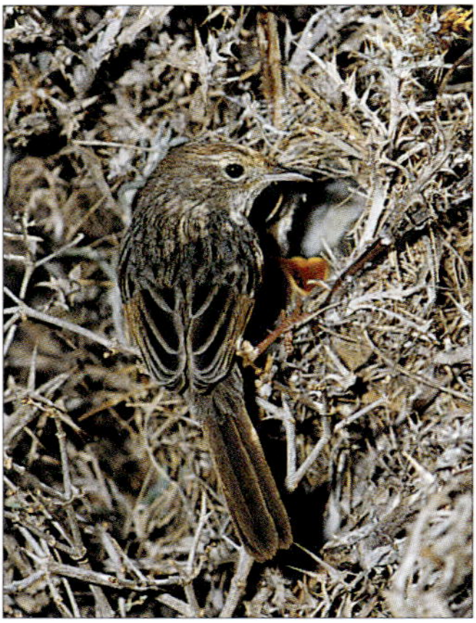

NICO MYBURGH

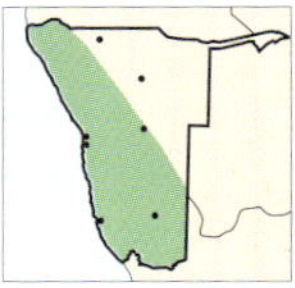

This cisticola has a *long tail, a grey back finely streaked with black, and a chestnut cap*. The immature is duller than the adult. During the breeding season the bird becomes conspicuous, engaging in aerial display and emitting a muffled 'prrrttt' call followed by a sharp 'phweee-phweee-phweee', which is given in a fluttery low flight over its territory. This is an uncommon, thinly distributed resident bird, and is found in scrub areas, on grassy hillsides and on grassy dunes.

Rattling Cisticola *Cisticola chiniana* (672) L 13 cm

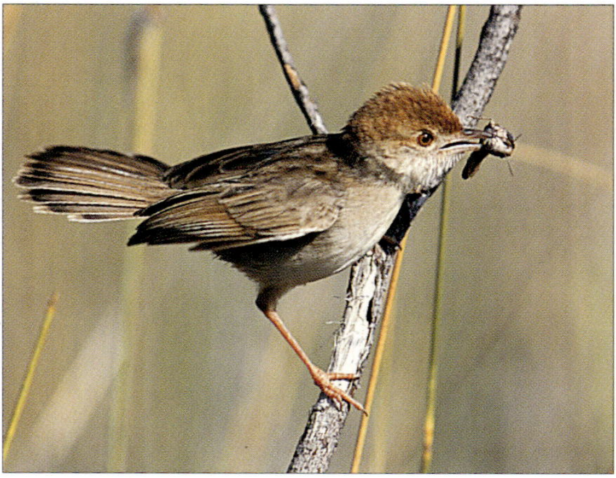

W R TARBOTON

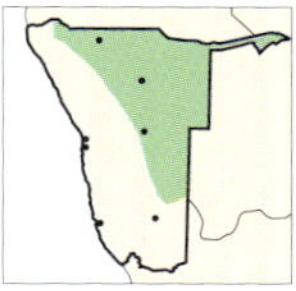

This is the most abundant cisticola of the thornveld, and probably the most conspicuous cisticola in the region. It is a *small, long-tailed bird with a chestnut cap* and is often seen perched openly on the top of bushes. The immature is yellower than the adult. When proclaiming its territory from an exposed perch it utters a 'chureee-chureee' song that ends in a diagnostic, *rattling 'cherrrr'*. Its alarm call is a bold, repeated, scolding 'cheee-cheee' note. This bird frequents woodland, savanna and scrub, and is a common resident of Namibia.

Blackchested Prinia *Prinia flavicans* (685) L 15 cm

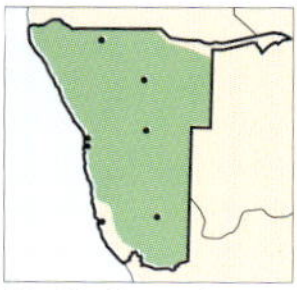

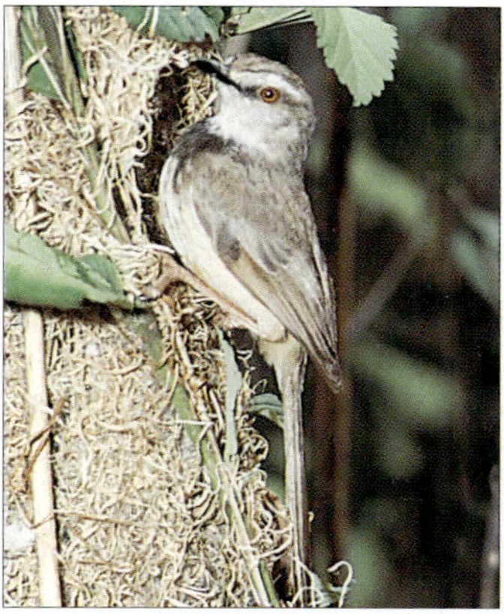

S M BLOOMFIELD

Unlikely to be confused with other prinias when in breeding plumage, this is the only prinia in the region with a *broad black breast band.* The band is usually absent in non-breeding plumage. The female has a narrower breast band than the male. Like other prinias, it has a long tail which is often held cocked at right angles. The immature lacks the black breast band and is very yellow below. The call of this bird is a series of loud 'zzzrt-zzzrt-zzzrt-zzzrt' notes. A common resident, it generally frequents arid scrub and thornveld.

Rufouseared Warbler *Malcorus pectoralis* (688) L 15 cm

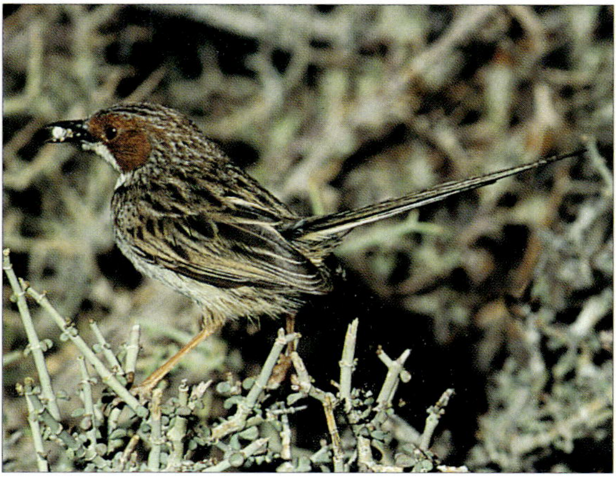

PHOTO ACCESS/P STEYN

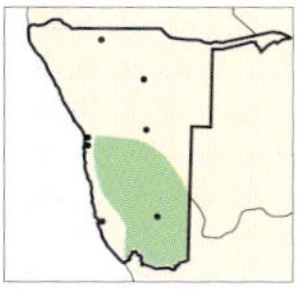

This warbler is prinia-like in appearance and habits, although if glimpsed foraging freely on the ground it might even be mistaken for a rodent as it scuttles swiftly from bush to bush. The *reddish ear coverts and narrow black breast band are diagnostic.* The male has a broader breast band than the female. The immature resembles the adult but lacks the distinctive breast band. It gives a harsh, scolding 'chweeo, chweeo, chweeo' call. This common resident of Namibia occurs in stunted and low semi-desert scrub.

Spotted Flycatcher *Muscicapa striata* (689) L 14 cm

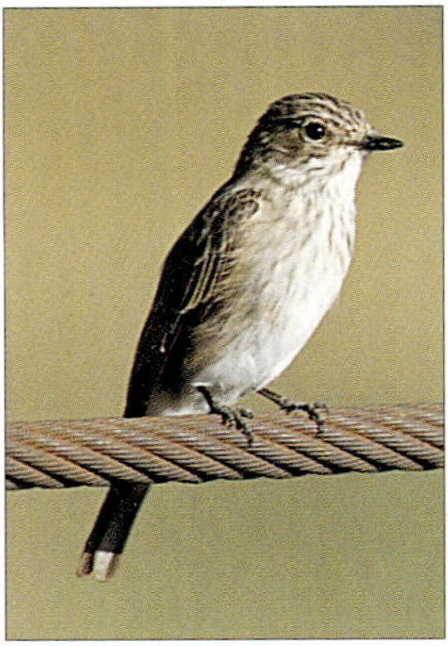

J J THERON

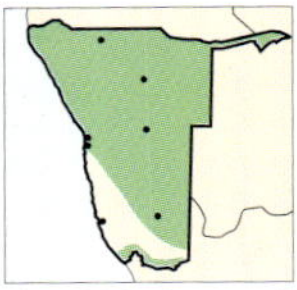

The diagnostic *streaked and spotted breast and forehead* of this small flycatcher should help to tell it apart from the larger, pale-breasted Marico Flycatcher. The immature is mottled brown and buff, but is not likely to be seen in the region. Mostly silent in Namibia, this common summer visitor occasionally utters a soft 'tzee'. It has a very upright posture when perched and frequently flicks its wings on alighting or when agitated. It usually returns to the same perch after a sortie for flying insects. It frequents a wide range of habitats in the region.

Marico Flycatcher *Melaenornis mariquensis* (695) L 18 cm

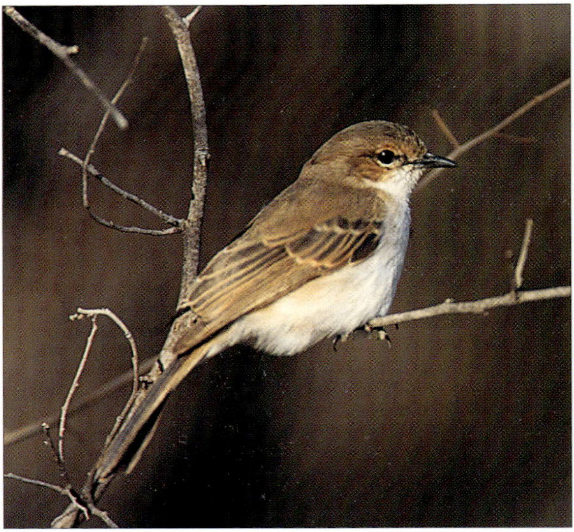

W R TARBOTON

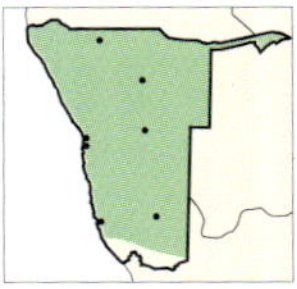

This is a nondescript flycatcher with *uniform buffish brown upperparts contrasting with clear white underparts*. The immature is heavily spotted with buff above and streaked with brown below. Its song is a soft 'tsii-cheruk-tukk'. This bird perches conspicuously along roadsides, hawking insects and often returning to the same perch. It is a common resident in Namibia, and is found in mixed thornveld and open, dry broad-leafed woodland.

Chat Flycatcher *Melaenornis infuscatus* (697) L 20 cm

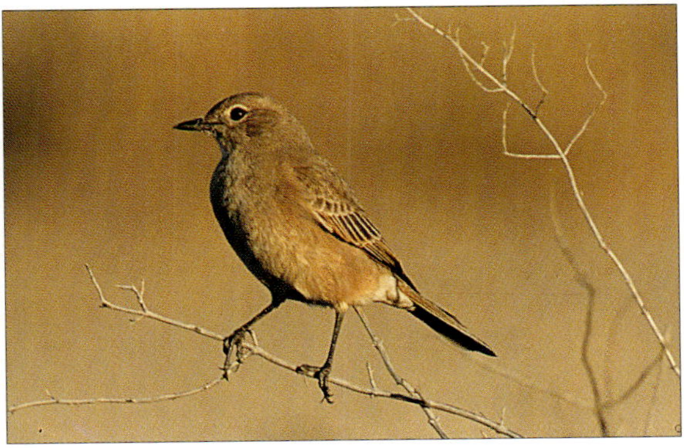

PHOTO ACCESS/T CAREW

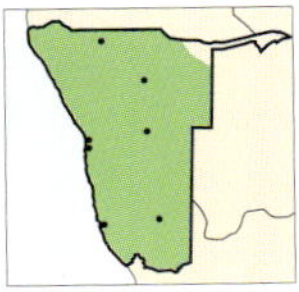

The plumage of this species is *uniform brownish above with paler underparts. A pale brown panel on the folded secondaries* should help to identify this large chat of thrush-like proportions. The immature is heavily spotted with buff above and below. This bird has a rich, warbled 'cher-cher-cherrip' song, interspersed with squeaky, hissing notes. A common but unevenly distributed resident, it occurs in pairs in desert scrub and stunted thornveld.

Pririt Batis *Batis pririt* (703) L 12 cm

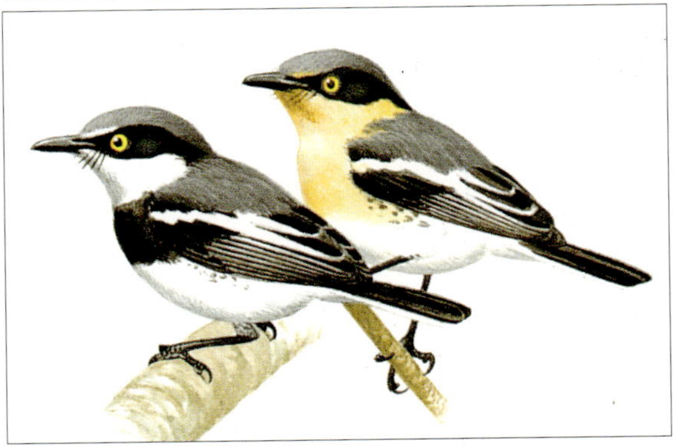

NORMAN ARLOTT

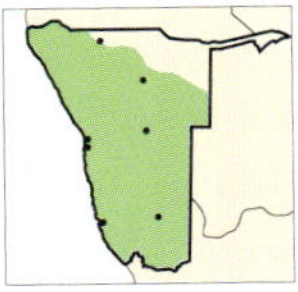

This is a *small, black and white* flycatcher, the female of which has a distinctive chestnut wash over the throat and breast. The male differs by having a broad black breast band. Both sexes have indistinct black markings on the flank. The immature resembles the female. Its call is a series of slow 'teuu, teuu, teuu, teuu' notes, descending in scale. This is a common resident of Namibia and is found in dry thornveld, broad-leafed woodland and dry riverine bush.

African Paradise Flycatcher *Terpsiphone viridis* (710)
L 23 cm (plus 18 cm tail in breeding male)

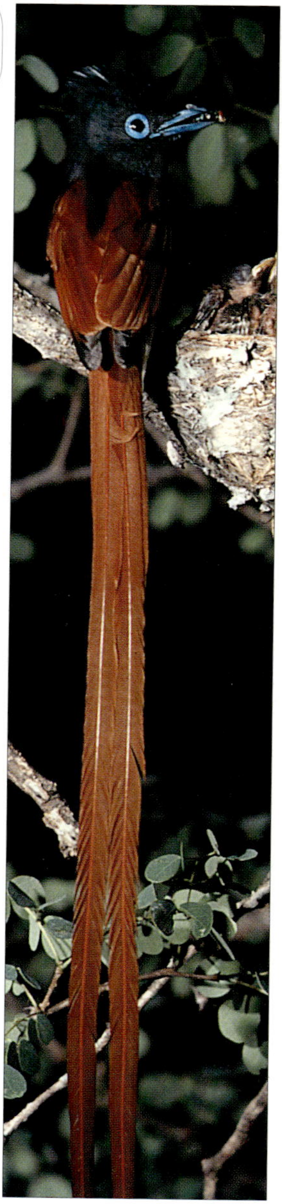

J VAN JAARSVELD

Male

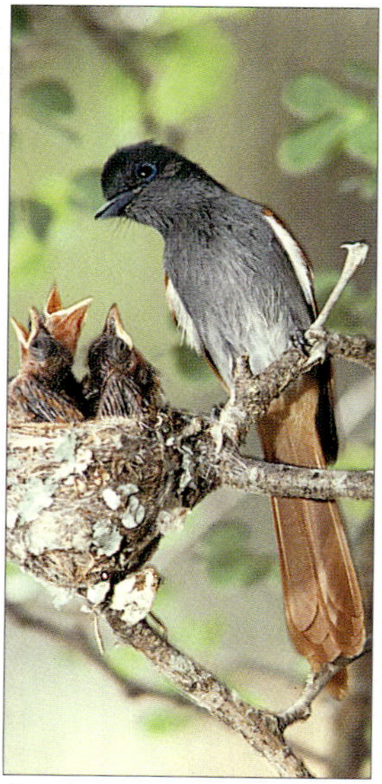

J VAN JAARSVELD

Female

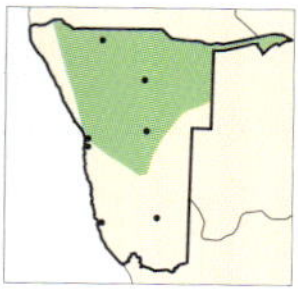

Both male and female African Paradise flycatchers are unmistakable and easy to identify. The adult bird has a *dark head and breast, bright blue bill and eye-ring,* and a *chestnut back and tail*. In breeding plumage the male boasts an extraordinarily long, chestnut tail. The immature is a duller version of the female. Both the female and immature lack the very long tail. This is an active and noisy bird whose harsh 'tic-tic-chaa-chaa' notes are often heard before the bird is seen. Its song is a loud 'twee-tiddly-te-te'. It is generally very active, dashing about in the mid-canopy chasing insects, and rarely settling at one perch for very long. It is a common summer visitor, frequenting moist areas in the north, riverine and broad-leafed woodland and suburban gardens.

Cape Wagtail *Motacilla capensis* (713) L 18 cm

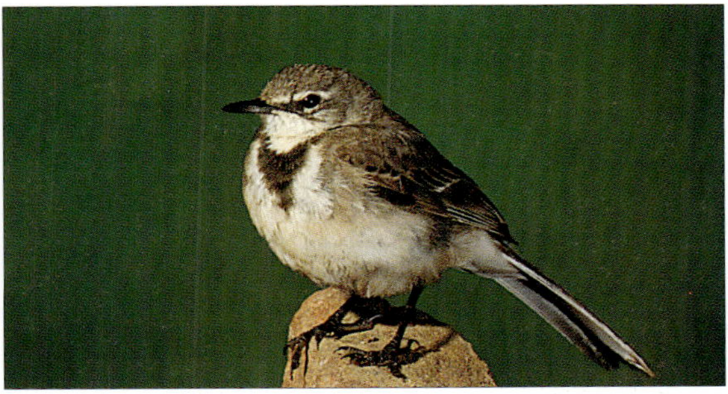

IAN SINCLAIR

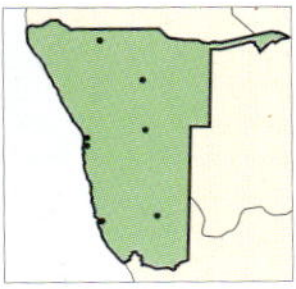

Its habit of continually moving its tail up and down when walking or at rest gives rise to its name. The *unmarked greyish brown upperparts, combined with the narrow black breast band*, are diagnostic. The immature is duller than the adult with a buff yellow wash over the belly. Its call is a clear, ringing 'tseee-chee-chee' and a whistled, trilling song. Uncommon and thinly distributed, it prefers damp and marshy areas. It is also found in city parks and gardens.

Grassveld Pipit *Anthus cinnamomeus* (716) L 16 cm

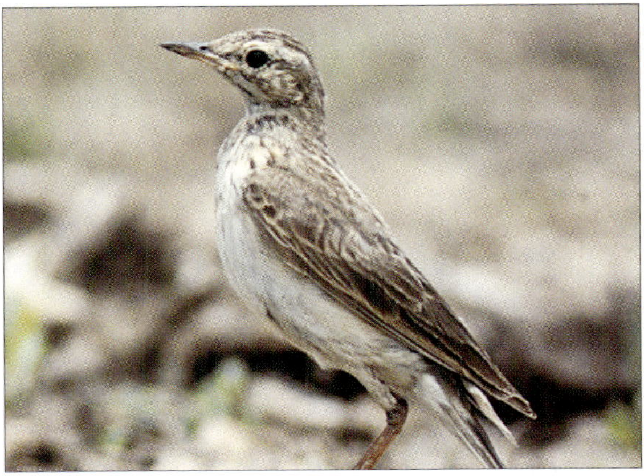

DR & MRS MANFRED REICHARDT

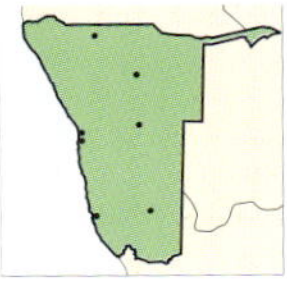

This fairly nondescript bird has *buff and brown plumage with streaking on the breast*. In flight the *prominent white outertail feathers* are visible. The immature is darker above and more heavily streaked than the adult. The song given during display is a 'trrit-trrit-trrit', and when flushed it utters a 'chisseet' alarm call. It feeds on the ground, running short distances before stopping to pick up food. This pipit is most likely to be seen in the open veld or grasslands near towns. It is common but thinly distributed in the region.

Lesser Grey Shrike *Lanius minor* (731) L 21 cm

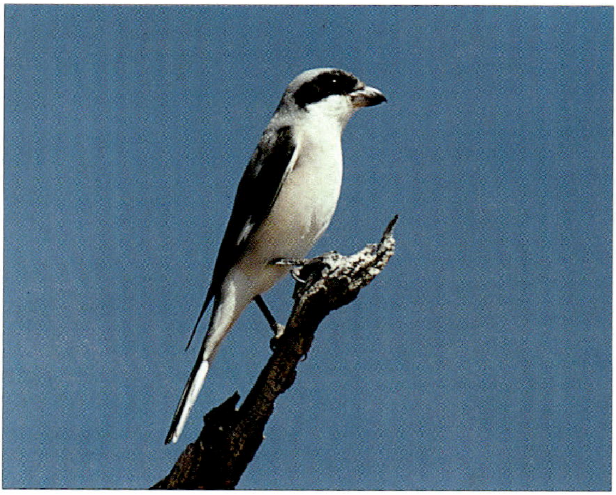

ABPL/CLEM HAAGNER

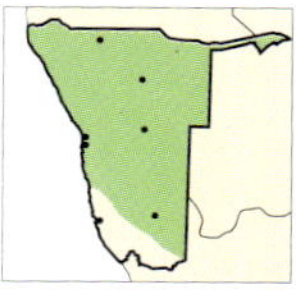

This bird is identified by its contrasting *white underparts, grey back and the extensive black mask which encompasses the forehead.* The female is duller and often has less black on the forehead. Immatures have buffy underparts with light barring. The soft 'chuk' and warbled song are rarely heard. Obvious along roadsides, where it perches on telephone wires and atop bushes and poles, it is a common summer visitor. This shrike occurs in mixed dry thornveld and semi-desert scrub.

Common Fiscal Shrike *Lanius collaris* (732) L 23 cm

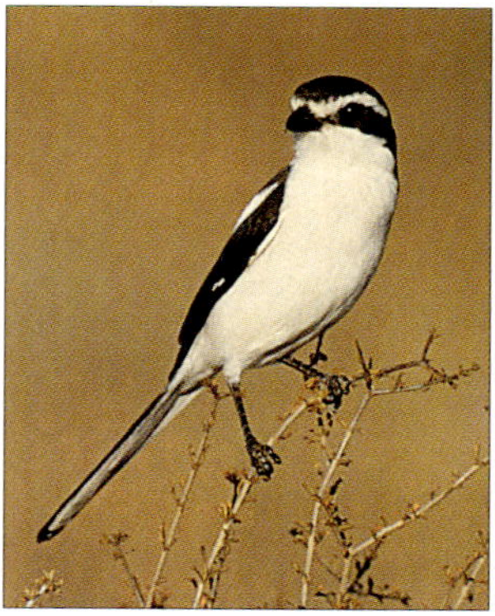

PHOTO ACCESS/T CAREW

Desert form

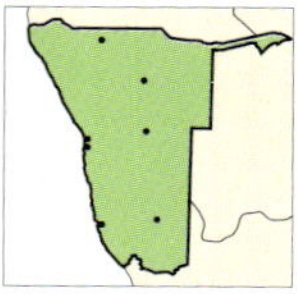

This shrike has *black upperparts and white underparts with prominent white shoulder patches.* The female shows a rufous patch on the flank. Birds of the more arid areas of the region are smaller, with a smaller bill and a prominent white eyebrow stripe. The immature is greyish brown with grey crescentic barring on its underparts. While other black and white shrikes are shy and furtive, this conspicuous bird hunts from exposed perches. A harsh, melodious, jumbled song is uttered while mimicking other birds' songs. It is a common resident, and is found in a wide range of habitats but avoids dense woodland.

Swamp Boubou *Laniarius bicolor* (738) L 23 cm

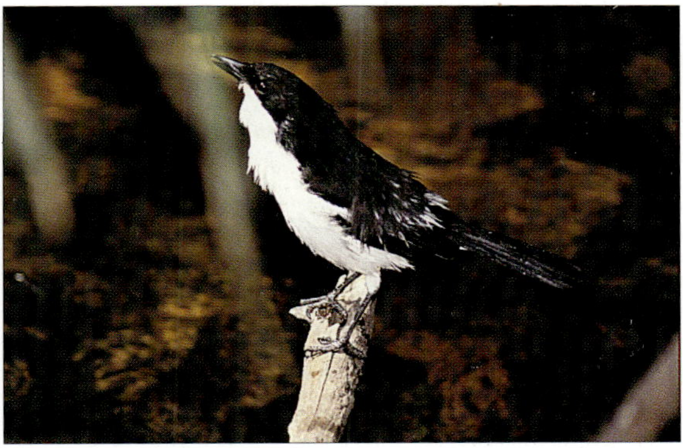

ABPL/BRENDAN RYAN

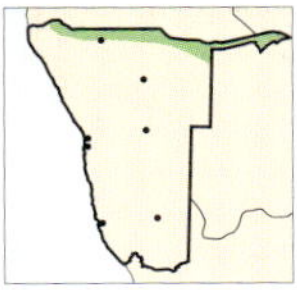

The *black upperparts with a white wing stripe and clear all-white underparts* (with no trace of rufous or pink coloration) help to identify this bird. The immature is spotted with buff above and barred below. Its call is a diagnostic, *clear and ringing 'hoouu'*, often in duet, followed by harsher 'kik-kik-kik' sounds. This shrike is a skulking inhabitant of thick tangles along rivers and in reed beds, and is common on the northern river systems of Namibia.

Crimsonbreasted Shrike *Laniarius atrococcineus* (739) L 23 cm

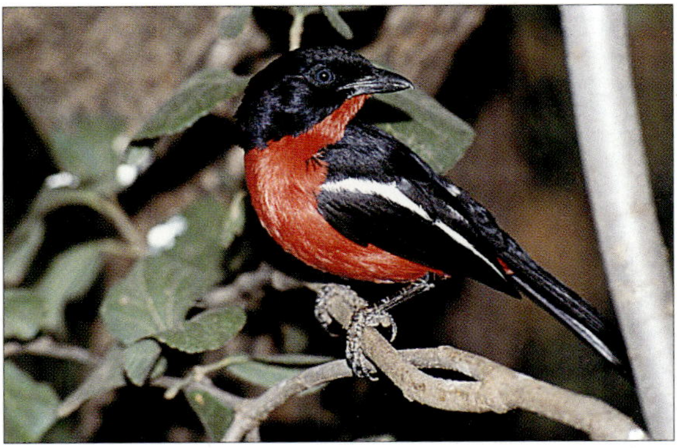

ABPL/BRENDAN RYAN

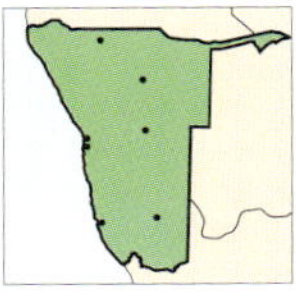

This is one of the most strikingly coloured birds of the bushveld. The *bright crimson underparts and black upperparts, offset by a white flash down the wing*, render this bird unmistakable. The immature is barred with greyish brown, showing varying amounts of crimson below. This bird's calls are an unusual clonking sound and a harsh 'trrrrr'. It is a common resident though not always easily seen as it tends to skulk in the undergrowth of thornveld and dry rivercourses.

Brubru *Nilaus afer* (741) L 15 cm

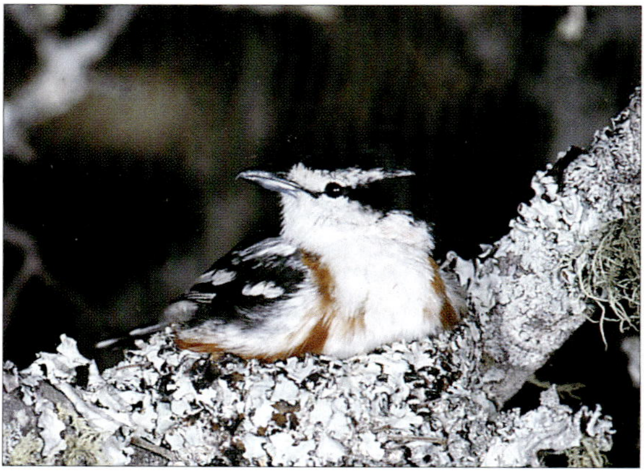

P J GINN

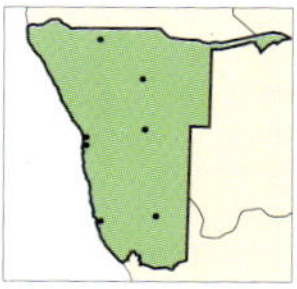

Although it could be mistaken for a batis, its large size and thick bill should obviate any confusion. Its diagnostic features are the *black and white chequered back, broad white eyebrow stripe and russet flank stripe*. The female is duller than the male. The immature has brown and white mottling below. Its call is a soft, trilling 'prrrr, prrrr' and a piercing, whistled 'tioooo'. Found in open broad-leafed woodland and dry thornveld, this is a common resident.

Threestreaked Tchagra *Tchagra australis* (743) L 19 cm

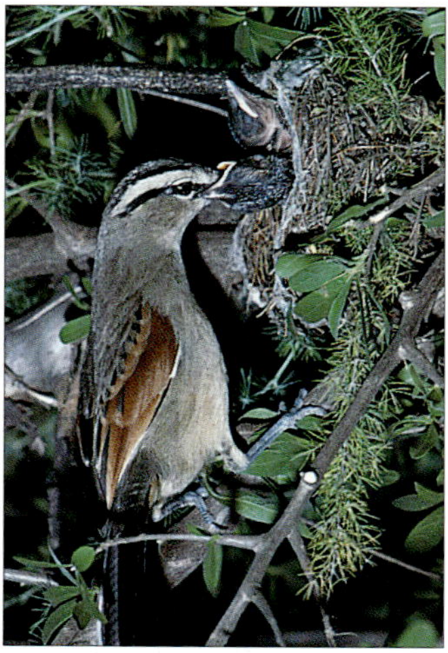

S M BLOOMFIELD

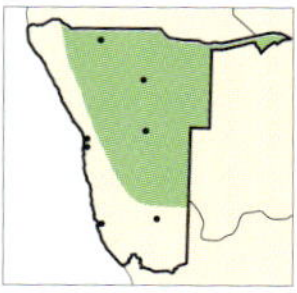

This is a shrike-like bird with *russet wings and a white-tipped tail*. Other identifying features include an *obvious black eye-stripe and a white eyebrow stripe*. The immature is a duller version of the adult. It tends to skulk in thick tangles and undergrowth in thornveld. During the breeding season, however, it is more conspicuous: in display flight it flutters into the air, then descends slowly, giving its 'weee-chee-chee-chee' song. This bird is a common Namibian resident. It is found in bushveld and forested areas of the region.

Bokmakierie *Telophorus zeylonus* (746) L 23 cm

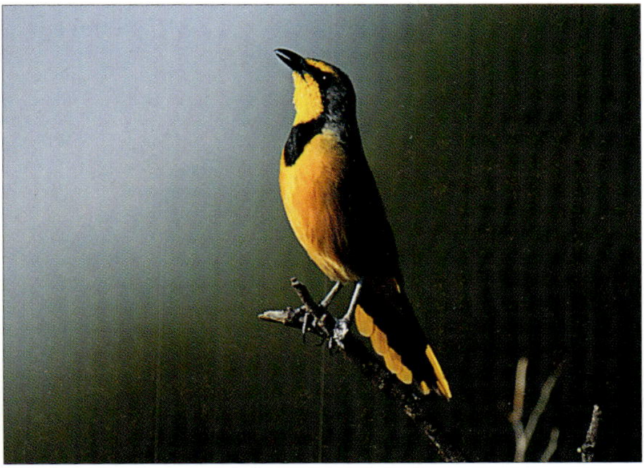

SIL/NIGEL J DENNIS

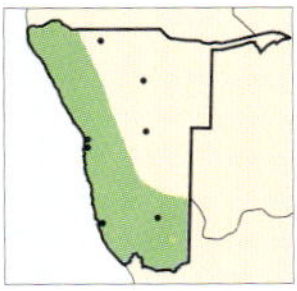

The *bluish grey head, bright lemon yellow underparts and broad black breast band* of this bird are diagnostic. In flight it shows a vivid yellow tip to the dark green tail. The immature lacks the breast band and is greyish green below. The Bokmakierie has a variety of calls but the name resembles the most frequently heard 'bok-bok-kik' call. It is an uncommon and thinly distributed resident of Namibia and is found in scrub-filled valleys in mountainous areas.

Whitetailed Shrike *Lanioturdus torquatus* (752) L 15 cm

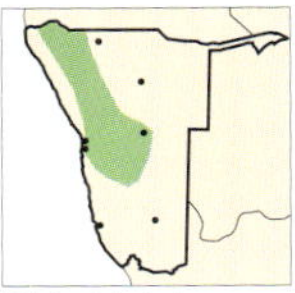

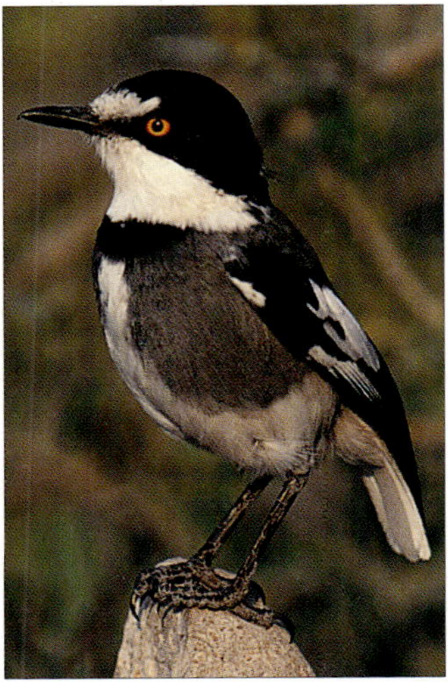

PETER CRAIG-COOPER

This bird is very striking with its *diagnostic contrasting black, white and grey plumage*. The *long legs and very short tail* are also diagnostic. It has a characteristic upright stance that makes it appear almost tailless. The immature is similar to the adult but has a mottled crown. The sexes are alike. The call consists of a series of clear, drawn-out whistles and harsh cackling. This bird is a common resident of Namibia, and is often seen on the ground or hopping over rocks in dry thornveld and scrub desert.

White Helmetshrike *Prionops plumatus* (753) L 20 cm

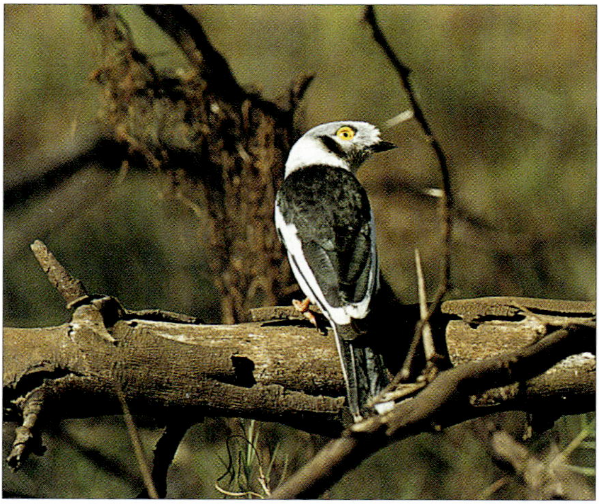

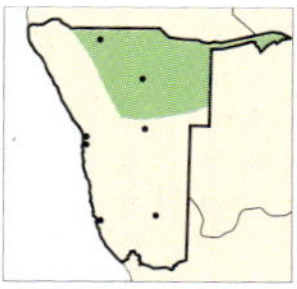

When in flight this gregarious bird shows a pied plumage with white flashes in the wings and white outertail feathers. At rest the *clear white underparts, grey crown, white collar, yellow eye-ring and black ear coverts* are visible. The immature is duller than the adult, and lacks the yellow eye-ring and black ear coverts. The call consists of a jumble of chatters and whistles. Small groups of this common resident are seen flitting through mixed woodland and thornveld.

Southern Whitecrowned Shrike *Eurocephalus anguitimens* (756) L 24 cm

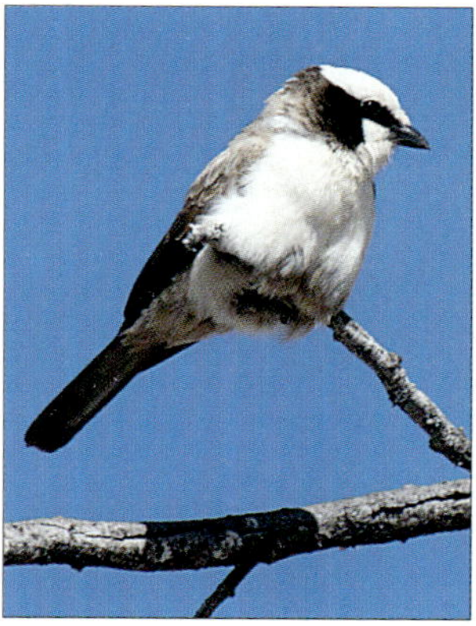

J THERON

Adult

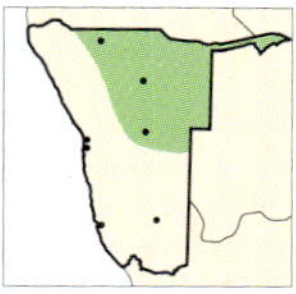

This large, robust shrike is easy to identify as it is the only one in the region to show a *white crown and white forehead.* The throat and breast are also white and the belly and flanks are washed with buff. The immature is paler than the adult with a mottled brown body. Its calls are a shrill, whistling 'kree, kree, kree' and harsh chattering and bleating. This gregarious bird is a common resident of Namibia and is found in thornveld and dry woodland.

Wattled Starling *Creatophora cinerea* (760) L 21 cm

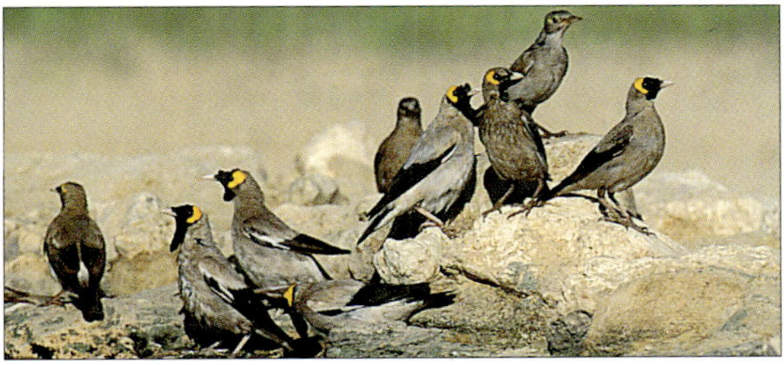

ABPL/NIGEL DENNIS

Breeding males

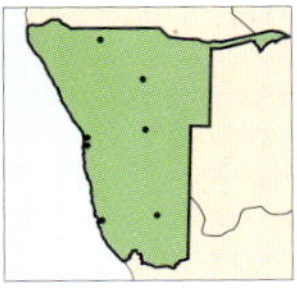

This greyish starling has *black pointed wings and a short black tail*. During the breeding season the male becomes very conspicuous with its black and yellow head and black wattles. The female has a whitish rump; the immature is brownish grey with the whitish rump. The call is a sharp 'ssreeeeo' note. It is nomadic and abundant when breeding, and is found in large flocks in open scrub areas, light woodland and grassland.

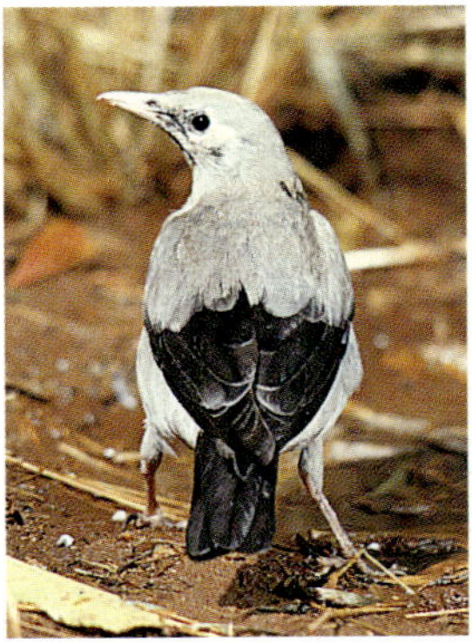

J VAN JAARSVELD

Non-breeding male

Burchell's Starling *Lamprotornis australis* (762) L 34 cm

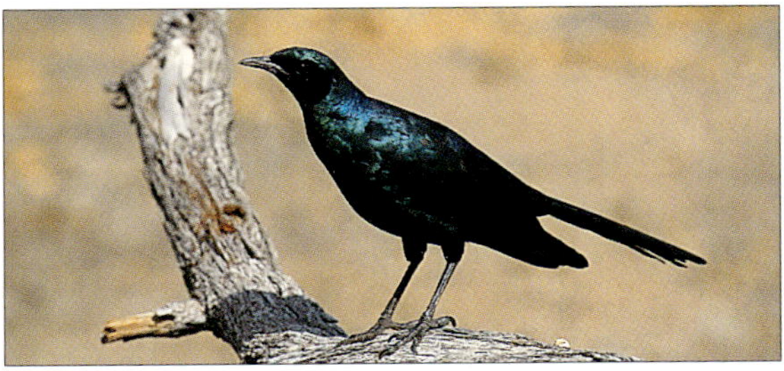

NIGEL J DENNIS

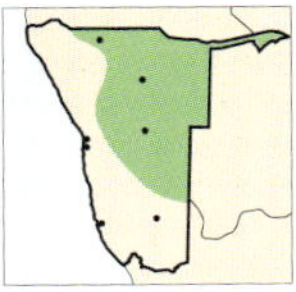

This is the largest starling in Namibia. A glossy species, it is regularly seen along roadsides where it lazily flies up from verges into trees or onto telephone wires. The tail is long and wedge shaped and the wings are rounded; the flight is noticeably laboured and floppy. The immature is duller than the adult. The call of this bird is a rough and throaty series of chuckles and chortles. It is a common resident of thornveld and dry broad-leafed woodland.

Glossy Starling *Lamprotornis nitens* (764) L 25 cm

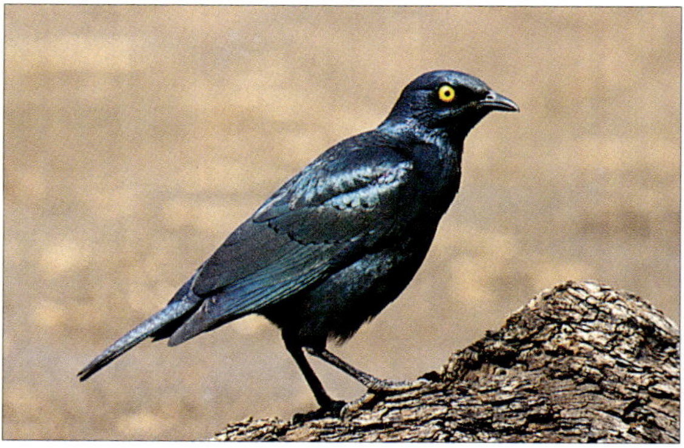

PETER CRAIG-COOPER

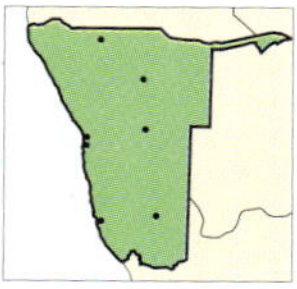

From a distance this short-tailed starling appears to be completely black and it is not until one is reasonably close to it that the *iridescent coloration* becomes visible. The ear patches, head, belly and flanks are all bright, shiny green. Its *bright orange eye* is wide and staring. Immatures are duller than adults with straw-coloured eyes. The song is a slurred 'trrr-chree-chrrrr'. Found in thornveld, mixed woodland and suburbia, this is the most common glossy starling in Namibia.

Palewinged Starling *Onychognathus nabouroup* (770) L 26 cm

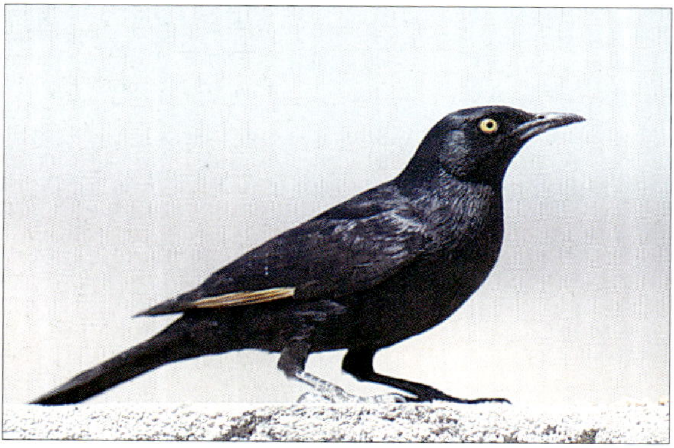

T D LONGRIGG

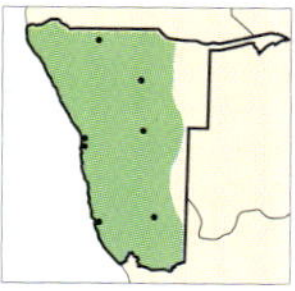

In flight this long-tailed starling shows a highly visible *white patch in the primaries* from which it derives its name. It has a *dark blue-black, slightly glossy plumage and a bright orange eye*. The immature is duller than the adult. Its call is a ringing 'preeeooo' which is given in flight, as well as warbling calls like those of the Glossy Starling. It inhabits rocky ravines and cliffs in dry and desert regions but has also colonized cities and towns. This is a common resident of Namibia.

Cape White-eye *Zosterops pallidus* (796) L 12 cm

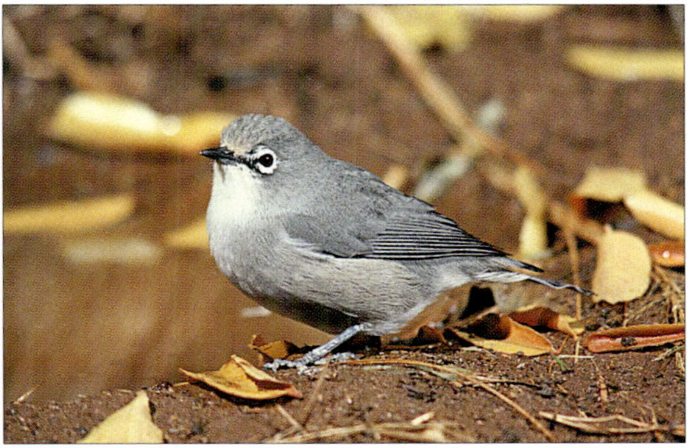

J VAN JAARSVELD

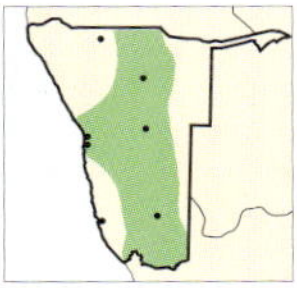

The plumage of this warbler-like bird is *greyish below and olive green above*. The *ring of white feathers around the eye* is diagnostic. The immature is duller than the adult. The soft, sweet 'tweee-tuuu-twee-twee' call is continually repeated by these birds moving in bird parties, as pairs keep contact with each other. This species is commonly found in groups in a wide range of habitats including suburban gardens. It is a common resident of Namibia.

Marico Sunbird *Nectarinia mariquensis* (779) L 14 cm

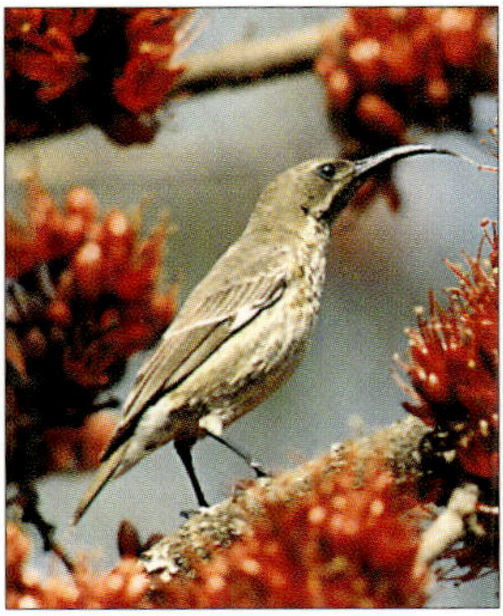

G CUBITT

Female

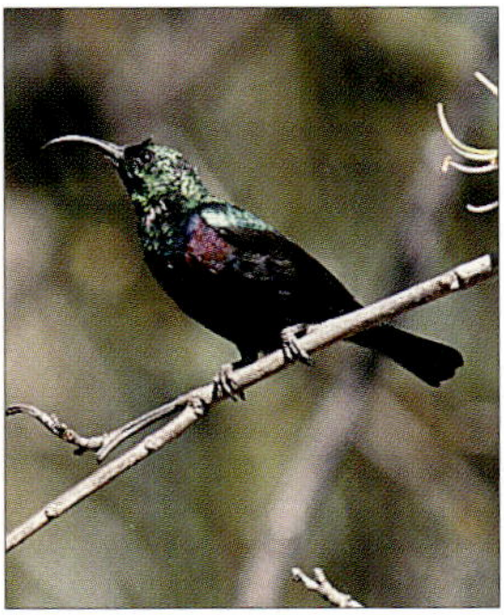

ABPL/BRENDAN RYAN

Male

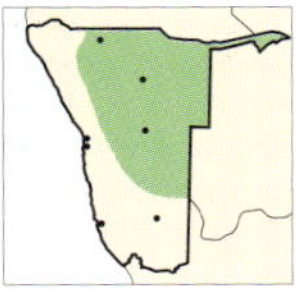

The male of this species has *an iridescent purple breast band that contrasts with the black belly, and a scarlet chest band*. The *head and back are metallic greenish blue*, and the *bill is long and decurved*. In comparison, the female has drab, olive-brown upperparts and pale, dull yellow streaked underparts. The female's distinguishing feature is a *long, robust and decurved bill*. The immature resembles the female. It has a typically chippering sunbird call. This common resident frequents thornveld and dry broad-leafed woodland.

Dusky Sunbird *Nectarinia fusca* (788) L 10 cm

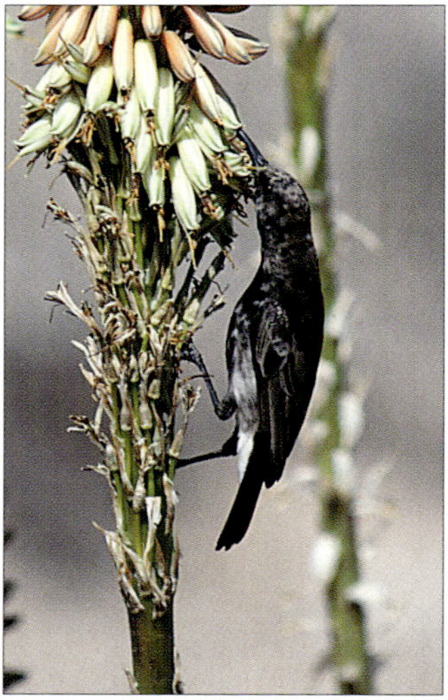

THEO BUCHHOLZ

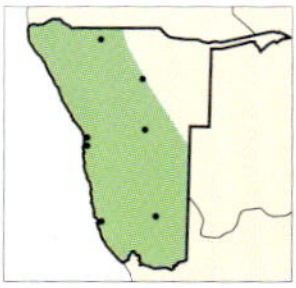

The *black head, throat and back, and contrasting white belly,* are usually diagnostic in the male of this species; plumage is variable in the male with sometimes only a black line running from the throat to the breast. The *pectoral tufts* in both sexes *are orange.* The female's upperparts are *light grey-brown and the underparts are off-white.* The immature resembles the female but has a black throat. This bird's short warbling song is interspersed with a scolding 'chrrr-chrrr'. It is a common resident of dry thornveld, dry and wooded rocky valleys, and scrub desert in the region.

Scarletchested Sunbird *Nectarinia senegalensis* (791) L 15 cm

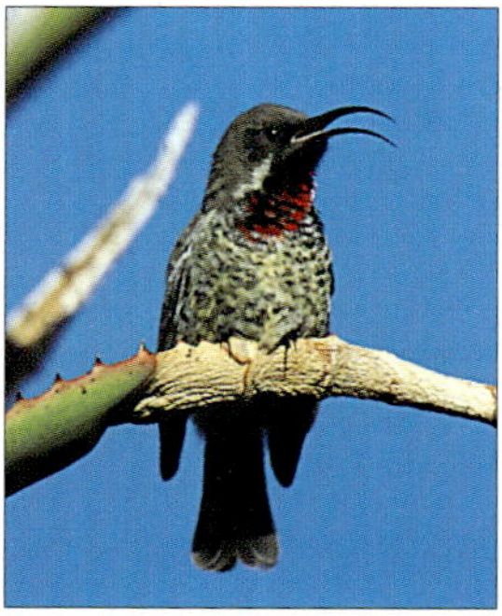

Male eclipse plumage

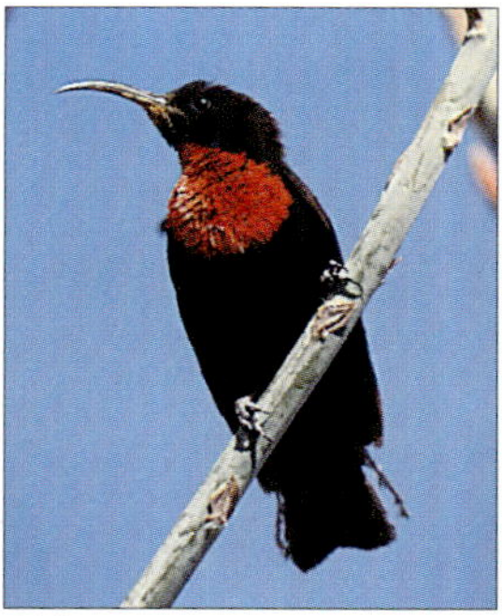

Male

P J GINN

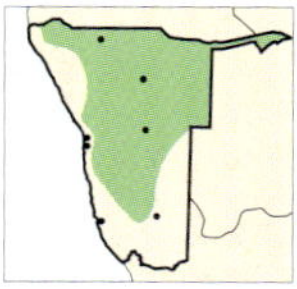

This large chunky sunbird is unmistakable. The male's *black body and scarlet chest* are diagnostic. At close range iridescent blue flecks on the male's scarlet breast can be seen. The female is *greyish olive above and very heavily mottled below.* The immature resembles the female. The song is a loud, whistled 'cheeup-chup-toop-toop-toop' call. The male is bold and conspicuous, chasing other birds from the territory. This common Namibian resident occurs in mixed dry and moist woodland, thornveld and suburbia.

Redbilled Buffalo Weaver *Bubalornis niger* (798) L 24 cm

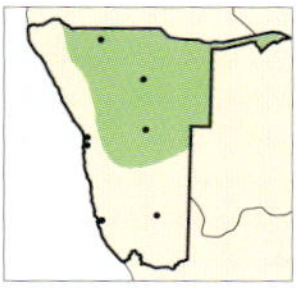

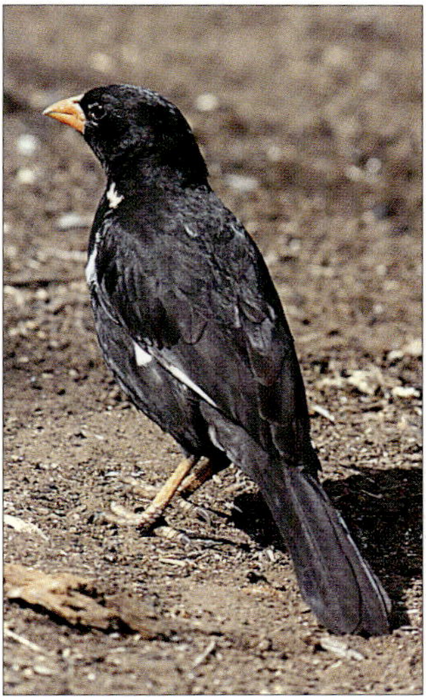

PETER CRIAG-COOPER

This is the only large, black, sparrow-like bird in the region. The *robust red bill, black plumage and white wing patches* are diagnostic. The female and immature are brown versions of the male. The song is a 'chip-chip-doodley-doodley-doo'. This common resident occurs in dry thornveld and broad-leafed woodland. It breeds communally, making a large, untidy nest from bundles of thorny sticks in trees or on electricity pylons.

Whitebrowed Sparrow-weaver *Plocepasser mahali* (799) L 19 cm

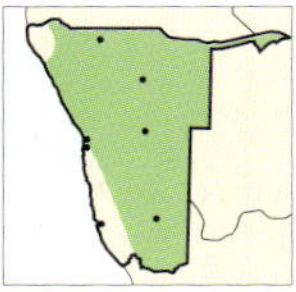

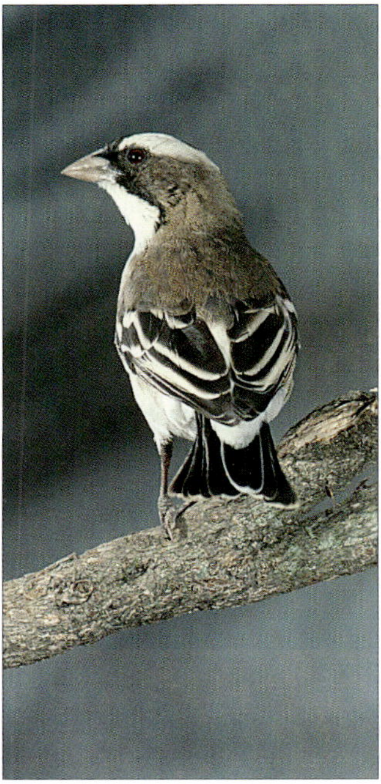

N BRICKELL

This is a large, plump, short-tailed weaver with a *distinctive broad white eyebrow stripe, a conspicuous white rump and a white wing stripe*. The male has a black bill; the female has a horn-coloured bill. The immature is similar to the adult but has a pinkish brown bill. These birds build many untidy nests from dry grass in the outside branches of a tree. The loud, liquid 'cheeoop-preeoo-chop' call is given from these colonies; a harsher 'chik-chik' alarm call is also given. It is a common resident in the region and is found in thornveld and along dry, scrubby river courses.

Sociable Weaver *Philetairus socius* (800) L 14 cm

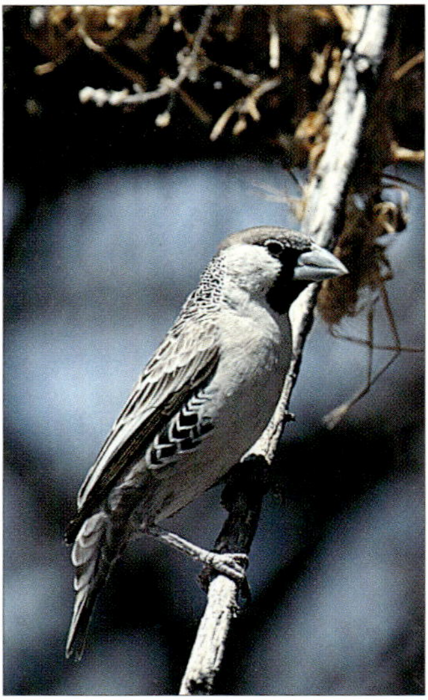

ABPL/NIGEL J DENNIS

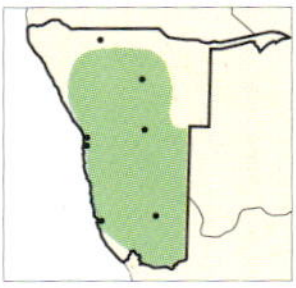

The *black chin, black-barred flanks, and scaly-patterned back* render this particular species unmistakable. The immature lacks the black face mask. In flight the bird gives a chattering 'chicker-chicker' call. These birds are gregarious by nature and build large communal nests, resembling small haystacks, which appear to 'thatch' the trees in which they are built. Small flocks of Sociable weavers are found roaming areas of dry thornveld and broad-leafed woodland in this region. It is usually a common resident in Namibia but becomes nomadic during years when there is drought.

Great Sparrow *Passer motitensis* (802) L 15 cm

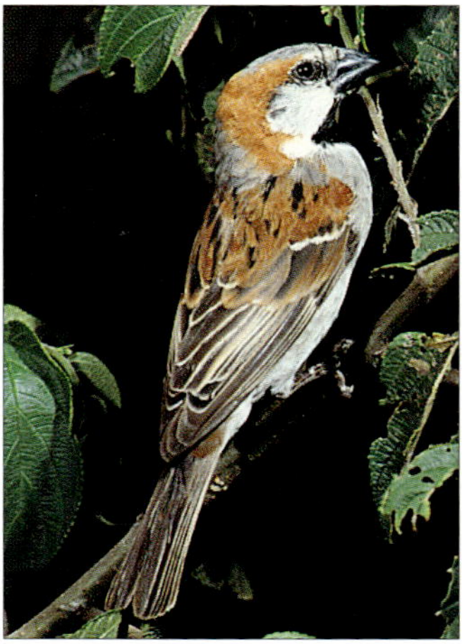

PETER CRAIG-COOPER

Male

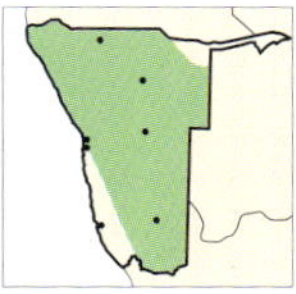

This sparrow differs from the smaller, but very similar, House Sparrow with its *bright chestnut back and sides of head*, but can be distinguished from that species by having a *chestnut, not grey, rump*. The female might be mistaken for a female House Sparrow but the Great Sparrow is much larger and much redder on the back and shoulders. The immature is similar to the female. The call is a liquid 'cheereep, cheereeu'. This sparrow is a common resident in the region and occurs in dry thornveld; it is not usually associated with human habitation.

Cape Sparrow *Passer melanurus* (803) L 15 cm

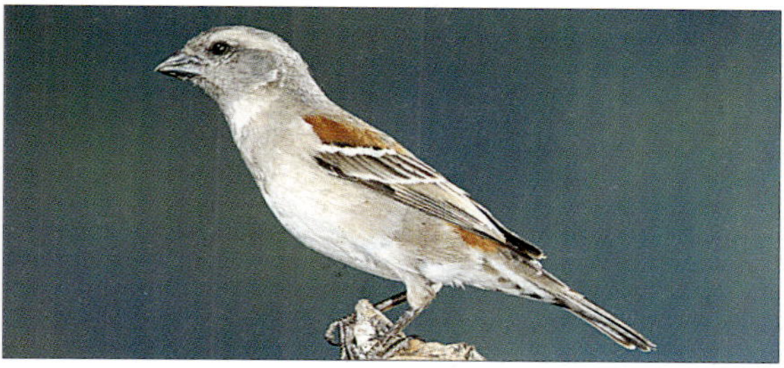

HEIN VON HÖRSTEN

Female

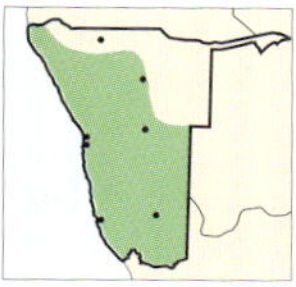

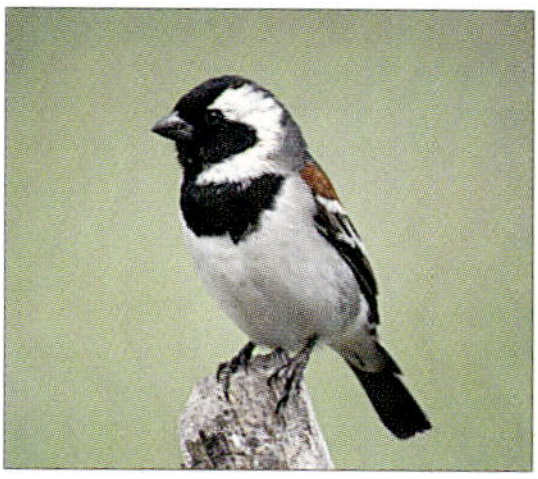

COLIN URQUHART

Male

The male of this species is distinctive, as it is the only sparrow in Namibia to have a *bold black and white head pattern*. The female has a *chestnut mantle and faint shadow markings of the male's head pattern*. The call consists of a series of musical cheeps. It is a common Namibian resident, and although it has adapted to human habitation it is frequently found in remote grassland areas.

Scalyfeathered Finch *Sporopipes squamifrons* (806) L 10 cm

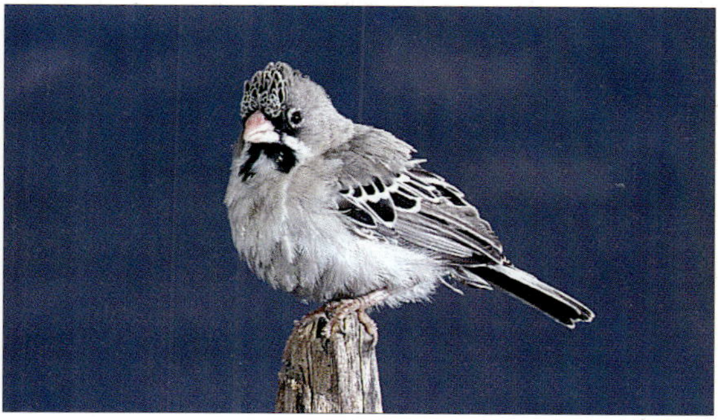

PETER CRAIG-COOPER

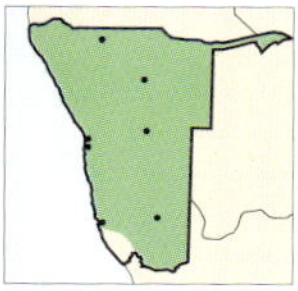

When seen at rest, this is an easily identified, tiny finch with *black and white malar stripes, a freckled black and white forehead, and white-fringed wing and tail feathers*; in flight it appears as a grey blur. When flushed it settles on an exposed perch. Immatures lack the malar stripes and the freckling on the forehead. In flight this bird emits an indistinct 'chizz-chizz' call note. It is a common resident found in dry thornveld and around cattle enclosures, watering troughs and farm buildings.

Chestnut Weaver *Ploceus rubiginosus* (812) L 15 cm

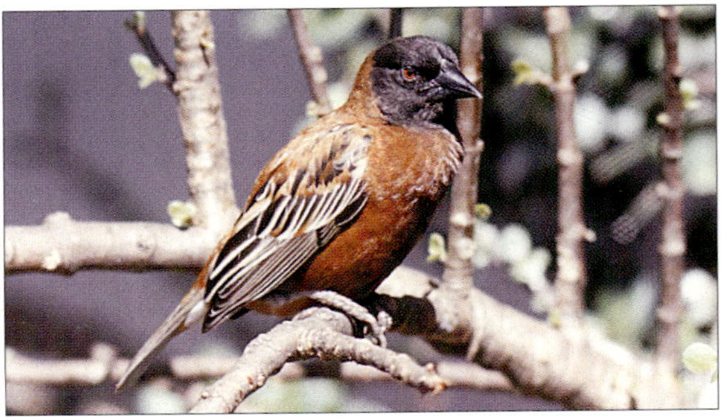

N BRICKELL

Male

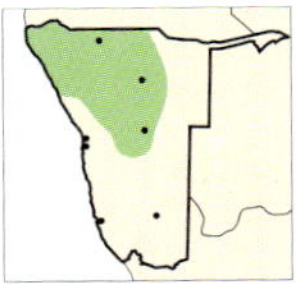

The breeding male of this species has a *black head* and a *chestnut back and underparts*. The female and non-breeding male are dull *grey-brown with a yellowish throat ending in a brownish breast band*. The immature is similar to the female but has streaking on the breast. This bird utters the usual 'chuk, chuk' and swizzling weaver-type notes. Occurring in dry broad-leafed woodland, thornveld and dry riverine woodland, it is common to abundant in years of good rain but otherwise nomadic.

Redbilled Quelea *Quelea quelea* (821) L 13 cm

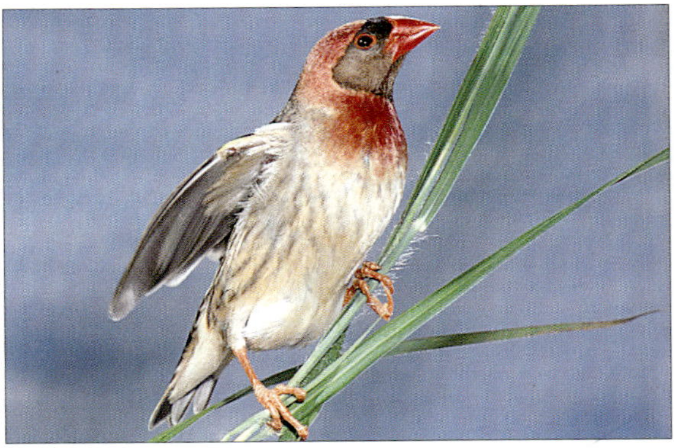

PETER CRAIG-COOPER

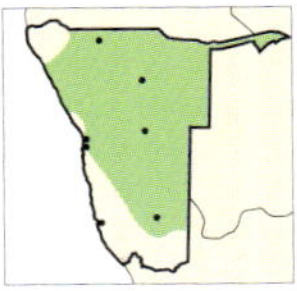

The male in breeding plumage is easily identified by its *black face bordered with pinky red, bright red bill and red legs*. The non-breeding male and female are drab birds but retain the *red bill and legs*. Females in breeding plumage show a horn-coloured bill. The immature resembles the female and has a yellowish pink bill. The song is a mixture of harsh and melodious notes. This species concentrates in flocks numbering hundreds and thousands. A common to abundant resident, it occurs in dry, mixed woodlands and savanna, and on farmlands.

Southern Masked Weaver *Ploceus velatus* (814) L 15 cm

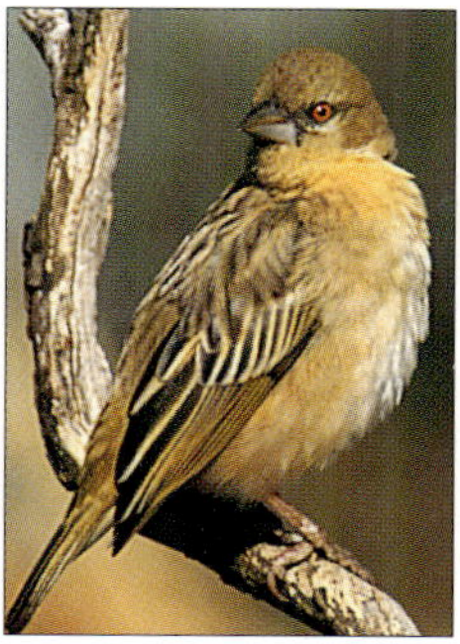

Female

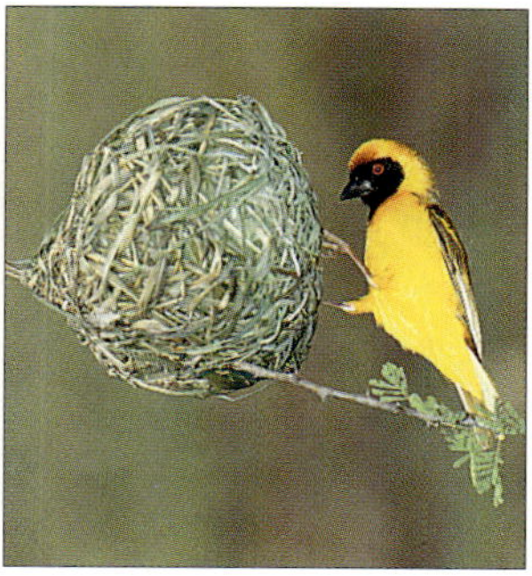

Male

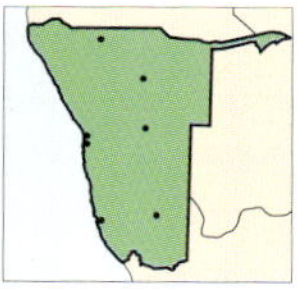

The breeding male of this species is easily confused with the Lesser Masked Weaver but differs by having *brown legs, a red eye, and a black mask which does not extend behind the eye on top of the head but forms a point on the throat.* The female, non-breeding male and immature are alike, having *yellowish underparts and olive-brown upperparts.* Its call consists of typical swizzling weaver notes. This common resident breeds in trees overhanging water, in thornveld, and in suburbia.

Lesser Masked Weaver *Ploceus intermedius* (815) L 15 cm

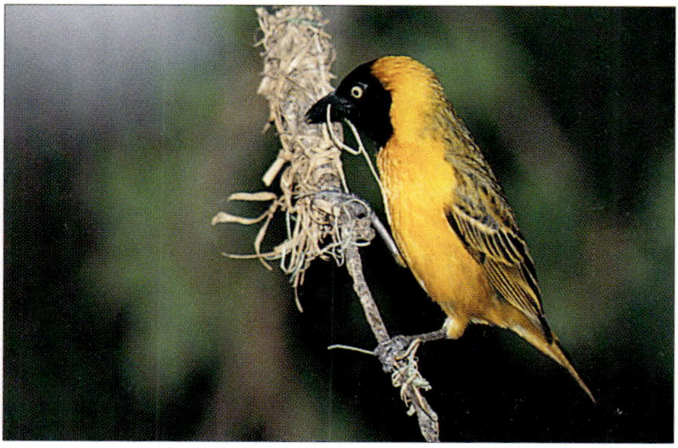

Male

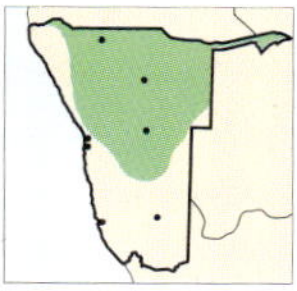

Slightly smaller than the Southern Masked Weaver, this weaver is identified in breeding plumage by the shape of its *mask which extends well on to the crown and comes to a rounded, not pointed, end on the throat.* It shows a *white eye and blue legs.* Immatures and females lack the mask and are yellow below. The call is a typical weaver 'chuk' and swizzling noises. It breeds colonially in trees overhanging water but also away from water; it is less common than the Southern Masked Weaver.

Southern Red Bishop *Euplectes orix* (824) L 14 cm

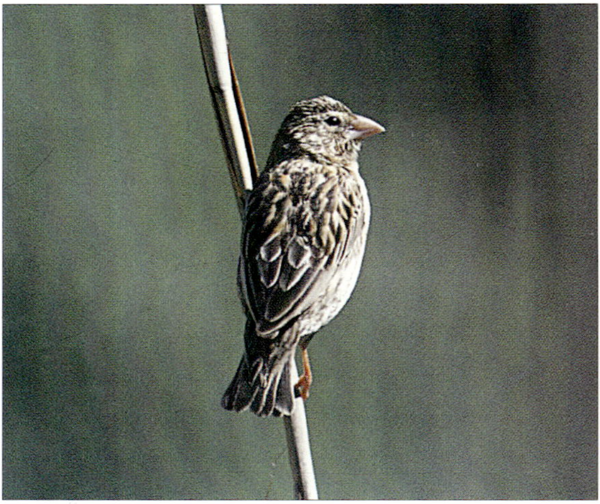

DR & MRS M REICHARDT

Female

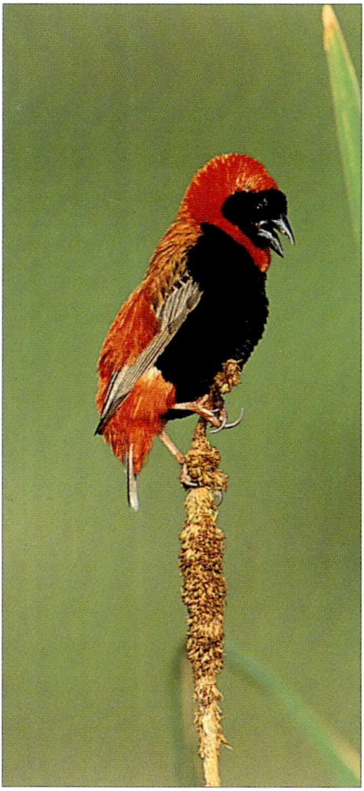

SIL/NIGEL J DENNIS

Male

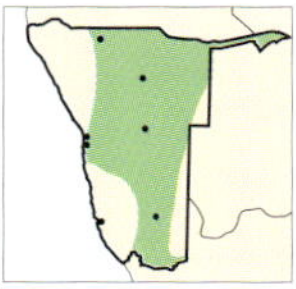

The breeding male of this species is very distinctive with its contrasting *bright orange and black plumage, and black forehead and crown.* The female and non-breeding male are *brown and buff with dark streaking on the underparts.* The immature resembles the female. This bird gives a 'cheet-cheet' flight call. The male performs a spectacular display flight in which he fluffs out his feathers and, with rapid wing beats, whizzes to and fro like a gigantic bumble-bee; a buzzing, chirping song is given in display. This widespread, common resident is usually associated with water and is found in reed beds adjoining freshwater and agricultural lands.

Golden Bishop *Euplectes afer* (826) L 12 cm

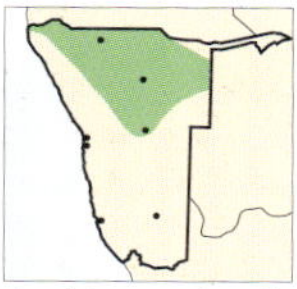

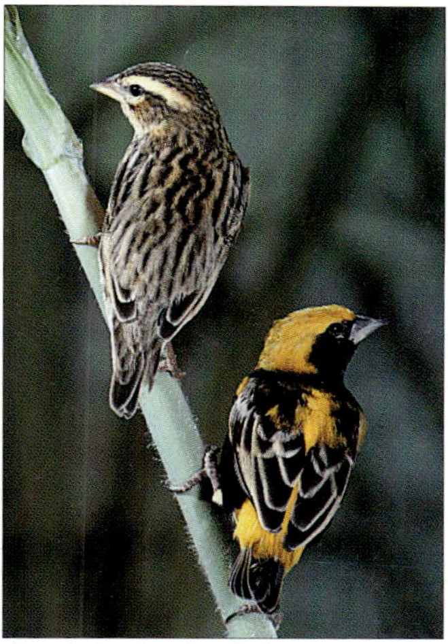

PETER CRAIG-COOPER

Female (top) and male (bottom)

In this species the breeding male is easily identified by its striking *black and yellow* plumage. In non-breeding plumage the male and female most closely resemble the Southern Red Bishop but differ by being noticeably smaller, more compact and paler with reduced streaking on the breast and flanks and a prominent yellow eye-stripe. The immature resembles the female. The call consists of a series of buzzing and chirping notes. It is found in reed beds and grasses near water, as well as on agricultural fields and grasslands. This is a common resident in the north of Namibia.

Melba Finch *Pytilia melba* (834) L 12 cm

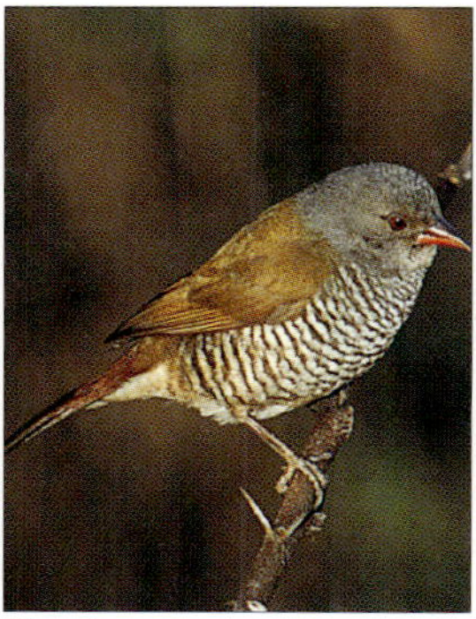

J J THERON

Female

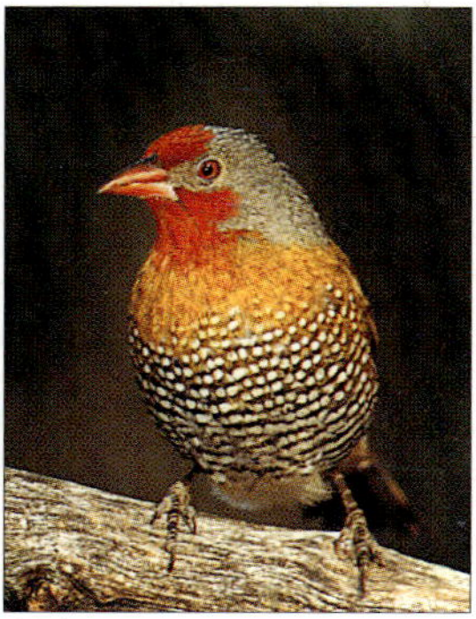

J J THERON

Male

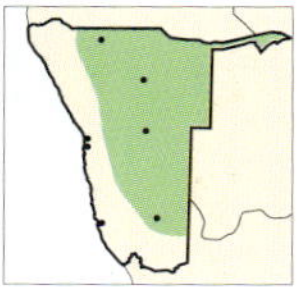

This is a brightly coloured finch, showing a *crimson face, bill and throat, a blue-grey nape, and a boldly barred belly and flanks*. The female has an all-grey head and breast. The immature is similar to the female but is more olive above and plain greyish below. This bird has a pretty, trilling song that rises and falls in pitch. It is also known to utter a short 'wick' call. This bird is a common resident in the region and frequents dry, broad-leafed woodland and thornveld.

Blue Waxbill *Uraeginthus angolensis* (844) L 13 cm

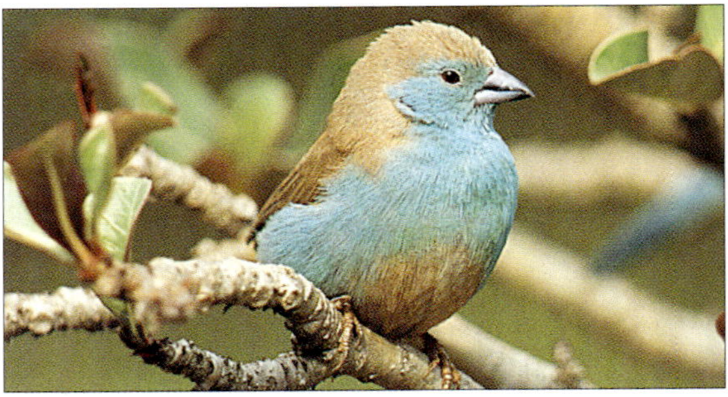

J J THERON

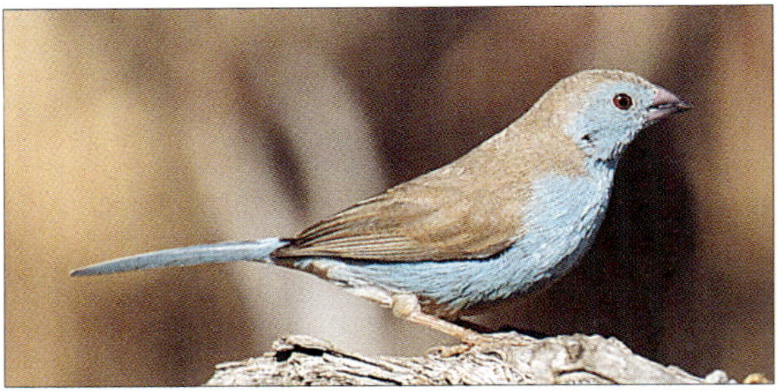

J J THERON

Top: female. Bottom: male

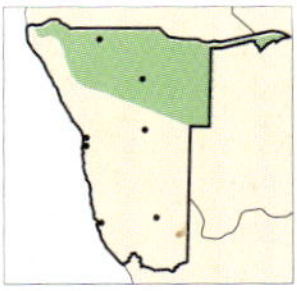

This waxbill is unmistakable with its *powder-blue face, breast and tail*. The female is paler than the male with less blue on the face and underparts; the immature is paler than the female. Its call is a soft 'kway-kway-sree-seee-seee-seee'. A common resident, it usually occurs in pairs or flocks in dry areas of mixed woodland and thornveld.

Common Waxbill *Estrilda astrild* (846) L 13 cm

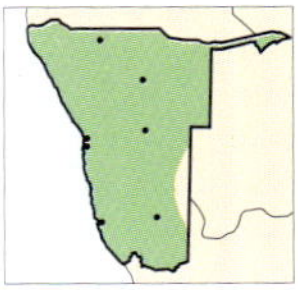

As the sexes of this long-tailed species are similar, it is best to identify it by its *bright red bill and face patch, and the small, reddish patch on the belly*. The immature is a duller version of the adult with a black bill. Its call is a nasal 'cher-cher-cher'. It has a 'ping-ping' flight note. This common resident prefers the long grass of damp areas, alongside rivers and in reed beds.

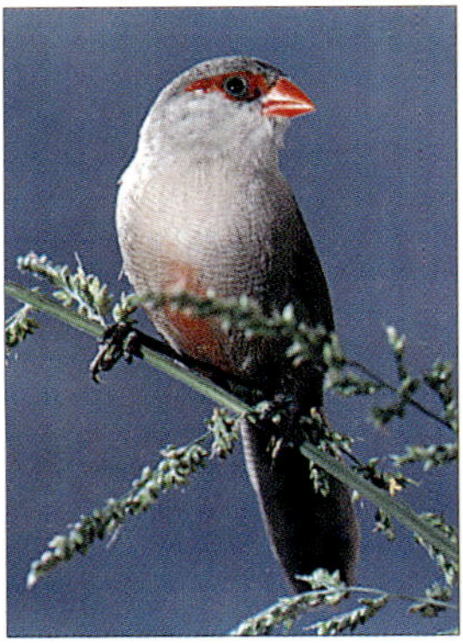

N BRICKELL

Blackcheeked Waxbill *Estrilda erythronotos* (847) L 13 cm

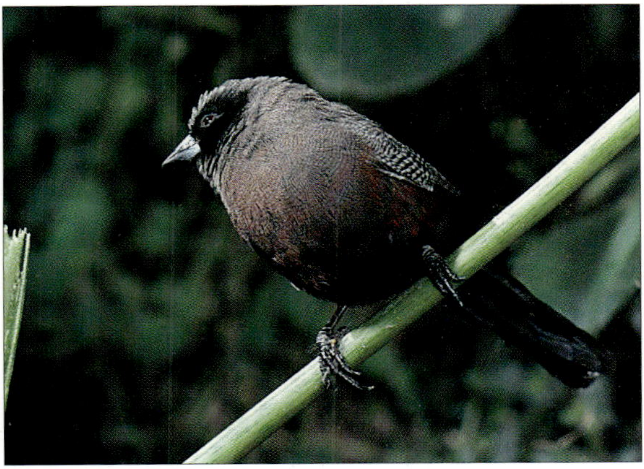

N BRICKELL

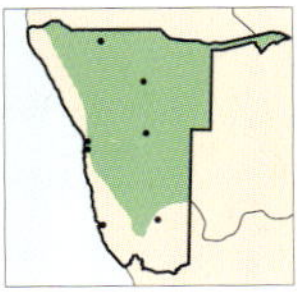

This waxbill is easily identified by its unmistakable *greyish brown body and head, conspicuous black face patch, and dark red rump and flanks.* The immature and female are duller versions of the male. Its call is a high-pitched 'chuloweee'. This is a common resident of Namibia, occurring in thick tangles in dry thornveld and grassy areas.

Violeteared Waxbill *Uraeginthus granatinus* (845) L 15 cm

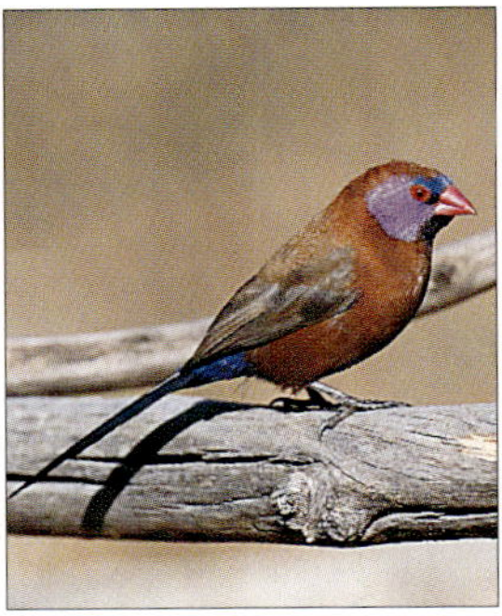

J J THERON

Male

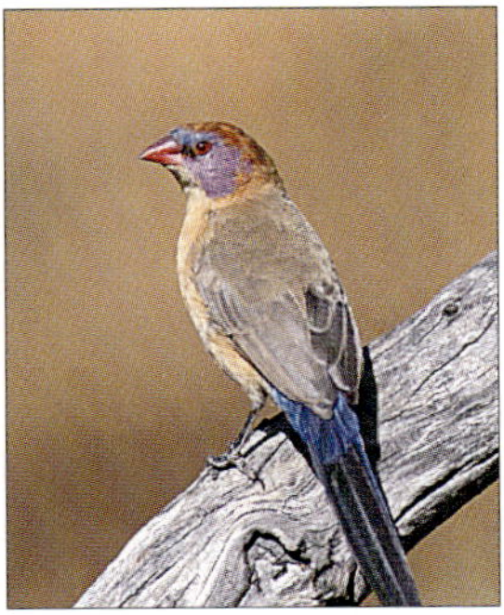

J J THERON

Female

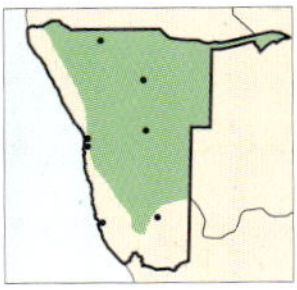

The male is the most colourful of all the waxbills in southern Africa, and has a *cinnamon body, iridescent violet ear patches, a brilliant blue rump, red eyes and a red bill.* The female is biscuit coloured and is identified by the diagnostic violet ear patches and the blue rump. The immature resembles the female but lacks the violet on the head. The call of this bird is a soft, whistled 'tiu-woowee'. This waxbill is a common resident that occurs in woodland and savanna, especially in dry thornveld, on rivercourses and on grassy roadsides.

Redheaded Finch *Amadina erythrocephala* (856) L 13 cm

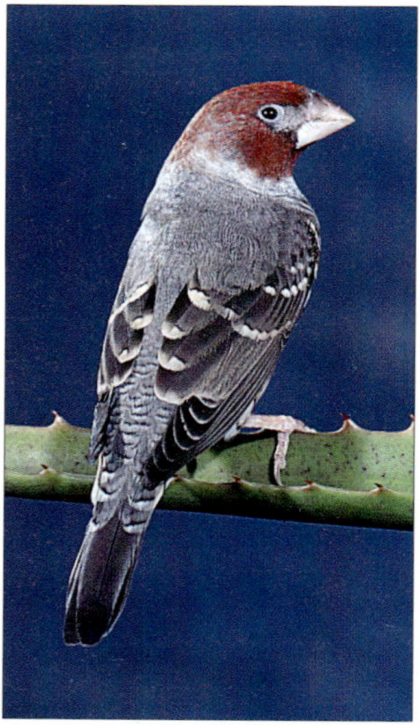

PETER CRAIG-COOPER

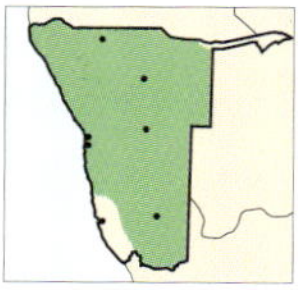

This is a small finch with a *bright red head contrasting with barred and mottled underparts*. The male of this species might be confused with the male Redheaded Quelea but it lacks the black face and has barred, not uniform, underparts. It has a soft 'zree-zree' flight call and a harsher 'chuk-chuk' call. This bird is often seen at Sociable Weaver nests and sometimes forms large flocks when not breeding. It is a common resident and occurs in dry woodland, thornveld and scrub.

Eastern Paradise Whydah *Vidua paradisaea* (862) L 15 cm (plus 23 cm tail in breeding male)

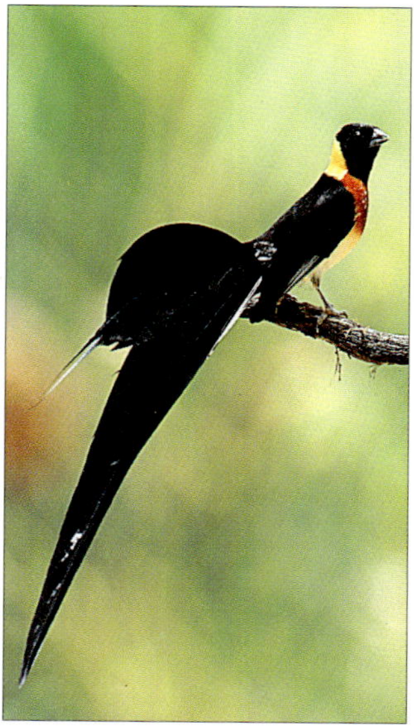

ABPL/NIGEL J DENNIS

Breeding male

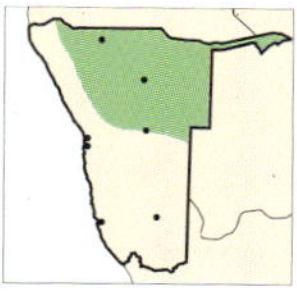

The breeding male of this species has a *long tail of stiff, downward-curving feathers, tapering to a point*. It has *black upperparts and a black head, a yellow hindcollar and yellow belly, and a chestnut breast*. The non-breeding male, female and immature all have a *black bill, an off-white head with black stripes, and grey-brown upperparts*. Its call is a sharp 'chip-chip' and a short 'cheroop-cherrup'. A common resident of Namibia, it occurs in mixed woodland, especially thornveld.

Shaft-tailed Whydah *Vidua regia* (861)
L 12 cm (plus 22 cm tail in breeding male)

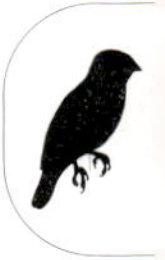

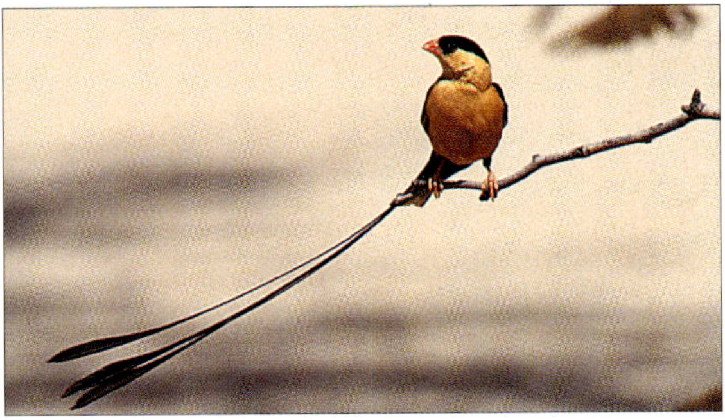

ABPL/BRENDAN RYAN

Breeding male

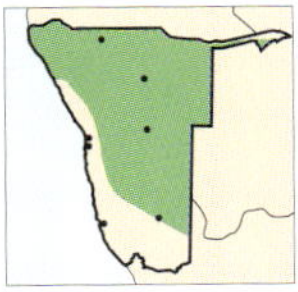

In breeding plumage the male Shaft-tailed Whydah is easily identified by its *buff and black plumage* and the diagnostic spatulate tips to its elongated tail feathers. The non-breeding male and female are slightly paler and have *streaked head markings*. The immature is dull brown with dark streaking on the back. Displaying males utter a harsh 'tseet-tseet-tseet' call. This common resident occurs in grassy areas in dry thornveld and broad-leafed woodland.

Blackthroated Canary *Serinus atrogularis* (870) L 11 cm

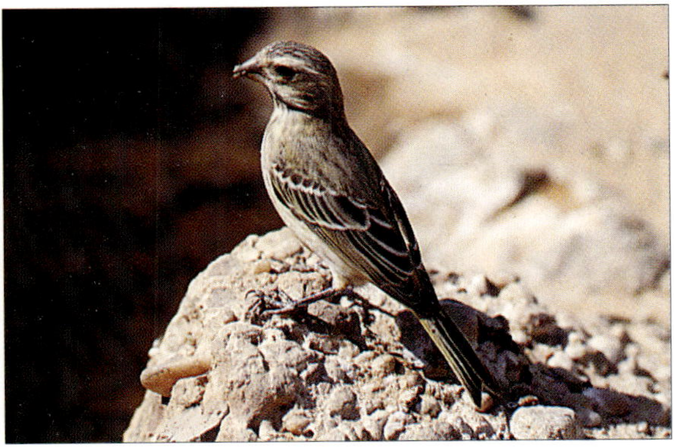

T D LONGRIGG

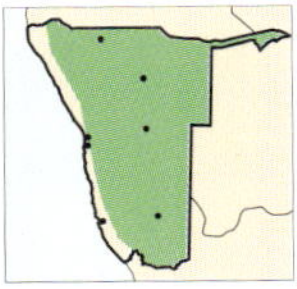

This is a small, nondescript, pale grey canary, heavily streaked dark brown on the upperparts. It has a diagnostic *black-speckled throat, and a bright yellow rump*. The female has less black on the throat. The immature is spotted on the throat. Its call is a prolonged series of wheezy whistles and chirrups. This species is the common, small canary seen in most parts of Namibia. It occurs near water holes in dry broad-leafed woodland and thornveld.

Yellow Canary *Serinus flaviventris* (878) L 13 cm

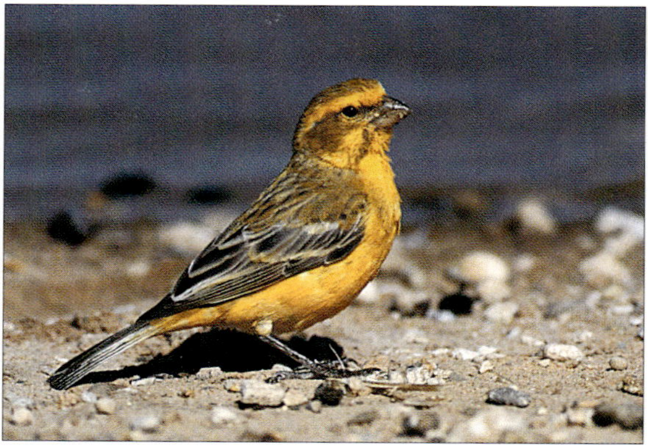

ABPL/TERRY CAREW

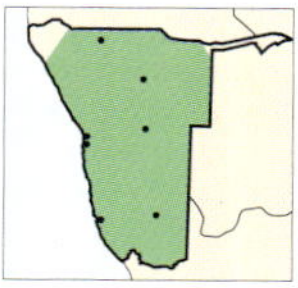

This is the brightest yellow canary found in Namibia. In bright sunlight the male appears *bright golden yellow* all over; it is much more yellow than any weaver. The female and immature are drabber and are more *greyish green with streaked upper- and underparts*. The call is a fast, jumbled series of 'chissick' and 'cheeree' notes. This canary is a common resident that occurs from desert-edge scrub to thornveld, and in well-wooded, dry riverbeds.

Goldenbreasted Bunting *Emberiza flaviventris* (884) L 16 cm

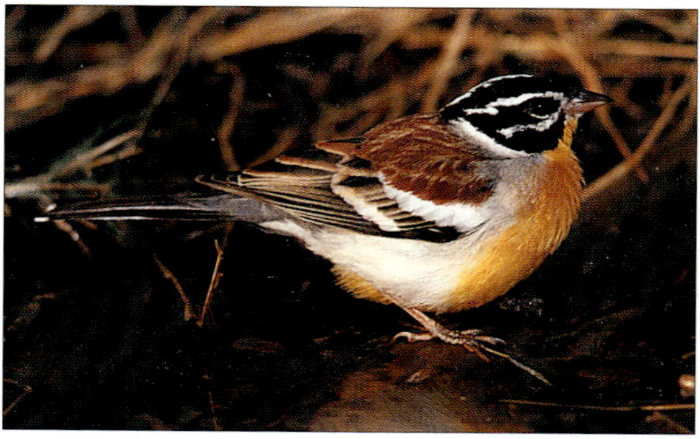

J VAN JAARSVELD

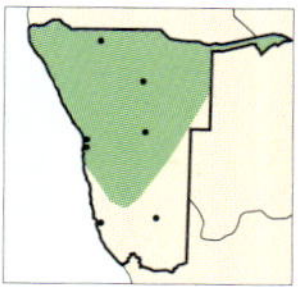

This bunting has a diagnostic *yellow-orange breast, a chestnut mantle and a black and white striped head*. The white wing bars are conspicuous in flight. The female and immature are duller versions of the male. It often reveals its presence by giving a nasal, buzzy 'zzhrrr' call or singing its varied 'weechee-weechee-weechee' song from within the canopy of a tree. Found in thornveld, broad-leafed woodland and exotic plantations, this is a common Namibian resident.

Cinnamonbreasted Rock Bunting *Emberiza tahapisi* (886) L 14 cm

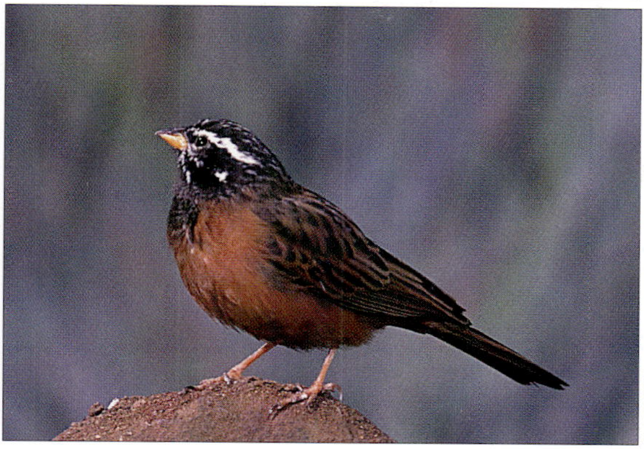

N BRICKELL

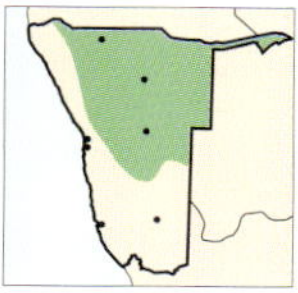

This species can be identified by its black throat, black and white head, and *diagnostic cinnamon underparts*. In the female and immature, which both show the diagnostic cinnamon underparts, the black and white head markings are less bold. This bird has a grating, rattled song and a soft 'pee-pee-wee' call. It is a common resident, nomadic when not breeding, and frequents rocky slopes in mountainous terrain, and mixed woodland.

Larklike Bunting *Emberiza impetuani* (887) L 14 cm

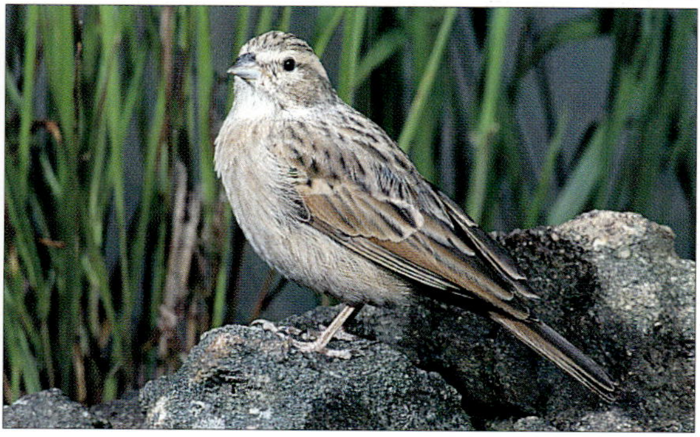

N BRICKELL

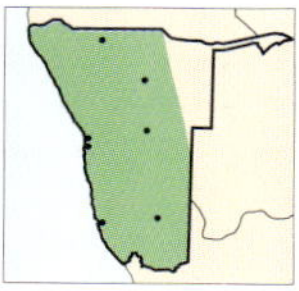

The *lack of any diagnostic field characters* in this drab and dowdy bird are clues to its identification. It might be mistaken for a lark but displays typical bunting behaviour, hopping over stones and grubbing around for seeds on the bare ground. The immature is paler than the adult. The contact call is a short 'tuc-tuc'. It occurs in drier areas in open plains, on the desert edge, and in rocky valleys. This species is nomadic, being very common in some areas before vanishing for long periods.

Birding etiquette

Once you are equipped with a pair of binoculars, a notebook and a fieldguide, you are on the road to birding and no other licence is required. Access to most game and nature reserves, wildlife sanctuaries and wilderness areas is allowed if the necessary permits are arranged prior to the visit, and admission fees, if any, are paid. Most other birding areas are on privately owned land and it is advisable always to seek permission from the landowner before you cross his veld. Enter fields through gates (and leave them open or closed, as you found them) or by climbing carefully through, not over, a fence.

The ever-increasing number of birders is placing pressure on the better known birding areas and, to avoid being denied access, birders should observe a simple code of etiquette. In their innocent pursuit birders can disturb and harm the very things that have taken their interest. Watching a flock of terns or roosting waders on a beach might seem harmless enough but if you put them to flight, you are causing a direct disturbance. This is tolerable if you do it only once, but repeatedly disturbing flocks causes distress and the birds subsequently move away altogether – this often happens if there is more than one birder in the area. Making any kind of close approach to breeding colonies of birds such as weavers, bishops, herons and seabirds can cause incalculable harm and may even result in the entire colony disbanding and deserting, with a total breeding failure in that season. Bird-viewing is simple if a quiet and careful approach is made or, even better, if you use a spotting scope and thus avoid too close an approach altogether.

It is easy to recognize the situations in which birds will flush. They become very agitated, sometimes giving off alarm notes, and will begin wing stretching. Respect these signals and leave the vicinity. General disturbance of any breeding birds should be avoided – with experience you will be able to tell if a bird is holding a territory and actively nesting. A nesting bird or a bird with young may feign injury, give alarm calls, or dive bomb an intruder in an effort to distract attention away from its nest or young. When you recognize these signals it is best to limit your time in the immediate area in case you cause the birds to desert.

A technique which is being employed more frequently is that of using a tape recording of a bird's call or song to entice the bird into the open for better viewing. This practice is useful for attracting the more furtive species and, in particular, nocturnal owls and nightjars. It does not do any harm if done very infrequently but most certainly will if the bird is repeatedly lured to a tape recording. A bird responding to a taped call is seeking out an invader of its territory and if it cannot find the intruder, it will inevitably become confused. If continually lured to a tape, the bird defending its territory will eventually abandon the area.

The key to 'unobtrusive' birding is to bear the bird's interests in mind. Remember all the time that the habitat in which you are watching the bird is fragile: take care not to damage it or to disturb the area.

Actively involve yourself in a local or national conservation society and draw their attention to areas near you that need conserving or that are being disturbed or developed. If added up on a national scale, the small areas of natural habitat which are rapidly being destroyed and cleared for development would cover a vast area.

Further reading

The following books may be of interest to those wishing to learn more about birds and bird-watching

Berruti, A. and Sinclair, J.C. 1983. *Where to Watch Birds in Southern Africa. Struik Publishers*, Cape Town.

Ginn, P.J., McIlleron, W.G. and Milstein, P. le S. 1989. *The Complete Book of Southern African Birds*. Struik Winchester, Cape Town.

Hockey, P.A.R. and Douie, C. 1995. *Waders of Southern Africa*. Struik Winchester, Cape Town.

Maclean, G.L. 1994 (6th edition). *Roberts' Birds of Southern Africa*. The Trustees of the John Voelcker Bird Book Fund, Cape Town.

Newman, K.B. 1987. *Newman's Birds of Southern Africa*. Macmillan South Africa, Johannesburg.

Sinclair, I. and Davidson, I. 1995. *Southern African Birds – a Photographic Guide*. Struik Publishers, Cape Town.

Sinclair, I. 1987. *Field Guide to the Birds of Southern Africa*. Struik, Cape Town.

Sinclair, I., Meakin, P. and Goode, D. 1990. *Pocket Guide Series: Common Birds*. Struik Publishers, Cape Town.

Sinclair I. and Whyte, I. 1991. *Field Guide to Birds of the Kruger National Park*. Struik, Cape Town.

Sinclair, I., Hockey, P.A.R., and Tarboton, W. 1993. *Sasol Field Guide to Southern African Birds*. Struik, Cape Town.

Sinclair, I. Meakin, P. and Goode D. 1990. *Pocket Guide: Common Birds*. Struik Publishers, Cape Town.

Sinclair, J.C., Mendelsohn, J.M. and Johnson, P. 1981. *Everyone's Guide to South African Birds*. CNA, Johannesburg.

Steyn, P. 1982. *Birds of Prey of Southern Africa*. David Philip, Cape Town.

Glossary of terms

Alien A bird which is not indigenous to the area.

Breeding endemic A species which breeds only in a particular region but undertakes movements or migrations during the non-breeding season such that a measurable proportion of the population leaves the region.

Cap Area encompassing the forehead and crown.

Casque A helmet or helmet-like process on the bill.

Cere Coloured bare skin at the base of the upper mandible.

Colonial Associating in close proximity, either while roosting, feeding or nesting.

Decurved Curving downwards.

Display A pattern of behaviour in which the bird attracts attention while it is defending territory or courting a female, for example.

Eclipse plumage Dull plumage attained during a transitional moult, after the breeding season and before they acquire brighter plumage.

Endemic Restricted to a certain region.

Eye-ring Circle of coloured feathers immediately behind the eye.

Feral Species that have escaped from captivity and now live in the wild.

Flush To rouse and put to flight.

Form Colour variation within a species.

Immature A bird that has moulted its juvenile plumage but has not yet attained full adult plumage.

Juvenile The first full-feathered plumage of a yound bird.

Migrant A species that undertakes long-distance flights between its wintering and breeding areas.

Moustachial stripes Lines running from the base of the bill to the sides of the throat (*see* malar region *in illustration*).

Near endemic A species whose range is largely restricted to a region but extends slightly outside its borders.

Parasitize When a bird lays its eggs in the nest of another species for the purposes of incubation.

Plumage Feathering of a kind.

Primaries The outermost major flight feathers of the wing.

Range A bird's distribution.

Resident A bird that occurs throughout the year in a region and is not known to undertake migration.

Rufous Reddish brown.

Secondaries Flight feathers of the wing, adjoining the primary feathers.

Shield Bare patch of skin at the base of the bill and on the forehead. Often brightly coloured.

Summer visitor A bird that is absent from the region during the winter.

Territory An area that a bird establishes and subsequently defends from others.

Vagrant Rare and accidental to the region.

Vent The area from the belly to the undertail coverts.

Parts of a bird

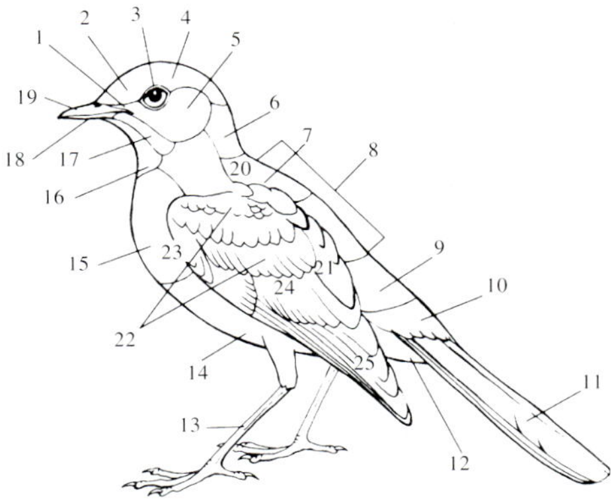

1 lores
2 forehead
3 eye-ring
4 crown
5 ear coverts
6 nape
7 mantle
8 back
9 rump
10 uppertail coverts
11 tail
12 undertail coverts
13 tarsus
14 belly
15 breast
16 throat
17 malar region
18 lower mandible
19 upper mandible
20 scapulars
21 tertials
22 wing coverts
23 alula
24 secondaries
25 primaries

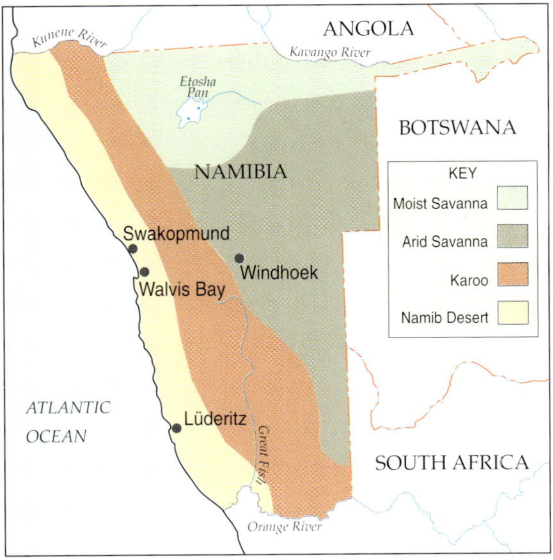

This map of Namibia shows the major vegetation zones. Distribution is contained by, and in many cases, restricted to specialized habitats within these zones.

Index

The page numbers refer to the page on which the species account appears.